FROM CZAR TO BOLSHEVIK

KERENSKY IN PETROGRAD

KERENSKY IN THE TRENCHES ON THE EASTERN FRONT,
JUNE 1917

FROM CZAR TO BOLSHEVIK

By E. P. STEBBING

ILLUSTRATED WITH PHOTO-
GRAPHS BY THE AUTHOR

University Press of the Pacific
Honolulu. Hawaii

From Czar to Bolshevik

by
E. P. Stebbing

ISBN: 0-89875-450-X

Copyright © 2001 by University Press of the Pacific

Reprinted from the 1918 edition

University Press of the Pacific
Honolulu, Hawaii
http://www.universitypressofthepacific.com

PREFACE

THE inquiry which took me to Russia last year had an economic rather than a political character. Within a very short space of time, however, it became evident that very little progress could be made with the former aspect until I had become conversant with the political conditions of the New Russia, so entirely at variance with the old, and thus be in a position to gauge their effects economically upon this country.

The study so made, as day by day the extraordinary kaleidoscopic events passed before the eyes, proved of absorbing interest, and left me deeply impressed with their extreme importance alike to this country and to Russia herself. The occurrences which led directly to the present position are set down in diary form in these pages. I have refrained from criticism. For the sequence of events appears to furnish its own answers to the thoughtful man.

But in the national interests the diary has a further object. It is of the highest importance that the true causes for the present appalling condition of Russia should be understood, and the question be regarded with that breadth of view and the clarity and coolness in passing judgment with which our race has become credited by the foreigner.

At present there is a strong feeling amongst the peoples of the Entente that Russia has " let us in."

That the loss of the Eastern front has proved a disaster of the first magnitude is obvious to all. As a direct consequence we are now engaged upon the greatest battle in history and fighting for our lives, or, which we value more, our national honour.

I leave it to my readers to decide whether, given the conditions which of necessity followed the gigantic upheaval caused by the Revolution amongst a totally uneducated people of so vast an empire, we could or should have expected Russia to be able to maintain her

v

fronts, which held up nearly half the Austro-German divisions, without direct help from her Allies.

Germany conquered the Eastern front by propaganda, not by force of arms. This propagandist campaign was carried on absolutely unchecked and unopposed by the Allies.

At the end of two and a half years of war German methods were well known. Should not the Entente have assisted their Ally in both the German fields of warfare— force of arms by force of arms and propaganda by propaganda ?

E. P. STEBBING.

Hawthornden,
Midlothian.
April 8th, 1918.

Since the above went to press I have deemed it advisable to add a few remarks on the present position of Russia. What is that position ? Germany is the master of Russia. She is already tearing up her peace treaties—more scraps of paper—with the Ukraine and Russia, and appearances point to Finland soon finding herself in a similar plight to the Ukraine. We hesitated to recognise the Finnish Republic. Sweden refused to help her against the Bolsheviks, and when the Entente in their turn were appealed to the same course was followed, and food cargoes were stopped from reaching her. Finland then applied to Germany, and armed help was at once forthcoming. Food was also promised, but of course it has not been sent. As a consequence of Entente inaction the new ice-free port at the head of the Murman railway is now imperilled.

As regards the present position of Germany in the East, Professor Troeltsch, of Heidelberg, recently described it as follows : " We have achieved a military tenable frontier for Central Europe towards the East and, on the other hand, we have created a girdle of buffer States which stretches from Finland to the Caucasus, follows the whole front of the Central Powers and, in the East, already stretches out to Persia as the last link in the chain." This is overstating the position, but it does not leave the

German aims in much doubt, and has a very plain significance for us. We have been carrying out an arduous campaign in Mesopotamia, sacrificing lives and treasure, with the object of putting an end to Germany's Berlin-Constantinople-Bagdad-Persian Gulf Railway scheme, with its direct threat to India. In this campaign we have been successful, and we had begun to regard that German dream as disposed of. But it has been replaced by a new one, which she is busily fashioning into a semblance of reality. With the loss of the Eastern front Roumania was left in the lurch and is now under the German heel, bound by the most callous, brutal and rapacious treaty ever conceived in modern times. Constanza, the fine Roumanian port, is thus at Germany's mercy. By the Brest-Litovsk treaty Russia was forced to concede to the moribund Turk the rich district of Kars and Batum. Germany had not given up her Indian dream! This province wrested from Russia, and Persia (where she is very active and has the Turks as her pioneers) are meant to take the place of her lost trade and conquest route to the domination of Asia. Her new route to the East is to be Berlin-Constanza-Batum-Baku, and then across the Caspian and through Persia to the Persian Gulf. To assist her in carrying out this purpose she is preparing to seize and retain for herself the rich mineral wealth of the Urals and Caucasus and to make the Caspian, like the Baltic, a German lake. Germany has a long way to go yet to realise her new object; but so have we to defeat it. It is therefore imperative that the British Empire peoples should realise her Eastern aims. For otherwise our Mesopotamian and other campaigns will have been fought in vain. Do we yet, as a nation, realise the position?

We, a World Empire, invented the expression " side-shows," by which we more or less contemptuously designated the Egyptian, Gallipoli, Mesopotamian and Macedonian campaigns. And the Russian front was the affair of the Russians. Co-ordination of fronts amongst the Allies, admittedly a difficult problem, was almost non-existent; if we except the first year of the war, when the

Russians in East Prussia and Galicia gallantly drew on themselves the brunt of the enemy attacks, and so saved the French and small British force from what might well have proved annihilation. We did not then understand that we were fighting an enemy with one front only. "Why waste money and lives on 'side-shows'?" was the phrase on every one's lips a couple of years ago, in ignorance of the fact that for our Empire these "side-shows" were of paramount importance, that the Eastern fronts were vital to our future existence as an Empire. Have we yet realised this?

That Germany can be left to enjoy spoils obtained by a false propaganda combined with a callous premeditated treachery; that she can be left to bring permanent misery and hardship into the homes of millions of men and women who are, or were, our Allies, is unthinkable. The Allies have played some wrong cards, but the rubber is not yet lost. But to win it the Germans must be ousted from Russia and the East.

The Bolsheviks have done the world one good turn. For they forced or entrapped Germany into showing her hand and displaying, yet once again, the treatment meted out to all who fall beneath the ruthless Prussian heel.

We have quitted Russia. Withdrawn our Embassy, evacuated our naval and military staffs from Archangel, Kola and elsewhere, and, with a few exceptions, recalled all Britishers, civilian, soldier and sailor, who were representing us and working for us and for Russia in that country. The American Embassy, in spite of Bolshevik and German protests, remained; the French military mission remained; and other foreign Embassies have since returned. Was it a wise policy on our part to leave Russia? Would it not have been wiser to have withdrawn to the south, to that part of the country occupied by our Russian friends—those friends who have been watching us with such anxious eyes: to have remained, even if at some risk? Is "playing for safety" the right kind of fight, even from the merely materialistic point of view, to put up after nearly four years of war?

Was it not, in the case of Russia, too much like waiting to see which way the cat would jump? Was it not an unfortunate miscalculation? True, we could never seriously have considered the possibility of allying ourselves with the present so-called "Government" who do not represent Russia, a "Government" who have destroyed all that human foresight and human skill (backward in Russia though they were) had built up. But we are now chiefly concerned with thwarting German ambitions in Central Asia and safeguarding the road to India, and every possible step should be taken to achieve this end.

The greater bulk of the Russians liked and admired us; and, as a nation, we have grown accustomed to regard ourselves as the champions of the oppressed and weak. Have we occupied this position *vis-à-vis* with Russia since she was confronted with the greatest moment in her history, in her destiny? We have still many friends in Russia, and it is of vital importance that we should, in order to retrieve our position there, leave no stone unturned to get into touch with them at once. The position bristles with difficulties : they need not frighten us. But these difficulties are only solvable on the spot.

The British peoples are almost entirely ignorant of the true issues involved in this Russian imbroglio, and Germany is making extraordinary efforts, by confusing these issues, to keep them so. The British do not understand the importance, the necessity to our Empire, of a strong and friendly Russian Empire. And yet a dismembered and Germanised Russia might well sound our death-knell as an Empire. For with Russia to exploit at her will, Germany would grow wealthy again in a comparatively short period, and would once again play, and this time, it is conceivable, play successfully, for the World Stakes. Is there any one, acquainted with the facts, prepared to say that this is an overdrawn statement of the position? Can the pacifist say so? Germany, we know, would make peace to-morrow on the Western front if the Allies agreed to recognise her so-called " peace " treaties (annexation treaties is the true term) on the Eastern front, and left her to work her own hard and ruthless will on the unfortunate peoples from whom she has wrung them.

It behoves us, then, to dally no longer, for we have a long leeway to make up, and it must be made up.

There are three points in Russia at which the Allies should act, and act with vigour. In the north at the ports of Alexandrovsk, at the head of the Murman Railway and Archangel, at the head of the Archangel-Petrograd Railway; in the south-east at Vladivostock, at the end of the Siberian Railway. In the north all true Russians would welcome Allied intervention and occupation of the two ports and as much of the railways as can be secured and held. The Germans have made no secret of their northern aims. These ports were not included in the clauses of the Brest treaty having reference to the Baltic ports, etc. But Admiral Kaiserling, who arrived in Petrograd in charge of the German Naval Mission at the end of last December, announced that he had been sent " to establish German naval bases at Alexandrovsk and Archangel "; from which, we may infer, to operate against ourselves and the Americans—in fact, to reproduce Zeebrugge and Ostend in this northern region. If the Allies delay much longer this great northern region will be occupied, and fairly easily held, by the Germans.

At Vladivostock in the far south-east the question of Japanese intervention has been simmering since August of last year. In this matter Germany has, by means of her extraordinarily well-organised propaganda, attained a success which must have been beyond even her hopes. She has successfully sown dissension, or, we will say, hesitation, amongst the Allies; brought forth the " Yellow Peril " bogey, and by its judicious use frightened, it would appear, the Allies as much as the Russians. Japan has been credited with motives and aims which her past loyalty to her Allies should alone have sufficed to discredit. How much longer are we going to hesitate ? It is perfectly well known that Germany is collecting together throughout Siberia her own and Austrian prisoners; and these are certainly being reinforced by the considerable and food-stuffs at Vladivostock which must not be allowed to fall into German hands. So far we have landed a handful of men at the port!

This war, as we now all recognise, can never be won without a co-ordination of the fronts in which all the Allies should work, each up to her greatest possible output of ability, men and material. If we accept this dictum, Japan's position and right to enter the land war is indisputable, and her point of entry, equally indisputable, since she is on the spot, is at Vladivostock. If we are still so divided in opinion (*i. e.* unwelded) as to make Japan's entry a matter of susceptibilities—and it is here that Germany has always played her strongest card in the past—the war to all appearances will drag on for a number of years, and may end in disaster as the outcome. Of one thing there can be no longer any doubt. Between the Bolshevik and the German Siberia will be lost to the Allies unless they take prompt action. We may accept it as probable that Russia, educated Russia, has learnt her lesson from the failures, dissensions and vacillations of last year, to which have been added the unspeakable horrors and misery of the Bolshevik regime and the callous perfidy of the German. We are not yet in a position to say how much of this lesson has been absorbed. But we do know the only way to save her. Before this last road is barred to us by the German, should we not make up our minds to take it?

With each of the three forces operating from the points mentioned, we should send men, as many as we can lay hands on, whose business would be propaganda—propaganda against the German. It will not be possible to give them any stereotyped orders. They must be trusted. Pick them out, give them the order " Propaganda " in one word, and leave them to do the job in their own way; and that way will be determined entirely by the nature of each difficulty as it arises on the spot.

The object before us is to save the Russian Empire from the German. If we fail in this the war will have to be fought out again in the future. E. P. S.

PREFACE

numbers who, I discovered for myself, were quartere[d]
the eastern parts of the Archangel and Vologda Gov[ern]
ments, which are linked up with Central Russia and [the]
Siberian Railway by the Kotlas-Viatka Railway [and]
waterways. These prisoners are being armed, and Ger[man]
officer prisoners are organising them into divisions [and]
corps. And whatever his other disabilities, we are [well]
aware that the German officer is very efficient at his o[wn]
job. In London and elsewhere efforts are being made [to]
belittle this danger. But it is useless waiting till it com[es]
to a head before recognising it, and then taking steps [to]
deal with it when too late. Up to now Colonel Semen[off]
and his gallant Cossacks have been left to wage [an]
unequal fight alone, but there are evidences that he [is]
gathering strength; for Russia now hates the Germa[ns]
as much or more than the Bolshevik. And the Czech[o-]
Slovak troops are now entering the arena. With the Allie[s]
advancing up the railway from Vladivostock there can be[]
little doubt that the position would alter for the better.
But this advance must be made before the prisoners of
the Central Powers are organised into a striking force
capable of invading Siberia. For if Germany gets her
grip on Siberia and secures command of the Siberian
Railway and the northern route via Kotlas and down the
Northern Dvina to Archangel (for which reason, amongst
others, she wants that port), she will secure at once a
great granary and store of food-stuffs. It will be well, in
view of the great organising ability of the Germans and
the surprises this war has held for the world, not to lay
too great stress on the difficulties of transportation which
would face them. It is safer to give the enemy the credit
of being able to organise this business. If it eventuated
it would mean the prolongation of the war for several
years. For when beaten in her present great offensive,
Germany could retire towards or on the Rhine " for strategic
reasons," sit down and dispatch large forces to the East to
exploit her conquests and obtain stores of food and raw
materials. Finally, the Allies have an additional incen-
tive for immediate action in the accumulation of munitions

CONTENTS

LIST OF ILLUSTRATIONS

FROM CZAR TO BOLSHEVIK

CHAPTER I

ACROSS THE NORTH SEA

There are few of us, I suppose, who do not believe that the Great War has been a blessing in disguise for the British race and for the British Empire. It has acted upon us much in the same way as our bitter nor'-easter—bracing us all up. A kill or cure business, eliminating the effete. And it is not, as has been mostly the case in former wars, only the youngsters who have been able to bear a hand in the game, as we are all by now well aware. Towards the end of the second year of the war I remember hearing a man, a big fleshy man (a civilian in peace time) of forty-five or thereabouts, who was wearing a captain's stars and serving somewhere in Britain, say to a friend : " Early in 1914 I had made up my mind that I was getting into the sere and yellow and that for active pursuits I was becoming *passé*." His opinion of himself had undergone a remarkable change in the two war years. He continued, " I now feel thirty once more, and do not propose to consider the sere and yellow stage for many years to come." To how many must the war have brought this realisation ! And it will be all to the good of the Empire that the softness of living which produced this early ageing, in mind if not in body, has been swept away.

This new aspect of the nation with regard to its physical and mental fitness as the outcome of the war formed the burden of a discussion which took place in a railway compartment in which several of us, bound for Petrograd, were seated last July. The journey to Petrograd is no

longer the luxurious trip of the old days of peace.   There
were not many direct ways of reaching the Russian capital
last year.   The best known during the past year or two is
probably the Archangel route.   I shall have something to
say later on about this Russian port and its extraordinary
development as a result of the war.   We were not travelling
via Archangel, and devoutly thankful we were.   Ammunition ships are not liners; nor does the Arctic Ocean com-
pare favourably with the Mediterranean, more especially
if you happen to get immersed in it !   We were at the
moment bound for Bergen, and were not troubling about
the rest of the land journey.   The first thing, in the
times we live in, thanks to the Bosche, is to get across
the sea which girts our island.   That accomplished, the
rest of the journey, whatever the destination, can be
regarded with equanimity.   We, born and bred on an
island, regard these crossings philosophically.   But Continental people view the matter differently.   On several
occasions in Petrograd, Russian friends expressed the
greatest horror of this North Sea crossing.   They appeared to be under the impression that the floor of the
North Sea was paved with German submarines who popped
up as occasion demanded, bagged their ship at leisure and
retired once again to their forms.   It was a pleasure to
point out that the Bosche did not find it quite so easy a
pastime as all that.

In due course we reported to the N.E.O. at the port and
an A.B. was told off to escort us to the ship, whose size,
from the landsman's point of view, the most cursory glance
showed to be far too small.   There must be many who will
remember the shortcomings of this little vessel for many
years after peace once again restores the amenities of
travel.   But our particular trip will remain in the memory
for reasons quite apart from the deficiencies of the little
ship herself.

In conformance with the action of her Allies in this
respect, the Russian Government last summer ordered all
its subjects to either join the British Army or to return
home and join up in Russia.   As a result of the order the

British authorities were clearing out London, the East End of London, and we were to travel with the first consignment. Our *compagnons de voyage* proved a most extraordinary crowd hailing from every corner of Russia's vast dominions, comprising types of all Eastern Europe and beyond. The vessel, as I have said, was a small one, with practically no deck space and one saloon in which first, second, and, I imagine from some of the gentlemen who sat at table, third class passengers eat together. I had returned to the hotel, retrieved my kit and brought it down on board; but hearing that we were not to sail before midnight at earliest, had determined to dine ashore. I succumbed, however, to the importunities of the head steward, who pestered me to take a seat at the second dinner. In view of my experiences in food matters during the next three months, I shall probably regret that hotel dinner for the rest of my days! And yet I would not have missed the experience which followed on my decision to dine on board. The dinner as a meal was as big a farce in its way as I felt my own position to be amongst the extraordinary collection, of humanity who sat in the saloon. The head steward in a disgusted voice said it was the first occasion they had carried such a crowd, and hoped it would be the last. I could well believe it, but knew his hopes would be falsified, as there were many more of this type to follow. I had not expected that they would be sent by this route, though. At table it was possible to inspect one's fellow-passengers at leisure. They consisted of prosperous small tradesmen, small clerks and book-keepers, artisans, labouring men and loafers. There were not much over a couple of dozen of ourselves in the crowd, naval and military men, King's Messengers and so forth, all in mufti; the naval youngsters bound for the submarines at Reval, half a dozen subalterns *en route* to Persia, and R.N.V.R. men for the armoured cars on the Russian front—striking evidence of our far-flung battle line. The bulk of this lot had wisely elected to dine on shore. Of women, there were five members of the Scottish Women's Hospitals bound for the late Dr. Elsie Inglis'

Unit in the neighbourhood of Odessa and three or four others.

The men seated round the table were Russians of more or less pure extraction—Ukrainians, Lithuanians, Poles, Czechs, Jews and so on. One point only had all these people in common : they were one and all wearing new boots. These new boots were significant. There would be no boots to buy in Russia. The choice varied with the position in life of the wearer, from the stout thick ammunition boot, through endless grades of the better-class army boot now procurable, to beautiful civilian boots in black, brown or patent leather. All were being worn to avoid paying the duty. I made subsequent acquaintance with the long boot queues in Petrograd. A lady there told me that a maid of hers had spent all her leisure hours for a fortnight in endeavouring to buy a pair of shoes, and then gave it up.

To return to the saloon. Opposite to me sat a gentleman of Jewish extraction, clad in a thick leather motor-jacket surmounted by a very dirty collar, blue breeches, and good new black boots and gaiters. He kept the whole of this kit on in spite of the stifling heat in the saloon. Hard by a man, an artisan apparently, was clad in a suit of yellow-brown gamekeeper's corduroy, buttoned to the neck. He had his double, black-haired and low-browed, similarly clothed, higher up the table. Next the former was a member of one of the London tea-shop orchestras, with long narrow hands and fingers, and a head of hair some six inches or more in length which had not made acquaintance with a comb for many a day. A fourth type next to me was obviously one of the small prosperous Russian traders who found London a good place to live in. He was well dressed, very content with himself, and extremely informative and boastful over his own affairs. Amongst other things he mentioned, for the benefit of the table in general, that he had never been short of sugar, that his small grocer, with whom he had dealt several years, had always let him have as much as he wanted. He also entertained the company with various other stories of a

similar nature, all illustrating the fact that we could well
do without this type of alien in our midst and let our own
people occupy their places.   As a matter of fact, no country
requires that type of citizen.   Another individual more
difficult to place was a fine specimen of a Frenchman of
the lower *bourgeois* class.   He had done two years'
fighting in France, wore several medal ribbons, and had
now, so he said, got his *congé* and was returning to his
wife and family in South Russia, where apparently he was
settled when the war broke out.   He was an engineer by
profession, and spoke English and Russian fluently and,
I gathered, several other languages.   Perhaps he was a
secret service man.   But he wore semi-military kit and a
Russian service cap on reaching that country.

At 9 p.m. drinks became permissible on board.   It was
close time at dinner.   The saloon filled up and soon became
reminiscent of the Café Royale in Regent Street if you
add, what you do not see there, a considerable proportion
of the lower-class aliens of the East End of London.
Dominoes, chess, cards and drinks were in requisition, and
a dense pall of tobacco smoke soon filled the place, together
with a babel of tongues of all Eastern Europe.   It was an
interesting community to watch, but half an hour drove
me on to the confined deck space and I entered the saloon
no more that voyage.   They were not exactly the class
of passengers to travel across the North Sea with, and I
remained in my cabin.   It was rough, and from the
reports I elicited from the cabin steward of the happenings on deck, for most of the passengers remained on
deck, being in mortal terror of Bosche submarines, I
congratulated myself on this decision.   We saw no
submarines.   A wild panic, had we done so and been hit,
was our verdict.

CHAPTER II

TO PETROGRAD THROUGH SCANDINAVIA AND FINLAND

THE Bergen-Christiania railway is said to be the highest in Europe, and it is certainly one of the most fascinating. Whilst breakfasting in the restaurant car the great climb is commenced soon after leaving Bergen, the train mounting up by fourteen steep zigzags through beautiful pine, spruce and birch forests, amidst which nestle the tiny neat villages, whilst deep lakes mirror the surrounding forest. At the end of the great climb the railway runs over rocky and stony barren fastnesses, for here we have got above tree level, still climbing, till the highest point is reached at Fiense, 4010 feet elevation. Fiense is a tiny settlement consisting of a handful of wooden houses amongst which the only prominent buildings are the station and hotel alongside, a wooden-built chalet-like place, with rather an attractive timber-roofed lounge hall. This remote village is dumped down in a howling wilderness of rock, marsh and snow, with marshy lakes, semi-frozen even in July, in which float great island-like masses of frozen snow and ice. In its wild austere barrenness Fiense is exceedingly picturesque. There are several granite obelisks here to the memory of Arctic explorers, mute witnesses to the chief interest of the inhabitants of Fiense, buried for three-quarters of the year in ice and snow. The latest set up is to Captain Scott, Dr. E. A. Wilson, Captain Oates, and Seaman Evans—a tribute to our gallant dead one liked to see. There is a good deal about this railway of high interest, especially the way the line is protected from snowdrift and avalanches—but better than any description I can give is an exhortation to go and see it. You will spend the whole day amongst mountain and forest, lake and river, howling wilderness intermixed with snow and ice; and if your good fortune gives you brilliant sunny weather it will prove one of the days set with a white stone in the memory.

In my compartment there were two Norwegian colonels and a middle-aged civilian. We had some interesting conversation. It naturally turned on the war. I was asked for my opinion, and gave it as one knew the position in July 1917. I naturally wanted to hear their views. In reply to my query as to how long they thought the Germans could go on manufacturing new big guns and the enormous amounts of munition now required, they were dubious, but were unanimous on the point that once the limit was reached in that production and the guns began to wear out and the shells to fall short, the infantry would refuse to advance. No infantry in the world would advance, was their verdict. They were exceedingly curious on the subject of the tanks, of which they had heard fabulous stories but knew nothing first-hand. In reply to a question about submarines, I described how the Turks had sown the Ægean Sea with mines just before the transport I was on had entered it the previous year. They expressed the greatest indignation at this tale, and also commented with heat on the Germans' submarine warfare. They expressed admiration for our great army, " but," said the senior colonel, " you were not ready and did not listen to Roberts." I agreed, but pointed out that we were not a military nation. Had never pretended to be one. Our job was on the sea and always had been, and there we were ready. We had never undertaken to keep up an army on the Continental scale or for Continental use. We had a crushing burden of taxes which we paid readily to keep up the navy in peace-time. We had not considered that our duty lay on the Continent. The colonel agreed to this. I said that many Frenchmen whom I had met and conversed with in the past two years admitted that they were not ready in 1914, as all the world knew. " Nor the Russians," he interjected. " No," I replied. " And yet both must have known of the danger. And now in three years we have an army on the Continental scale plus the largest navy the world has ever seen. We considered we were doing our full share and policing the North Sea for all in addition!" I must say my audience listened with the greatest attention, interpolating shrewd remarks on both the German and Allied tactics on various occasions. We shook hands most effusively at parting, promising to meet again after the peace. It will take several years' journeying round the world to fulfil all the promises of this kind made since the war started, but this last is one which I hope to make good.

Christiania was very gay and very full, but we were only concerned to get out of it and on the next stage to Stockholm. We were greatly struck by the pro-Ally spirit exhibited by the people generally. The Britisher is liked here. In the book and picture shops English books and English pictures and picture postcards with English descriptions on them were strikingly abundant, in marked contrast to Stockholm, where they were conspicuous only for their absence. In the Swedish capital almost every shop of this kind had series of enlarged photographs (as also had the tobacconists) depicting German scenes— battle pictures of Germans capturing Allied trenches; columns of French prisoners marching between German guards; Germans behind the lines in Belgium, the soldiers playing with Belgian children—set pieces, from the expressions of soldiers and children, for the delectation of neutrals; or scenes in Germany in the Unter and Thier- garten in Berlin showing frivolous crowds parading about and enjoying themselves. The latter were undated, so one was permitted to surmise that they had been raked out from happier times. The people depicted were too well fed. Not all the German food substitutes together would quite produce those expressions! Of course our illustrated papers show the same type of war pictures—all in our favour. No self-respecting nation can be expected to do anything else. But we do not ask or expect neutrals to exhibit them in the shop windows of their capitals.

The other little incident in Christiania worth recording is the Queen of Norway's potato patch. The Palace demesne stretches down to one of the main streets, quite unfenced; it here consists of a stretch of park with grass and scattered clumps of trees. An area which abutted on the road had been ploughed up and carried a fine crop of potato plants. The Palace head gardener, we were told, had had the temerity to demur on receiving the order to prepare a queen's potato patch in full view of her admiring subjects. But the Queen was adamant and would not have it hidden, and the reluctant servant had to obey the order. The nearest analogy to this patch in London would be the formation of a potato patch on the region of the New Mall in the vicinity of the Queen Victoria Statue opposite Buckingham Palace. Other loyal subjects in Christiania had copied the Royal example—not always with like success. In one case where the sloping lawns were heavily shaded with trees the only result of turning them into a potato patch was the production of tall four foot six inch straggling plants which had been dug up and thrown away by October. Queen Maud had a heavy crop by then.

We received bad news here. Our Legation told us that there was a strike on the Finnish railways and that we would not be able to get to Petrograd. Also that the Russians had lost all the ground gained in the brilliant advance brought about earlier in the month by Kerensky's eloquence. Things looked black, all the more so because it was impossible to say how much was truth and how much rumour. At Stockholm next day, however, the Finland railway crisis proved to be false. The strike alluded to was the old one we had read of in the English papers before we had left home. It was over. But that the Christiania Legation should not have known this shows how slow news is in filtering through.

One of our party was an oil-company manager. He had only just managed to escape from Bucharest with his wife and year-old child during the retreat, had taken them to England, and was now on his way to the Caucasus to take charge of a business there. He was enthusiastic over the future of the oil industry in Russia, and said it was going to become one of the most important in the world. As an indication of how the Revolution has upset the old order in Russia, neither this man nor another of our travellers, who had been born in Russia and spent nearly all his life there, but had been in England since the Revolution, could express an opinion on the present position in the country; nor could they form any estimate of the conditions they would go back to.

In Stockholm I first made acquaintance with the bread-card. It was at breakfast an hour after our arrival. The rather grim-looking lady in the restaurant almost smiled when I said I had never heard of a bread-card. Apparently I ought to have got it on the train. Some one had come round, but I must have been asleep. She procured the bread for me. I had forgotten the incident, but it was recalled at lunch. I had missed a companion at a place he told me to go to, and so sat down by myself. A very pretty girl came up to take my order, and to my relief spoke broken English. " Bread-card." " No, I had none," I blushfully stammered as she bent down insinuatingly and asked me for it. I suppose they are used to it, for she laughed, as did the nearest of the guests. Again the bread was forthcoming. I don't know how they manage it. But I provided myself with the indispensable card after this. These cards consist of tiny little slips of stiff paper divided for travellers into nine divisions lasting three days—three a day. Each one allows you one very thin small slice of white bread, one brown ditto, and a thin longish brown rye biscuit as hard as a brick. You can eat all your cards—I mean the bread allowed for them —up at a sitting if you like, but you then go breadless for the rest of the three days unless you can beg divisions from companions; the usual procedure, this latter, I found. Sugar was as bad as at home, both in quality and allowance. It was different in Norway, where white bread, rolls, and butter were plentiful, as also sugar—white loaf sugar, a thing I had not seen for months. Also the prices for food were higher in Sweden than in Norway. But there did not appear to be any lack of money in either capital.

Had the Finnish railway been closed I had meant to have gone on from here to Harparanda, even though I was warned that there was no accommodation and no food, the place consisting of a few wooden tin-roofed huts, an outcome of the war (few had ever heard of the place before, I believe, and yet it has had the distinction of sending forth Russian telegraphic news to an expectant world). But there is a spot near Harparanda, an elevated tableland, from which, for a fortnight, at about this time of the year, the sun is visible at midnight, and I had a mind to see that if possible.

The method of feeding the passengers on the railway when there is no restaurant car on the train is simple and effective. A big centre table in the station restaurant is loaded with hot and cold dishes. The passenger goes to the bar, pays the price of the meal, receives in return the requisite number of plates, and then helps himself and eats as much as he can or as time will permit, whichever gives out first—the best plan I have yet met with.

I do not propose to describe the scenery, but as an economic point of importance in after-the-war reconstruction work, and for some considerable period with us, it is worthy of mention that although the scenery seen passing through Norway and Sweden is chiefly interminable forests with grand rivers and innumerable lakes, by far the bulk of the old forest in both countries has been felled, cut up in the numerous saw-mills and sent to the European timber markets. These latter cannot hope in the future to see for many years to come, or only for a very short period, anything like the quantities they have been receiving for the past half-century or so.

Sweden is a wonderfully neat country to see and travel through. Perhaps the most interesting feature is to note the very full use they make of their water power. In fact, the Swedes say the Americans have copied them in this respect, and that many of the supposed American devices are merely enlarged copies of the Swedish ones. I am unable to offer any opinion on this head, not being an engineer. But I listened to many arguments on this subject between an American and a Swede, both versed in engineering, on my return journey through Sweden. All Sweden is lighted by electricity generated from water power. And the rivers and lakes are utilised to a high degree for floating timber and for cutting it up in the saw-mills. In our own country in this matter of utilising water power we can learn much from the Swedes, and it is to be hoped that when reconstruction sets in after the war we shall not be above doing so.

The biggest town in the north is Boden, a strong garrison town which has its counterpart on the opposite side of the Gulf of Bothnia in Uleaborg in Finland, which is her largest northern military cantonment. I believe the defences of Boden have been entirely remodelled on the lines indicated by the present war, and that it is now almost impregnable. We arrived at Boden at 10 p.m. in broad daylight. The big unfenced station formed the after-dinner promenade of the élite of the town, whilst the fine station restaurant was filled with officers just finishing dinner. All the girls were parading about in thin, flimsy white creations, and though to us from the south the air felt quite fresh, to them it was apparently a fine balmy night.

Harparanda is on the Swedish side of the Tornea river at the head of the Gulf of Bothnia, with Tornea opposite to it on the Finnish side. The extension of the railway to Harparanda is quite recent. Before that passengers had to detrain at Karunga and drive up to Harparanda to cross the river; and a rough time they had of it by all accounts in the winter. The rise of Harparanda is, it may be imagined, purely ephemeral — a by-product of the war which will largely disappear at the peace, especially as a big railway bridge is in process of construction here to join up the Swedish and Finnish railway systems. The Swedes have finished their half and are now completing the Russian section for that country. Tornea, on the other hand, is a very ancient, curious old town of historic interest, which would doubtless boast of tourists in peace-time were it not for its hopeless inaccessibility, situated as it is within a score of miles or so of the Arctic circle.

The transit from Harparanda to Tornea was a lengthy business, taking from 6 a.m. to 4 p.m. The Swedes were very polite and nice over the formalities, and the business was put through expeditiously compared to the delay on the other side. It was the waiting which took the time at Tornea, for the Russian officials were as friendly and nice as possible. They told us that the frontier was to be closed for several days—the time indefinite—and that we were the last lot to be let into Russia till it was reopened. We were in luck. Between the lengthy periods of filling in forms containing all one's family history for a generation or two, being interviewed, and repacking one's kit after it had been through the Customs people's hands, there were some things of interest to see. Wounded prisoners, Russian, German and Austrian, are exchanged up here once a week. A hospital train was slowly drawing into the station at Harparanda as we left, and we met a couple of enormous house-boat barges as we crossed the river. The men are supposed to be *grands blessés* only, but it was difficult to place not a few of the Germans and Austrians we saw in that category. The Russians had crossed the day before, and we saw a number of them in the afternoon. They were appallingly emaciated and thin and ill, and were, so a medical man with us said, more than half starved. Poor devils ! They were dressed in vivid-coloured shirts of the crudest of scarlet, pink, and yellow, a distinctive hospital kit which does not make for beauty.

Prisoners' parcels on a considerable scale go via this route, and to facilitate transit and lessen delay an immense overhead wire-rope railway has been erected over the river, the length of wires being supported on open trestle supports forty to fifty feet high. There are four separate wires, and all day long the big bales, looking exactly like large white flour casks, went creeping backwards and forwards over the wires. The wires were

entirely confined to presents sent by their friends to
prisoners of war.   It was worth seeing and reflecting upon.
Whilst on this subject of prisoners : I had the good fortune
to obtain some very interesting information anent our own
war prisoners in Germany.   A young American joined my
coupé at Tornea, I having been alone so far.   This American
had spent two years in Germany with the American
Mission who had undertaken the work of looking after
the welfare of British prisoners.   He himself worked in
Wurtemburg and Baden.   The Mission had a staff of
fourteen on the job and ran the business pretty much on
the lines of our Y.M.C.A., providing games, books, etc.;
getting up entertainments and supervising the receipt
and distribution of the parcels of food sent out to the
prisoners.   Such contradictory accounts have been received on the subject of the treatment of our prisoners in
Germany that I naturally took such a heaven-sent opportunity of obtaining first-hand information.   I record below
what he told me just as I jotted it down in my diary after
the American had gone to sleep (the conversation occurred
after dinner), whilst we rumbled and jolted our way
through the desolate forest-clad country of North Finland.
Here is the extract—

" The American made a statement well worth recording.   He said that, on the whole, within his charge
(where he was at work for two whole years) the prisoners
were well treated and that with the food parcels received they had plenty to eat within his area.   In fact, he
said, the prisoners did better than himself, as he was often
hard put to it to satisfy his hunger; for he was treated
as a German civilian and only got the latter's rations.
That he would have had a very poor time of it had it not
been for the British officers.   The latter gave him tins of
food of which, said the American, they usually had large
and often excessive supplies owing to the great number of
food parcels sent them.   As to the treatment of prisoners.
He admitted that there were, of course, bad cases of ill-
treatment on the part of a commander of a prison camp
who happened to be a brute by nature.   Also on the part

THE EPHEMERAL "WAR" TOWN OF HAPPARANDA, AS SEEN FROM TORNEA

RUSSIAN SOLDIERS AND SAILORS BUYING RASPBERRIES FROM CHILDREN AT A WAYSIDE STATION
IN FINLAND

of the German N.C.O.'s in striking prisoners—treating them, in fact, as if they were their own soldiers. But on the other side, as must always be the case with armies on the present gigantic scale, there were cases of glaring insubordination on the part of individual prisoners which had to be treated severely, and the Germans' ideas on the subject of treatment differ from ours a good deal.

" This American says that he used to go into the Germans' military training camps, which are now placed near the prison camps, to save soldiers required for guarding the latter. He said the German officers were always anxious to show visitors their methods of training recruits, of which they were very proud. Unfortunately he did not possess the military knowledge which would have enabled him to describe them to me. He used to have meals with them in the German officers' casino. He told me that the military authorities have now swept Germany clean of all men to get her last two millions of reserves, and that so far as man-power goes she has no more at her back. That in this last sweeping are included numbers of men who are really incapacitated by physical infirmities —literally, as he expressed it, ' the blind, the diseased, the halt and the lame '; for partially disabled men were included. That all these were not left in Germany, but were sent to the front or to work behind the lines. That all sentries save the essential ones on the prisoners' camps have been taken off and sent to the front. Also all hospital men orderlies, and so on. That all the office work and other work of the country and towns is done by women, who even do sentry-go round the Palace and public buildings in Berlin and other cities and towns. That a sentry corps had been formed for this purpose, the women being put into uniform.

" As to food, he says the civil population are in very low straits—find it difficult to exist, and that he himself was very run down and low when he left Germany last April owing to America joining the war. He said that the grain crops this year (1917) are very poor owing to the drought, and that he himself expected a sudden collapse. Soldiers

c

are well fed up at the front. The food scarcity in Germany is chiefly in the large cities and towns, especially in the north. That in the country there is more food, as the farmers and peasants will not sell it. The civilian population, even in good hotels, may see a small piece of meat—about two mouthfuls, he expressed it—once a week; for the rest weak soup of cabbage and turnip is the staple food. The bread was the best article of food, as it is all of one uniform quality throughout the country; only five slices a day per person were allowed—about $3\frac{1}{2}$ inches in diameter (they are circular), and $\frac{1}{4}$–$\frac{1}{3}$ inch thick. The discipline in the nation is still good, and he thought that the people liked the Emperor and would maintain some form of the monarchy; that they wished to do so, but with a free parliament and the franchise. When war was imminent with Germany and the American Embassy left, twelve out of the fourteen Americans supervising the prisoners' camps left with the Embassy entourage. He and another man remained to instruct the neutrals, Swiss, Swedes, and Norwegians, who were to carry on the work of supervision. The Americans wished the work to be continued, as they had considerable funds and a large amount of equipment and material connected with entertainments, and so forth, for the prisoners in the country. They had found it difficult to get the class of men required, the absolute neutral neither pro-German or pro-Ally, to take over the job. As the American said, it is absolutely essential to have men who have no political bias at all for this work, and he was doubtful if the world could produce such men nowadays. He doubted whether many of the men they had been trying would be able to carry on the job. He might have added that it will, at any rate, be difficult to replace the efficient Americans at this juncture. His companion had remained on when he left in April. He was treated well by the Germans during his two years. At first all his papers were taken from him and he was not allowed to move about; but after a time these restrictions were removed and he was allowed to travel everywhere free of all restrictions, save the viséing

of his passport. He showed me this latter, a remarkable document, simply black with the *visé* stamps and
signatures. It was a most interesting conversation."

This closes the extract in my diary.

We saw plenty of the new revolutionary soldiers and
sailors *en route* through Finland. They swarmed in
crowds on all the station platforms. But they were not
the soldiery one associates with war-time or, in fact, with
any other time. They were merely an undisciplined mob
in uniform. The Revolution has by no means improved
them, and they are very different from the fine Russian
regiments I had seen in Macedonia the previous year.
There are now four types : (1) The swaggering loafer
who cares for nothing but a full stomach, plenty of
cigarettes, no drills (and, of course, no fighting), and to be
allowed to have his own way. (2) The dull-faced, totally
illiterate man who has only as yet grasped one thing—
that he is to have plenty to eat, to do no drills, and not
to salute or pay any attention to his officers, but must still
obey the Soldiers' Committees and vote as they tell him
to on any question. He understands nothing of the
present situation, but obeys the Committees so long as
there is no chance of his being sent up to the front—
he is in the majority. (3) The sullen, obstinate, strong-
minded ultra-Socialist who is the leader of the Soldiers'
Committees and the mainstay of the Council of Workmen
and Soldiers. He is the dangerous man of the present
time, purposely rude and threatening to all officers and
bourgeoisie, as all who are educated and wear a black coat
are termed, and out to get his rights, *i. e.* equality for all,
equal division of property, and he to rule the new country
and be obeyed in everything. (4) There is a fourth class—
a small minority—the old type of Russian soldier (it is
said it is less abundant in the navy), courteous and
deferential and polite to all he has always recognised as
his superiors. He exists in the cavalry and artillery, who
have mostly remained loyal to the Provisional Government
and Russia, and to a far lesser extent in the infantry.

Two examples of the new state of affairs struck us as

we left Tornea for the south. A Russian troop train had
come up north and was standing at a siding, the wagons
decorated with branches, etc., the men happy at having
got so far from the front. A Russian officer in our train
thus addressed three of the men who were walking between
the trains : " Heh, my friends ! Where are you going to,
colleagues ? " One of the men turned his head and curtly
replied without halting or saluting, speaking not even as
to an equal, but as if he considered the officer an inferior—
as he probably did. The second incident occurred in the
evening in the first-class restaurant car. Two Russian
privates lurched in, sat down in two of the places, and
proceeded to eat the same dinner as we had, partaking of
it mostly with their fingers; they were in a line with my
companion and myself across the alley-way, and made
horrible noises. At the end of the meal one of them produced a Finnish hundred-mark note and tossed it to the
attendant. I was told that a month or two ago they
would not even have paid the bill. But they have plenty
of money nowadays, and can get more when they want it—
those who are of use to the Soldiers' Council. And the
Russian private now gets seven and a half roubles a week
instead of eighty copecks as heretofore ! Think of an
army computed at twelve million men paid at fifteen
shillings a week—and that in Russia !

Finland is chiefly a forest country, a poor duplicate of
Sweden. The climate is too rigorous and the soil too poor
to ever make agriculture a paying business. The class of
arable land seen and the type of crop, including the
miserable little hay crops they were garnering in July,
was a matter of surprise to any one accustomed to the
crops reaped in more equable climates and on more highly
productive soils. The forests, though not of the same
class as the Swedish ones, in the northern half of the country
at any rate, are valuable and will have an increasing value.
In fact, the country will be likely to obtain a fair if not
large income from this source in the future. Lakes and
water power are as plentiful as in Sweden, if not more so.

We reached the frontier between Finland and Russia

at 11 p.m., and after an hour and a half of formalities here finally arrived at Petrograd at 1 a.m. All the prophesies that there would be no droskies and that if there were any they would demand forty roubles to take us to our hotels were falsified. There were lots of these pirates of the Petrograd streets, and I secured one for the drive to the Hotel Europe at a moderate figure. The capital was quiet and wrapped in slumber, and showed no evidence of its past few months of excitement.

CHAPTER III

RUSSIA AFTER THE REVOLUTION (APRIL—JULY)

RÉSUMÉ OF CHIEF EVENTS—RUSSIAN OFFENSIVE ON THE
SOUTH-WESTERN FRONT

A BRIEF *résumé* of the chief events which took place
during the three months following the Revolution is a
necessary preliminary to a narrative dealing with the period
which ended with the fall of the Provisional Government
in November 1917, and the seizure of the supreme power
by the Bolsheviks under Lenin and Trotsky. The Czar
abdicated on March 15th, the Duma then becoming the
controlling authority of the country. The Duma, whose
members mainly consisted of the *bourgeoisie*, set up the first
Provisional Government, a Cabinet of Ministers, who then
became the legal governing authority. But they quickly
found a rival in the Council of Workmen and Soldiers
who represented the Socialists. This body had grown
out of the Petrograd Council of Labour first formed during
the Revolution of 1905. In the early days of the March
Revolution some of the socialistic workers in Petrograd
revived this Council, and in order to give it added strength
brought soldiers into it, the body thus constituted styling
itself the Council (Soviet) of Workmen and Soldiers. This
Council very soon claimed all the honour of having made the
Revolution, and from the first, although it was not at once
recognised, dominated the Provisional Government. The
Prime Minister of the latter was Prince Lvoff, who held
the portfolio of the Interior. The other Ministers were Miliukoff, Foreign Affairs; Shingareff, Agriculture; Gutchkoff,
War; Tereshchenko, Finance; and Kerensky, Justice,
the latter a Socialist and vice-president of the Council of

Workmen and Soldiers. The president of the latter body was Tchkheidze, a man of considerable personality, and one destined to play a leading part in the months to come. The Council had at their back from the beginning the labour classes and peasantry. Within a few months they secured the support of masses of the troops in the rear.

The Provisional Government initiated radical changes in the administration of the country. Decrees granted full amnesty to all political prisoners, removed all the Romanoffs, and those known to favour them, from official posts, issued a Manifesto completely restoring the Constitution of Finland, emancipated the Jews, and addressed a rescript to the Poles stating that Russia regarded an independent Polish State as a pledge of a durable peace. The Government then abolished the death penalty, one of the steps which were ultimately to cause its downfall and led to untold misery in Russia. The Government declared itself in favour of Woman Suffrage, and agreed to the suggestion that all the land should be distributed amongst the peasants. But the method of distribution they left to the Constituent Assembly, a body which was to be elected by universal suffrage and which would ultimately decide the form of the Government of the country. International problems, questions of nationality rights, so soon to assume a formidable place in Russian politics, agrarian and labour legislation, and the abolition of titles, classes, etc., were also to be left for the decision of the Constituent Assembly. The origin of the Council of Workmen and Soldiers in Petrograd has been described. Similar councils were formed throughout the towns of the country, and these soon arrogated to themselves the positions of the Zemstvos Committees which had done such excellent work during the war. Throughout the country the old police were replaced by a militia, an inefficient force of very little use for the most part.

A later step taken by the Provisional Government was the issue of the " Soldiers' Charter." This charter was drawn up with a view to removing many of the gross abuses of power which existed in the army under the Czar, and with a view to democratising the army. But it went too far. This charter was not the work of Gutchkoff, first War Minister. Finding, even in these early days, that it was impossible to work with the Council of Workmen and Soldiers, he had resigned, as had Miliukoff for the same reason, though a different cause. Kerensky was now War Minister, and issued the charter. Under its provisions the soldiery were accorded equal citizens rights, freedom in religion and speech, equal freedom with other citizens in matters relating to correspondence and receipt of printed matter (subsequently taken full advantage of by the German propagandist), permission to wear civilian dress off duty, abolition of servile terms in addressing officers, abolition of saluting officers or serving them as orderlies, and abolition of corporal punishment.

To the issue of this charter, the abolition of the death penalty, both the work of the Provisional Government, and the famous Prikaz (Order of the Day) No. 1, published by the Council of Workmen and Soldiers, which resulted in the formation of the Soldiers' Committees, must be attributed the subsequent break up and ruin of the Russian Army. The Prikaz was the first of the three to be issued, and its history is as follows : Whilst the Revolution was in progress the allegiance of the soldiers was made to the Duma, which assumed the authority laid down by the Czar. These soldiers included some of the most famous of the Russian regiments, as also the Cossacks. The Duma had in its ranks many of the ablest men in Russia, but they did not act with the promptitude and firmness the times required. One of the first acts taken by some of the Bolshevik military members of the Council, immediately after the triumph and whilst the nation was intoxicated with its new-found freedom, was the issue of Prikaz No. 1, which practically resulted in the abolishment of discipline in the army. The draft of the Prikaz was carried by some soldiers to the President of the Military Commission of the Duma, who refused to accept or issue it, a decision in which he was supported by the Provisional Committee of the Duma. This was on March 14th. " Very well," said the soldier delegates, " we will issue it ourselves." It appeared the following day. The main provisions of the Prikaz were the election of the subaltern officers by the soldiers themselves, retention of their arms by the soldiers, and the superintendence by Soldier Committees of the administration of their own units. In practice it put the private on an equality with his officer, whom he addressed as tvaritch (comrade). In times of peace this must have bred trouble. With the nation at war and the subversal of discipline which followed, its consequences have been incalculable.

The political parties in Russia are subdivided as in other countries, and these subdivisions have led to curious misconceptions amongst foreigners as to their aims and objects. It must also be admitted that the opinions of the subdivisions underwent some considerable modifications or the reverse as time went on. Generally speaking, the Cadet or Constitutional Democratic party consisted of the intellectual classes, the *bourgeoisie*. With the exception of the socialist Kerensky they formed the first Provisional Government. This party contains a large number of very able men, and before the Revolution they were aiming at a Constitutional Monarchy, and for a short time subsequent to the upheaval. But at a Congress held early in April the delegates voted unanimously for a Democratic and Parliamentary Republic. The Socialists consisted of two main groups, Social Democrats and Socialist revolutionaries. The chief aim of the first was to ensure that labour should dominate capital; of the second to secure the land for the peasants. Both these groups were, however, subdivided within themselves. The Social Democrats consisted chiefly of Bolsheviks with a smaller Menshevik group. The Social Revolutionaries were subdivided into Maximalists and Minimalists. The ranks of the Maximalists included the Anarchists and Terrorists of the old regime. Many of these had been bribed by the old police to enter the Terrorist party in order to act as spies on it. These men still remained, and were a grave menace to the country, since their old source of income was gone. As the Bolsheviks also believed in violence, the Bolsheviks and Maximalists formed an alliance. It is known that many of the old Terrorists were Jews, clever unscrupulous men who made a profession of this business. They were now in power in the Petrograd Soviet or Council, bearing Russian names. The best known to foreigners are Lenin (real name Zederblum), Trotsky (Bronstein), Tchernoff (Feldmann), Parvies (Helfand), Bogdanoff (Seffer), Martoff (Zederbaum), Kameneff (Rosenfeld), Goreff (Goldmann), Sukhanoff (Himmer), Stekloff (Nahamkes), the latter the reputed author of Prikaz No. 1, and so forth. The Mensheviks, with Tchkheidze and Tseretelli at their head, with the Minimalists (under Kerensky), wished to allow the Duma to govern the country until they felt they had sufficient backing to dominate the Provisional Government and perhaps seize the power. The Bolsheviks and Maximalists, on the other hand, wished to push through their creed early and by force, and with this object they systematically set to work to wreck the army, the one power they feared as long as it retained its discipline. In this they were immensely helped by the horde of German spies and by German gold, both of which were placed plentifully at their disposal.

It was the fight against the rot setting in in the army in the rear that first brought General Korniloff, the Cossack General who escaped whilst a prisoner in Austria, into notice, he having been appointed to the command of the Petrograd military district. After carrying on this unequal struggle for a time, he asked to be relieved and given a command in the field.

One of the administrative pieces of work which occupied the attention of the first Cabinet was the question of the finances of the country. It was realised that Russia could only be financially rehabilitated by developing her great resources, and to this end they wished to invite foreign capital into the country. In this they were opposed by the Socialists, who did not believe in economic expansion.

KERENSKY CARRYING THE FIERY CROSS ROUND THE FRONT IN JUNE, 1917

KERENSKY ADDRESSING THE TROOPS AT THE FRONT IN JUNE, 1917

KERENSKY IN THE TRENCHES IN JUNE, 1917

Miliukoff's resignation came about through a difference of this kind. He had advocated the annexation of Constantinople as an economic necessity for Russia. The Socialists were against all annexations, and the Council of Workmen and Soldiers at once protested. The Prime Minister explained that Miliukoff's statement was only an exposition of his own views on the matter—not those of the Government. But the Government were forced by the agitation set on foot to issue a declaration denouncing all aims towards annexations and war indemnities. This step was taken to save the Cabinet, but it was taken unwillingly. Miliukoff sent this declaration of the Cabinet to the Allies with a note : " It is understood, and the annexed document expressly states, that the Provisional Government, in safeguarding the rights acquired for our country, will maintain a strict regard for its engagements with the Allies of Russia." This note gave rise to an outburst from the Socialists, aided by the German spies who were swarming in the capital. The Bolsheviks led this campaign, headed by Lenin, who had recently arrived at Petrograd from Switzerland via Germany. Lenin went too far, and was not supported in his pacifist campaign by the Council of Workmen and Soldiers. The aim and hope of this body was in effect a revolution amongst the workers of Europe, with the object of overthrowing all the European Governments and secret diplomacy and governing through the masses. The policy of conquest was to be suppressed, but they would fight to save their own country from invasion. To this end they appealed confidently to the workers in the enemy States to rise and overthrow their rulers. A crisis supervened, and Miliukoff resigned.

A national Congress of the Councils of Workmen and Soldiers from all over the country followed shortly after the Cadet Congress. At this Congress the policy of maintaining a firm control over the actions of the Provisional Government was definitely announced, in order to prevent it from siding with the counter-revolutionary forces, and to assist the Government in obtaining a peace based on a free national development for all peoples and without annexations or indemnities. The Congress appealed to the whole revolutionary democracy to rally round the Council and to support the Provisional Government, so long as its foreign policy was free from all desires for territorial expansion and provided that it maintained the Revolution. The democracy was also asked to aid the Council in preventing the Government from endeavouring to weaken the control of the democracy, or renouncing any of the pledges made to it.

The actions of the Soviet had not left the army untouched. The pernicious influence of the committees and propagandists had a startling effect on the previously well-disciplined masses of soldiery at the front, whilst the rear degenerated even more rapidly. At the front the creed of no annexations and no indemnities naturally left the soldiers wondering what they were fighting for. The Germans, after breaking the Russian lines on the Stokhod with ease, ceased fighting and commenced fraternising instead, an occupation they steadily pursued for some time. General Alexeieff, who had been appointed Commander-in-Chief after the Revolution, worked hard but without success to stem this deplorable tide.

After the Government's declaration of no annexations, etc., the Council of Workmen and Soldiers stated that their policy of no annexations had now become an international question and that democracy had thereby scored a great victory. It was, however, as it turned out, a great blow at the efficiency of the army.

Gutchkoff followed Miliukoff into retirement, and the first non-socialistic Government gave place to a coalition containing several Socialists. Lvoff remained Premier; Kerensky became Minister of War and Marine instead of Justice; Tereshchenko, Foreign Affairs instead of Finance; Shirgareff, Finance instead of Agriculture ; and Konovaloff, Commerce and Industry. Five Socialists entered the Ministry. Tchernoff, Agriculture; Skobeleff, Labour; Tseretelli, Posts and Telegraphs; Pereverzeff, Justice; and Peshekhonoff, Munitions. The Duma appeared officially for the last time at a Conference which preceded the formation of this Cabinet. From now onwards it disappeared before the socialistic advance. The soldier's charter was Kerensky's first act in his new position. It had effects which may or may not have been anticipated. Generals Alexeieff and the Commander of the Central Front, Gurko, resigned (the latter being then degraded by Kerensky), Brusiloff taking the former's place, and the veteran Ruzsky was dismissed from the Command of the Northern Front. It appeared as if the army would then and there crumble to pieces. But Kerensky now took a step which had extraordinary results. He went round the front with a fiery cross and an intense enthusiasm, his great oratorical gift assuring him a hearing wherever he went. Though he himself deplored the fact, when some one asked him whether he imagined that all his soldier audiences could understand him, that probably not more than one man in a hundred could so do. This fact mattered little for the moment, however, as the enthusiasm his mere appearance aroused was contagious. He preached an offensive, and the last brilliant and meteoric advance of the Russian Army came off. But in acting in this fashion, Kerensky, who ever placed his country above his socialism, was far from carrying out the wishes of the Workmen and Soldiers' Council. Tchernoff, speaking to delegates from the front, actually said : " A peace must be concluded in which there shall be no victors and no vanquished. Appeals have been published for an immediate attack, but the army should take advantage of the present calm at the front to organise itself, and then it will not need any prompting, as it will know itself what to do." At this juncture the Cadet Minister of Commerce, Konovaloff, declaring that the class war being fomented by Tchernoff and Skobeleff would result in a catastrophe, resigned. But even the Soviet was carried away by the general enthusiasm when the advance of the armies commenced.

The bait by which the Council attracted the workmen to their support was a six hours' day and constant increases in wages; that for the peasants was the division of all land amongst them, of which Tchernoff was the chief exponent. During the period under review the Moderate Socialists joined with the Bolsheviks in debauching the three classes of the masses—the soldiers, workmen, and peasants. It was not till much later that the Moderates, realising the peril the country had been placed in, split definitely with the Bolsheviks—and then it was too late.

The Ukrainian question, the first of the nationality questions which were to result in, it is to be hoped, a temporary dismemberment of the Russian Empire, now came into view. Soon after the Revolution a Council, or Central Rada as it was called, was formed at Kieff which said it spoke for the Ukrainian nation. It decided to call a Constituent Assembly into being in order to settle a form of government for the Ukrainians. The local Socialists were alarmed at this move, but were told that the Provisional Government had sanctioned it. Soon after a Congress of Representatives voted for autonomy in a federal Russian Republic, and the area to be governed by the Ukrainians was extended to Poltava, Kharkoff and Odessa. Kerensky visited Kieff, and promised that if they would wait till the Constituent Assembly met most of their wishes would be granted. But the Rada asked for more than this promise, and a Congress of soldiers and peasants sitting at Kieff voted for far more than the Rada was asking for. The Provisional Government endeavoured to compromise with the Rada, the Council of Workmen and Soldiers backing them up. But the Rada refused to be put off with promises, and issued a statement saying that they would henceforth manage their own affairs. They proceeded to form a General Secretariat with Vinnichenko as President. Tseretelli and Tereshchenko appear to have concluded an agreement with the Rada without the knowledge of the other Ministers, and this agreement, based on the grant of certain rights to the Rada, subsequently produced a Cabinet crisis. The Rada had refused to admit that the Secretariat should in any way be responsible to the Provisional Government, and the latter gave way for the moment. This conflict was to wage through the later months of the sway of the Provisional Government.

The food and financial situation grew steadily worse. In spite of the network of Food Committees the Government had set up, food was very irregularly distributed, and the amount available in the north grew steadily less, owing to the deterioration in the working of the railways and to the holding up of supplies by the peasants. Demoralisation and disorganisation had commenced to take a real hold on the country. The financial question was aggravated by the enormous increases in salaries and pay all round, and already the State bank was issuing 50 million roubles of paper money daily.

The Moderate Socialists predominated in the capital, as was evidenced by the elections held in June for the District Councils in Petrograd, in which the soldiers took part. The Socialists obtained 299 seats, Cadets 185, and Bolsheviks 156. This was followed by the All-Russian Congress of Soviets in the middle of the month under Tchkheidze and Tseretelli. These two leaders had prepared beforehand the resolutions which were to be passed by the meeting.

Kerensky delivered an oration and was warmly applauded. There was a great deal of talk by the members. Tseretelli held that a separate peace was impossible. Lenin said that Kerensky's efforts to bring about an offensive were treason to the cause of international socialism, and intimated that his party, which Kerensky alluded to as " an isolated and unorganised group," could and would save the situation. It was this Congress that Ramsay McDonald was to have attended. It is perhaps a pity that more effective measures were not taken to ensure his presence. Our Labour representatives who had been previously sent out from home were too moderate in their opinions for the most part to appeal to the Bolshevik, and even the bulk of the other members of the Soviet. Mr. O'Grady, M.P., appears to have made the greatest impression on the soldiers when he visited them at the front. I had an interesting conversation in August with a Russian corporal who had been in England for several years. He had heard O'Grady speak on several occasions, of course with an interpreter. The corporal said : " I was able to understand both speech and interpretation, and also the remarks of my companions. They liked O'Grady. If you had had a number of O'Grady's at our front and had kept them there things would be easier now." That was the mistake. We should have sent more propagandists and kept them there.

The Bolsheviks asked the meeting to devote their efforts to compelling the Imperialistic Governments of Great Britain and France to adhere to the principles proclaimed by Revolutionary Democratic Russia. The Congress at length passed the resolutions appealing to the people to refrain from armed demonstrations " without the consent of the Soviet," and with reference to the war, " that it could not be ended by the efforts of international democracy." " The breaking of the Russian front would mean the defeat of the Russian Revolution and a fatal blow to the cause of international democracy."

But the Congress went further, and touched on other points which were to appear in many forms during the next few months; and therein lies the importance of this meeting. They spoke directly to the democracies of the Allies and enemy nations, telling them that the lack of energy exhibited in their protests against recent statements of their Governments with reference to their annexation war aims was placing the Russian Revolution in a very difficult position. They asked for a socialistic conference of the Allies and neutrals, and protested against the difficulties which the Imperialistic Governments (England and France, the latter being an efficient republic !) were placing in the way of the assembling of such delegates; and wound up with the statement that the diplomatic service should be democratised. In order that it should be on hand if trouble ensued, the President of the Duma, Rodzianko, had summoned all the members to be present in the capital. The Congress looked upon this as an attempt at a counter-revolution, and decided that the Duma should be abolished—a step they had not the power to enforce, nor did it take place for several months, although it ceased to be an active factor in politics.

A Cossack Congress had assembled in Petrograd at this time. The Cossacks had remained loyal to the country— one of the most astonishing things about the Revolution. They decided to support the Duma, to fight the enemy without and the enemy within, and to reconstitute a Cossack army on the old lines. They also expressed themselves freely on Lenin and all traitors, saying that they should be proceeded against; and unanimously decided that all the land now belonging to the Cossacks would remain in their possession. The Government could feel that in the Cossacks they had a body of troops on whom they could depend—provided they treated them fairly.

The one aspect of the Revolution which has most struck the foreigner was the extraordinary little bloodshed which accompanied it. The officers suffered the most heavily, if we omit the hated police. At Helsingfors and Kronstadt massacres of officers took place in the Baltic Fleet, assisted largely by Bolsheviks, Finns, Swedes, and German Socialists. These massacres were ghastly, the officers being hunted round the ships like rats. The army also suffered severely in this way. But the toll of civilian life was extraordinarily small, almost negligible, in fact, when the magnitude of the upheaval is taken into account. July found the situation in Petrograd already extremely bad, but there was hope and faith still extant in the army and navy, in spite of the Bolshevik and German propaganda which was permeating it and had already demoralised the masses of soldiers in the rear, especially in the north near Petrograd and Kronstadt. The Black Sea Fleet up to now had remained unaffected. It was sailors from this fleet whom Kerensky took with him on his crusade round the front.

The result of Kerensky's fervid oratory and patriotism was now to bear fruit. The proposed thrust was decided for the south-western front, as being the furthest from the demoralising influences of Petrograd. Further south, in Roumania, although the Roumanian troops were ready and thirsting for the fray, the Russian troops on that sector were more than a doubtful problem. They could not be counted upon to assist the Roumanians. Galicia and Bukovina

D

were to be the theatres, then, of the first offensive, to be followed, if successful, by a thrust in the Vilna direction and a third in Roumania. Owing to the railway disorganisation the south-western offensive was delayed, the work of agitators amongst the troops having also to be controlled. In this latter the Soldiers' Committees gave the Generals great assistance, these committees at this period on the south-western front working loyally in the best interests of the army; and in the subsequent attacks many of these men fell at the head of the troops—men whom their country could ill spare. If this example had been followed by the committees on the other fronts the Russian Army would have maintained its traditions. General Gutor was in command of the three armies, the 11th, 9th, and 8th, which were to undertake the offensive, and military experts appear to agree that his stragetic dispositions were at fault, in view of the fact that the troops under his command were partly demoralised by the insidious propaganda pervading their ranks. His central attack was a frontal one in the dense forests round Brzezany, instead of being made in the open. The armies were well equipped with artillery and had an abundance of ammunition, and the British armoured cars under Commander O. Locker Lampson, M.P., D.S.O., assisted and did magnificent work. It was said that they held up the whole German Army in this sector for several days later on in the big retreat. The offensive started on the morning of July 1st against the strong Brzezany position, and in the two first days the Russians took prisoners 300 officers and 18,000 men, 29 guns, and 33 machine-guns. But by this time the troops were proving very unreliable, and refused to stop in the front-line trenches more than twenty-four hours at a time, and then only to act on the defensive. Even Kerensky's fervid orations passed unheeded, and the soldiers even threatened him with violence. Korniloff's 8th Army was the only one which more than carried out the objective set it. It did not go into action until a week after the offensive started. His army was east of Stanislau, and it met with such success that it is said that had he been more strongly supported he could easily have reached Rohatyn from Halicz, turned the strong Brzezany position, and reached Dolima south of Lemberg, thereby severing the enemy's communications and isolating some of his forces. This success could have been attained, say the Russian experts, had the main attack been thrown on the Korniloff wing. Korniloff did brilliantly, retaking ground lost in the retreat of 1915, including Halicz, a bridgehead of high strategic value. With the recognition of Korniloff's success, reinforcements were sent up to him, but they came too late to be of use. The main attack at Brzezany, where the troops fought gallantly at first, was held up by the impregnable nature of the position. And the heavy losses here resulted in indiscipline which was fomented by the Bolshevik agitators in the ranks.

The offensive brought about entirely by Kerensky's impassioned eloquence and fervid patriotism was at an end.

CHAPTER IV

PETROGRAD IN THE LATTER HALF OF JULY

July 16*th*–18*th*.—The meteoric advance of the south-western armies brought about by Kerensky united all parties for the moment in a common enthusiasm. But the indiscipline and inactivity which arrested the offensive were soon reflected in the capital, and Socialists and Cadets each accused the other of being the cause; whilst the Bolsheviks, in agreement with the German agents, matured their plans which had as object nothing less than the overthrow of the Government, the seizure of the power by themselves, and the signing of peace. It was to this end that they brought about the arrestation of the advance on the south-western front. The bolt fell with the sudden rising in Petrograd on July 16th, an attack designed to coincide with the German plan for an advance against the armies who had been engaged in the Russian offensive. The Ukrainian question had led to the resignation of the Cadet Ministers on the previous day. The confusion in the Cabinet was therefore an opportune moment for the Bolshevik plot, which was as follows : The garrison were to arrest the members of the Cabinet; the Baltic Fleet was to move to Kronstadt and thence reinforce Petrograd with the disaffected element from the former place. Lenin, who was at the head of the movement, having captured the capital, intended to at once open peace *pourparlers* with Germany, so as to ingratiate himself with the army and workers and intrench himself in the position secured. This plan was foiled by the Cossacks. For three days, from 16th to 18th, the capital was in a turmoil, at the end of which period the Government had put down the rising and captured a number of those implicated, including Trotsky, Kameneff and Stekloff, the rest escaping into Finland. Lenin disappeared. So far as Petrograd was concerned the matter was over for the moment. But it was responsible for a disaster of far greater magnitude. The Bolsheviks had sent a wireless message before the rising to their agents in the south-western army, instructing the latter to spread the news that the Government had been deposed, the capital captured, and that peace was to be signed. Its effect, with disaffection so rife in the ranks, can be imagined. Before the false news could be denied the mischief was done. It had its direct result in the opening of the Russian front, a result fully anticipated by Germany, whose Machiavelian policy had brought about the conditions for which she was prepared.

The extracts from my diary commence here.

July 20th.—Kerensky has formed a temporary coalition Government, and has himself become Premier. He is having a remarkable career. Minister of Justice, Minister of War, and now Premier all in four months. The rising of 16th to 18th has had one result. The Council of Workmen and Soldiers, who for the most part are not in sympathy with the Bolsheviks, are almost as frightened as the Government at the outbreak, during which some hundreds of people were killed in the firing, including five Cossacks. The feeling in the capital is very high, and if it can only be maintained the Bolsheviks are little likely to be able to bring off another *coup*. According to the papers they have also alienated the sympathy of the country as a whole. Tchernoff was one of those arrested by the soldiery as implicated. Whether he was guilty or no is apparently doubtful. He has been released. The Cadets are very bitter. They point out the dastardly nature of the attempt made at the hour when the Russian Armies were achieving victory over the enemy in the field. They demand the arrest of Lenin and all implicated, and their trial by the ordinary courts; that the Government should no longer be influenced by men who have not the welfare of their country at heart, and that the civil liberties and life itself should no longer be endangered by a handful of criminals. A firm and undivided authority is necessary, they say, to carry the country peacefully on to the Constituent Assembly.

" If democracy is to rule the world of the future it must be an educated democracy; and education can only come slowly and must be built up gradually. Unless this is clearly understood and the world makes up its mind to recognise the danger to civilisation of an undisciplined, uneducated and unintellectual democracy grasping the helm, the upheaval, chaos, misery, and death produced by the present war will be as nothing to the menace which will face the world after the war is over." This was the expressed opinion of some who have closely studied the matter within twenty-four hours after our arrival in Petrograd, during which hours we had been receiving our first doses of a democracy run mad. The incident amongst others which originated the discussion was the following—

We arrived at Biels ostrov on the Finnish-Russian frontier at 11 p.m., and were all requested to leave our carriages and proceed to a small room there to fill in forms and to await our turn to be examined. A deputation of Russian sailors from the fleet at Helsingfors had arrived here *en route* to Petrograd. They were about fifteen in number, representing various ships, and had apparently left the fleet without orders, or any other order than that of one of the committees in existence. A series of telegrams on the subject of these men had been received at the passport office here from the Provisional Government, ordering the men back to their ships and stating that they were on no account to be allowed to continue their journey to Petrograd. These men were collected in a knot in the *salle d' attente*, and showed, by the surprise exhibited on their faces, that they were dumbfounded at the order communicated to them. The lower ranks of both army and navy had become so accustomed to having their own way. This order was explained by one of the military passport officers, who had come out from the inner room into which the passengers were called in turn for examination. When they had grasped the purport of the officer's remarks, surprise quickly gave place to anger, and I have rarely seen uglier looks on men's faces. They disputed loudly and hotly with the officer, and attempted to invade the inner room by force. They were prevented from doing this, but two got in only to be sent out again immediately. Then the officer began arguing and expostulating with the men, and explaining the telegram, and his demeanour throughout called for commiseration. Obviously his orders were to get the men to listen to and accept the ultimatum, and I did not envy him the job. He assumed a most conciliatory air, tried cajolery, appealed to the private soldier assistants and orderlies of the passport office to confirm what he said; resorted to begging the sailors to listen, and spoke at times as an inferior to superiors. To a remark he went inside the office and returned with a sheath of telegrams which he offered to several of them to read for themselves. It was a painful business to watch, and one withal of the most dangerous. And the men— some shouted and tried threats; others scowled; a few exhibited perplexed worried faces, showing plainly that they only dimly realised what was taking place; that their brains, in fact, were incapable of understanding a tithe of the arguments the officer was using in the interests of his country, and of the Revolution itself, which they were so gravely imperilling by their insubordination. One face stood out from the rest and riveted the attention. A fine, strong, almost open seaman's face, but marred by a set, defiant, obstinate look, the thin lips compressed in a straight line. This man uttered no word. But it was not difficult to guess at the thoughts passing behind that face. He was of the true revolutionary type, possessed of the one fixed idea that all the power should be in the hands of the people, with equal division of property. Yet he lacked the training and education which would have shown him to what such a creed must lead to with totally uneducated masses. He was out to be a leader of the mob, but would exact the obedience and discipline he would not give himself, and would brook no deviation from his own narrow creed and hard-and-fast ideas. He was the most dangerous of the party. When some of the men had disappeared to harangue the crowd outside—we saw them at it later—he remained still and icily cold, took the papers from the officer without a word and read slowly through some of them with darkening and lowering brow. A deep-chested, broad-shouldered, powerful man, he had the appearance of having been a magnificent sailor before the Revolution had come to throw his great country into chaos, and unsettle such minds as his with visionary chimeras. He and his type are a positive menace to their country. Difficult men these to deal with in the Russia of to-day, men whom oratory alone will not sway as it does for the moment the rest. Men whom the world will hear of before long, unless a strong man arises in Russia to quell and dispose of them. And that man will have to be both strong and ruthless. Outside the passport office three officers of high rank stood on the platform. One was a fine tall officer of Cossacks, the second in the uniform of some Circassian regiment, whilst the third was in the dress of the infantry of the line. The passing soldiers took no more notice of them than if they had been railway porters—in fact less. The officers were evidently discussing the attitude of the sailor deputation, and their faces were very grave. It was easy to read that the seriousness of their country's position, coupled with the grave news from the front that the Russians were in retreat, was filling them with anxiety. And who could wonder! The sailor deputation did not leave on our train.

July 25th.—The Russians have broken their front in the neighbourhood of Tarnapol. The break commenced on the 19th at Zwyzen, north of Zborow, the 6th Grenadier Division deserting and fleeing. The disaffection of this division left its neighbours in the air, who in their turn broke and fled. Every day has since widened the breach, and the Germans and Austrians, previously prepared, it would appear, are advancing rapidly. From the reports in the papers the whole of the armies in this part of the front appear to have become stricken with panic, the soldiers leaving everything behind them and fleeing for their lives. As yet there do not appear to be any large forces against them, whereas the Russians are known to have had a concentration of troops at this point. Under the influence of Bolshevik propaganda the men seem to have lost their senses, and generals, officers, the commissaries and the military committees, are all apparently, according to the reports, powerless to stay the rout. The details in the papers are most disheartening to read; the more so that there are glorious episodes, vain sacrifices by regiments and individuals, in the effort to stem the tide of retreat and disgrace. The panic-stricken soldiery in their mad flight are sacking the towns and villages they pass through, towns and villages of their own homeland, violating women and killing the children. Our armoured cars, as also those of the Belgians, are performing prodigies of valour in holding up the enemy and enabling guns, etc., to be got off, but from accounts little is being got away and the enemy are likely to pick up immense booty. There are still hopes that the widening of the breach may be stopped, but the reports on this head are conflicting. It is a maddening record to read, and must put the eastern front in serious jeopardy.

There has been a serious mutiny in the Baltic Fleet. This mutiny was in connection apparently with the recent rising, some of the ships, whose crews are of Bolshevik persuasion, designing to aid the movement. Admiral Verderevsky, in command of the fleet, was ordered to despatch some submarines with instructions to blow up any of the ships which left Helsingfors for Kronstadt. This order the Admiral could not carry out, and several ships arrived at Kronstadt, but too late to take part in the rising, which by then had been quelled. The Provisional Government have arrested the leaders and deputation from the Baltic Fleet which recently arrived in Petrograd. The following Prikaz has been issued by Kerensky—

(1) The immediate dissolution of the central committee of the Baltic Fleet, and the election of a new one.

(2) All individuals implicated in the recent rising in Petrograd, and in the stopping of our offensive on the front are to be removed from the fleet and sent to Petrograd for trial.

(3) The detachments at Kronstadt and the battleships *Petropavlovsk*, *Republic*, and *Slava* are to arrest the ringleaders of the mutiny within twenty-four hours and send them to Petrograd for trial. If this order is not carried out, the Kronstadt detachment and crews of the ships will be branded as traitors and will be proceeded against.

July 26th.—Tarnapol was occupied by the enemy on July 22nd. A riot took place in the town before it was taken, but an officers' battalion, one of the " Battalions of Death " as they are called, formed entirely of officers whose regiments have deserted, or who have themselves been dismissed from the regiments by the Soldiers' Committees, quelled it by shooting down the soldier rioters. They also set fire to as much of the accumulation of stores in the place as possible. Commander Locker Lampson's armoured cars are reported to be doing marvellous work in assisting the Russian Generals in their endeavour to stop the wild panic and introduce some order into the retreat so that it may be stayed and fresh positions in the rear be taken up. Although the death penalty had been abrogated by Kerensky, Korniloff, who has been placed in command with orders to stop the retreat, has reintroduced it on his own responsibility. The following is his order to army commanders and commissioners : " I consider the voluntary retirement of troops from their positions as equivalent to treason and treachery. Therefore I require that all commanders in such cases should, without limitation, turn the fire of machine-guns and artillery against the traitors. I take all responsibility for the victims on myself. Inaction and hesitation on the part of commanders I shall count as neglect of duty, and such officers I shall at once deprive of their commands and commit for trial." Korniloff notified the Provisional Government of his action.

Brusiloff, to whom the telegram was also sent, supported Korniloff in an urgent communication despatched to the

Government. Korniloff received from the Provisional
Government on the following day an authorisation to
employ any and every method he deemed advisable to
stop the rout and restore order. The Cabinet, it is obvious,
are now thoroughly frightened at the position of affairs.
The Government accorded the men the power to form committees, to hold meetings and to discuss whether they
should, or should not obey orders received from their
officers. Such meetings were held at the beginning of the
great retreat and have been held throughout, so we are
told, wherever a unit held together. This is the result!
In confirmation of the sanction accorded to Korniloff
the Government have issued a Prikaz. It is signed by
Kerensky, Efremoff, Minister of Justice, and General
Yakubovitch, and restores the death penalty in the army
during the war. In this Prikaz the crimes punishable by
death are enumerated, as also the composition of the
military revolutionary courts to try offenders. They are
to consist of three officers, and three soldiers chosen by lot.
The verdict to be in a majority of votes. If the voting is
equal the prisoner will get the benefit.

July 29*th*.—Petrograd is settling down again. The
rising is a thing of the past. On the surface the capital
has much the same appearance it presented in the days of
the Czar before the war. The same cosmopolitan crowd,
intent on its own pleasure and amusement, fills the Nevski,
but though the bulk of the soldiery have a loafing, brazen
or furtive look about them, there is still a residue who
salute their officers in the streets of the capital. That
much is to the good, at any rate, and might easily prove
significant of a change for the better. The one change
for the bad is in the food and prices. The latter are preposterous, and the former of poor quality and small in
quantity. At the Hôtel Europe, where they did you *en
prince* in old days, in this respect there is a great change.
The waiters have imbibed the revolutionary spirit and
their service for a first-class hotel, as this used to be, is
beneath contempt. Coffee, black bread and butter (when
present, or a minute dole of jam if absent), costs 2.50;

A REVOLUTIONARY PROCESSION PASSING THE BRITISH EMBASSY IN PETROGRAD

KERENSKY ADDRESSING OFFICERS AT THE FRONT IN JUNE, 1917

KERENSKY DISCUSSING THE PROPOSED OFFENSIVE ON THE
S.W. FRONT IN JUNE, 1917

lunch, which is *à la carte*, gives you a choice of soup at three roubles, fish and meat courses at five roubles apiece, small portions only; and *compote* of fruit at four roubles; coffee 1.50 (they give you *jam* with black coffee when there is no sugar !). Dinner of four courses—soup, fish, meat and *compote*, all attenuated dishes, costs ten roubles (one rouble equalled two shillings before the war). The bread is black, very badly baked—a nauseous mass like putty in consistency, and very sour to the taste. If you pick up three or four slices laid together and throw it at the wall, it drops as one piece with a dull thud. This stuff never varies. It is always exceedingly nasty. Occasionally there is a little browny yellow bread slightly better to the palate by comparison. There is, of course, nothing to drink except a vile mixture in cream, yellow and black called kwass. I tried it to-day for the first and last time. It tastes like rotten fruit and decaying fish mixed together. Soda water, nasty tepid stuff, is a rouble per bottle. There is no wine or spirits. They say champagne is to be had by the initiated at fifty to eighty roubles a bottle, and cognac at twenty to forty. I have seen none, however. I had been warned of the outlook in these matters before me, but they are exceeding by a good deal my most pessimistic forecast.

A very impressive funeral was accorded yesterday to the five Cossack soldiers who were killed in the three days' outbreak. This funeral was attended in state by all the high dignitaries of the Church and State, and was an imposing religious ceremony.

It was intended as a rebuke, I was told, to the Red Socialist groups who had organised the funeral of the victims of the Revolution. These latter were buried in the centre of the Champ de Mars, and the graves are now covered with grass. The bodies were enclosed in red coffins and were escorted to the burial-place by a giant multitude waving thousands of red banners; but no clergy were permitted to officiate, and there was no religious ceremony whatsoever. It is said that several of the relations engaged priests to conduct private services over the graves subsequently. It is also an open secret that others carried off the bodies of their dead before the funeral took place, rather than have them buried in this sacrilegious fashion. And that in consequence many of the coffins carried to the grave with such revolutionary fervour were filled with bricks in default of bodies. Perhaps the day will dawn, however, when the last resting-place of those who gave their lives in the birth throes of the Revolution will be marked with a monument which will represent to generations yet unborn the event which will bring a real freedom to the country.

But yesterday's ceremony presented a very marked contrast to the " red burial."

July 30*th*.—I hear the troops on the northern fronts have announced that they are not going to fight any more till next spring. The soldiers propose retiring to recoup and reorganize. They do not appear to have yet taken into consideration the probable move of the Germans if they carry out this plan. Rumour has it, that there has been a considerable slaughter of Russian soldiers, who have started carrying out this retirement, by officers and men who have remained loyal to their country.

The drosky wallah was amusing with all his extortionate ways and his inability to have any fixed price to take you anywhere in the old days; but if you knew your way about he was then cheap—very cheap and gave you plenty of thrills for your money. You get as many thrills, even more, now if you care to pay the price; for he has degenerated into a pirate pure and simple. His demands are simply amazing, as amazing as the bundles of rouble notes he produces from his voluminous garments. · The prices he demands nowadays are laughable by reason of their colossal impudence. Five, ten, fifteen, twenty roubles, he now asks for a moderate journey, and he won't come down if he can help it. The cheapest drive I had during my stay was the night of my arrival, for I never had another like it. Of course his outgoings for feeding his pony must be heavy; but the latter are scarecrows to what one remembers of the past, and very few have a real fast-trotting nag to bowl you along as in the old

days, though a few are still on the roads : and a perfect
terror they are. For the militia police, who have taken
the place of the old police of the capital, are very inefficient
and pay no attention to the traffic, which goes its own sweet
way and runs itself.

The town is full of rumours of happenings on the south-
west front, but the position appears a little better. At
present there is no Government, all the Ministers having
resigned.

July 31*st*.—Tarnapol fell on the 22nd. The fall was
followed by the evacuation of Stanislau on the 25th,
Kolomea, where Korniloff had his headquarters, on 27th,
and now we hear that Czernowiez, the capital of the Bukovina, is to be, or has been, abandoned to the enemy.
But the armies, according to the telegrams and rumours,
are at last coming to a stand in their disastrous retreat.
Korniloff's strong action in ordering the deserters and
bolters to be shot down has borne fruit. It shows the
type of man that he should have taken the step on his own
initiative and braved the Provisional Government, and
the Council of Soldiers and Workmen, who are, of course,
bitterly opposed to the re-establishment of the death
penalty. The armies are said to be making a stand on the
Zbrnez river, and the Germans have not yet obtained a
footing across it.

The central group of armies between Krweo and Smorgon
did not commence their offensive till July 20th. They
started by capturing some positions and 1000 prisoners,
and then decided that they had had enough fighting and
desisted. Still less has been done by the armies of the
central and northern fronts where Bolshevism is rampant.

In the south, the Roumanian Army, which is said to
be well organised now and full of fighting, had commenced
a great advance, capturing positions, guns and prisoners
in fine style. The Austrians do not appear to have been
able to stand up to them at all. But the Tarnapol retreat
has necessarily put an end to this forward movement
and their position is likely to become precarious.

One hears that the trains for the south are going out of

the capital literally packed to the roof; for in the absence of all effective police supervision there is no control. The roofs of the carriages are invaded by the would-be travellers, and they must pass an exciting time packed together in so perilous a position. A friend of mine said he had paid seventy-five roubles as a *douceur* to get a ticket by the afternoon train to-day. This baksheesh business has a familiar ring about it. The Revolution, one had heard, was going to stamp out all bribery and corruption, but by all accounts it is as rampant as ever.

I hit upon the place to-day where the recruits of the women's battalions are drilling. They have been recently raised. A crowd was watching them, and this crowd interested me. The women in it had an eager, proud look in their eyes as they watched some of their own sex taking on so seriously the job peculiar to man—the stern preparation for fighting. As for the men, the soldiers looked on with a mixture of contempt and amusement, at the back of which lurked shamefacedness. And well they might, for they say that their women have lately been telling them something of what they think of them; and the Russian woman, when on her mettle, is more than a match for the average Russian soldier, so it is said. There is a story going the round now which throws a light on this new aspect. A number of soldiers were overcrowding a tram, travelling free as has been their custom since the Revolution. Said the conductress, a young girl, by no means impressed by these uniformed, slouching, stay-at-home warriors: " Call yourselves soldiers, you ! You've got a soldier's coat on your back but nothing inside it ! " One of the soldiers muttered : " It's a shame to talk to a poor wounded man like that." " You a wounded ! " replied the girl with withering scorn. " If you have been wounded it was in the left nostril, and the bullet which did it was the cork of a bottle." A laugh went round at this smart sally, and the soldiers took the first opportunity of quitting. A little of this sort of thing will do more good than volumes of oratory to shake from the Russian soldier the absurd mantle of arrogance he now parades about in.

The Provisional Government is again in the melting pot, all the Ministers having placed themselves in the hands of Kerensky, who is now practically a dictator, trusted by all. The Cadet party are accused of being the cause of the trouble. They want to get rid of certain men from the Government, and will not come in to the Government unless their demands are acceded to. Tchernoff, Minister of Agriculture, is apparently their chief *bête noire*. Another rumour has it that Tereshchenko, the Foreign Minister, is to go. This, one hopes, is not true, as one has heard he is an able man. Kerensky returned to Petrograd this afternoon, and the names of the new Ministry are awaited with keen interest.

In connection with the land question, the Minister of the Interior has despatched a telegraphic circular to all the Provisional Government commissioners, ordering that no arbitrary occupation of private lands is to be permitted, and asks all local organisations to assist the commissioners in this matter.

Rodzianko, President of the Provisional Committee of the Duma, addresses a strong appeal to the country to-day. He says : " The Russian Army is in retreat. On the field of battle the Russian Army has incurred a disgrace which has never before rested on it. It is the outcome of what is taking place in the interior of the country. This is due to the assumption of power and interference of irresponsible political organisations, to the existence of a double Government in the capital, and the absence of all Government in the provinces. We are menaced with bankruptcy. Chaos in the country spells the ruin of the Russian Armies, which means the end of Russia. We require a strong central power which will exact from each one of us his duty to Russia."

CHAPTER V

PETROGRAD IN AUGUST 1917

THE PRESENT POSITION OF RUSSIA—THE NEW CABINET

August 1st.—The Russian Press of the present time is a most interesting study. Nowhere in Europe to-day exists a Press with so great a liberty. All shades of opinion are reflected, and each paper says exactly what it thinks about the Government, its opponents, both newspapers and parties, and about the existing position. All the papers are giving a *résumé* of the three years of war in more or less detail. But of more importance are the articles devoted to the position of the Russia of to-day. The grave crisis in the nation's outlook is pointed out, and the fact that the whole of the objects the Revolution was to bring about are in jeopardy. Several articles unhesitatingly attribute this position to the Council of Workmen and Soldiers. They point out that the latter quite erroneously assumes to itself the whole success of the Revolution. That it was not to be expected and never can be expected, that a set of ill-educated men with no knowledge of public affairs, or of business affairs on the large scale, should ever be able to conduct the affairs of a great nation. That chaos was, and always will be, inevitable, and that economic chaos is in view. Professor Oxiérow, an economist, says that all those competent to manage the economic life of the nation have been eliminated owing to the jealousy of the Council and Socialists against the *bourgeoisie*. Every man of affairs is actually branded with the mark of Cain. And yet without the *bourgeoisie*, he points out, there can be no economic life. Rather should the Council of Workmen and Soldiers and the Socialists have got together

E
49

all the business men to conduct the distribution of the supplies of the nation, in order to bring down the preposterous food prices, prices which should never have obtained in view of the gigantic amounts of grain Russia produces. A considerable section of the Press brand the new men. They admit that Kerensky and Skobeleff are abandoning some of their old visionary ideas. But the grave danger is there. The moderate papers of all shades of opinion exhort the Provisional Government and all the different parties to throw overboard their own preconceived opinions with reference to the government of the country, and to combine together to form a strong Government, in which all parties shall be represented in order to prosecute the war with vigour after re-establishing a strong discipline in the army, and to bring order out of the dangerous economic chaos at present reigning. It is said that the new members of the Ministry will be settled to-day, and they hope that the men who enter the Ministry will work with this sole end in view.

Petrograd is busily engaged in getting in its stock of winter fuel, or the firewood portion of it, which by all accounts will have to form the major part next winter, as both coal and oil supplies are likely to be very short. The wood burnt is birch, and most of it comes from the great forests many hundreds of miles away. It is brought into the capital by water transport in great flat-sided, deep, shallow-draughted barges eighty feet or so in length. These are towed in strings down the great rivers, lakes, and through the canals which link up these latter. Russia's water-ways are excellent and numerous, and of course enormously aid the very inadequate railway system the country possesses. The quays lining both banks of the Neva and most of the canals, are conjested with serried rows of these barges, from which the fuel billets are now being transferred by soldiers and civilians to the neighbouring pavements and roads. Women for the most part fill up the shaggy-horsed carts, which carry the material away to be stacked on the squares and in the courtyards of houses throughout the city.

FUEL BARGES IN A CANAL IN PETROGRAD

THE "LIBERTY LOAN"—SELLING BONDS FROM THE BOAT KIOSK IN THE NEVSKI, AUGUST, 1917

August 4th.—The state of Russia has ceased to be the uppermost thought amongst her would-be rulers. All parties have spent the last few days in mutual recriminations in their efforts to capture the Ministerial posts. One has almost felt that one was reading home papers at a juncture when party feeling runs high. But here it is even more pitiful, as the country stands on the brink of an abyss. The Cadets by all accounts are now the chief offenders. On the subject of the reconstruction of the Cabinet one of the leading papers writes : " The *pourparlers* continue. At the eleventh hour the Cadets appear disposed to enter the Cabinet. They have ceased from naming individuals they will not serve with, and will not even insist on the resignation of Tchernoff (Minister of Agriculture). The Cadets will have four portfolios." But no Ministry has yet been formed. The Ministers, those who have not resigned, to-day went to the Winter Palace, which is to be used as the future headquarters of the Provisional Government—that Palace so interwoven with the regime of the Czar. A part of it has long been used as a Red Cross hospital, and now the red flag of Revolution waves over the historic building.

The trouble with Finland has been growing, and the Provisional Government have to-day dissolved the Finnish Diet. The notification will be sent by the Senate to the Diet to-day, and the elections are to take place within two months. This means trouble. Many members are already talking of resisting the Provisional Government, and more bloodshed is likely.

Petrograd does not show many signs of the war if we omit the hordes of loafing dirty soldiery. The streets are brilliantly lit at night, and theatres, cinemas, cafés, etc., are all filled to overflowing. Many buildings fly the Red Cross flag, for most of the big military hospitals of the north are in the capital. The red flag of the Revolution flòats everywhere—on all the public buildings, including the Fortress of Peter and Paul, the Admiralty, and so on; and from a number of private houses, restaurants, and shops, big and small, who thereby save their windows from being smashed, if no worse. Very little damage was done to buildings, monuments, etc., in the capital at the Revolution, which is curious in its way, but is due probably to the cosmopolitan character of the place; for the reverse was the case in the provinces. Some revolutionist of a humorous turn of mind took the trouble and risk of climbing up the great monument of Catherine II, just off the Nevski, and inserting in the outstretched hand a short stick to which was attached a red flag. If corpses have the power to turn in their coffins, surely hers must have done so.

The Imperial Golden Eagles came in for the chief attention. During the revolutionary days a mob of soldiers and workmen went down the Nevski, and took down all the eagles over the chemist and other shops. They then went on to the Winter Palace. There is a garden on the west side of the Palace, between it and the main road running to the Palace Bridge over the Neva. The garden is surrounded by a ten-foot wall surmounted by another eight feet or so of heavy ornate railing. At intervals all along this railing immense wrought-iron gilded double-headed eagles were fixed. The soldiers erected ladders against the wall and then proceeded to try and remove the great eagles, which were clamped on to the giant railing, by means of pocket knives, bayonets and ineffectual instruments of this kind. Great crowds watched them and offered advice. Whilst the soldiers were engaged on their futile efforts some one in the crowd shouted out, " We won't destroy them, we'll put them in the museums." The eagles were quietly taken down by the Government later on and stored away. I went to look at some of these insignia of a fallen royalty. Who would have said a few years ago, when I was last here, that such could be a possibility? But, needless to say, the capital is still full of eagles—for they were placed or stamped on everything, including the lamp-posts, and had perforce to be left.

There is plenty of fruit on sale in the streets and of good quality, raspberries, strawberries, pears and nectarines being the chief kinds. Queues are of course plentiful and long.

There was some fracas in one the other evening, or it may have been a meeting, which some of the new mounted militia police were endeavouring to break up. My curiosity was not sufficiently strong to make me mingle with the crowd to see the *dénouement*, especially as nowadays bullets so often come out of crowds.

I had an interesting conversation with a member of the Anglo-Russian Chamber of Commerce to-day. We discussed the question of employing foreign capital to open out the great undeveloped natural wealth of Russia. "At present," he said, "the intense jealousy between the various parties make it difficult to obtain concessions, even if to the advantage of Russia, to open out her undeveloped resources. If socialistic Ministers were to advocate such arrangements, their followers would at once accuse them of being counter-revolutionists; whereas, if the Cadets were to move in this direction the Socialists would start the cry that the country was being sold to capitalists. And yet," he said, "we all know we want capital with which to pay our debts and for our future development. Russia wants all the capital and all the assistance she can get, and this capital must come from the wealthy foreign nations. The whole country is in such a state of disorganisation that we can do nothing ourselves for a long time without help. But the people at present will not work. All departments and grades are affected by the rot which set in after the Revolution. I have a girl typist here. She now only types an average of four letters a day, whereas she used to do thirty. When questioned, she says she is ' so tired.' If I sent her away I should not get another who would do more. Why," he asked abruptly, "are not the Allies here to assist us?" "In what way?" I queried. "Men," he said, "soldiers— an army. The British and French must know our position —that our army is breaking up. Why do they not send an army to our front? The Germans would have done it—have done it constantly when Austria or Turkey showed signs of weakening. An army would save us and our front—where soon there will be no army and no front.

An Allied army, even a small one, would have done, would do, more for us than sending Socialists to talk to our Socialists, who were inebriated with the strong doses of liberty they had been taking." " We had our hands pretty full," I commented. " Yes, but how if you lose your eastern front, our front ? What then ? " " Is it as bad as that ? " " Fully as bad, I fear," he said gravely. I ventured no remark on what would be obviously a disaster of the first magnitude. But I wondered whether they understood at home the seriousness of the position out here. Yet it was impossible to doubt that we know. " And you know there will be a serious grain shortage in Russia for some time. How long it is impossible to say. But there will be little corn for export after the war. It is not being grown and will not be till this land question is settled, for the peasants will not sow. Our only hope of obtaining money is to make early arrangements to cut our forests. We have lots of wealth in them. The Press has been pointing out this possibility, as you will have probably noticed."

Tchernoff has resigned, but Tereshchenko is still Foreign Minister. This may clear the air a little. But the attack and counter-attack of parties still continues, and no Cabinet has yet been formed. Korniloff has been appointed Generalissimo of the Armies. This General has had a remarkable career. Born of humble Cossack parents in Western Siberia in 1870, he is self-taught, entering the Cadet Corps at the age of eighteen, and the Artillery College at twenty-four. After a brilliant career there, he made some daring trips in Afghanistan and Persia (in connection with our Indian frontier in all probability), often disguised as a native, and accomplished some valuable scientific work. He commanded a brigade in the Russo-Japanese War and displayed high military talent, being subsequently attached to the Staff. He was in command of the 49th Division in the conquest of Galicia. In the ensuing retreat he sacrificed his division and himself to save the left wing south of Tarnow. Wounded himself, he fought with a small rearguard till all had fallen, and was then taken prisoner by the Austrians. He is now considered to be one of the foremost soldiers of Russia. Two stories are told of this General. On reaching Petrograd after his escape from Austria, he obtained an audience with the Czarina. After describing his adventurous journey back to Russia, he detailed in moving terms the cruel suffering and hardships to which the Russian prisoners were being subjected in Austria, and begged the Czarina to exert her influence with the neutral nations to get better treatment for her poor soldiers who had fought so bravely. After listening impatiently for a short time, the Czarina coldly intimated that the interview was at an end. The General was furious. By the irony of fate, as the General commanding in Petrograd after the Revolution, it fell to Korniloff to inform the Czarina of the abdication of the Czar, and the decision of the first revolutionary Government as to the future treatment of the Royal family. The Czarina, dressed, in black, with proud, cold, impassive features received him standing. He commenced reading the proclamation. When half-way through she haughtily motioned to him to cease, signifying that she would hear no more of it. Out of kindness of heart the General stopped and hesitated. Was it necessary to further torture this woman who had paid such a heavy price for her folly? Then the memory of the sufferings of his poor soldiers, prisoners in Austria, swept over him, her people whom she had refused to help. He read the proclamation through to the end.

I dined with some English friends to-night. The cross currents of Russian and British opinions as to the existing state of affairs are of extraordinary interest. The disorganisation and its effect on transport are naturally matters of extreme importance, since the daily bread of the community is entirely dependent on them. Graft and bribery have increased a hundredfold, and are far worse than in the days of the Czar. Questioned on this matter, a high official in one of the departments said he was fully aware of this fact, but what could he do? Apparently all officials, especially in the lower grades, consider the position of the Government and their own so precarious that they say they must take bribes, and make as much out of them as possible whilst they are in office, in order to make provision for their families against a bad time in future should they lose their posts. The following rather amusing story is to the point. Wagons for the transport of merchandise form one of the great sources of this illicit traffic. A merchant who urgently wanted a number of wagons, saw to it personally that all the necessary officials from the stationmaster and so on downwards were heavily bribed. The wagons were then forthcoming, loaded up and despatched. After leaving the goods sheds they were, however, shunted on to a side track. Again and again the merchant went to the stationmaster and others, whom he had made " safe " at a heavy outlay, but was invariably told that all the orders had been issued and the wagons would go off. After a harassing week the reason for the non-departure of the wagons was finally traced. An obscure wagon-wheel greaser, who had been overlooked in the general disbursement the business involved, had omitted (*i. e.* refused) to grease the wheelboxes. Each time he was asked to pass the wheels, he said they were out of order and could not be passed by him. As the wagons could not proceed under the standing " running " orders of the railway till the wheels had been passed by this lowly *deus ex machina*, they were held up. The man's devotion to duty and loyalty to the railway having been satisfied by some palm oil, the wheel-boxes were duly filled, the wheels passed and the wagons despatched ! Another serious matter is the appalling deterioration of rolling stock of all kinds (including the Petrograd tramcars, for instance), owing to the short hours and inferior work being given. Trains are being taken off, and those running are very erratic, and only carry half-loads. And the general opinion is that things must get very much worse before they can improve, and that the food question will become very much more acute ; in fact, that famine will make its appearance in these northern parts of Russia. I mentioned that I understood that there was plenty of food in the south down Odessa way—plenty of flour and white bread. " Yes, there is plenty there," I was told. " It is the lack of transport, or rather the hopeless way it is being dealt with, that prevents it getting here. The soldiers in Petrograd have plenty of flour, meat, etc. You will have seen the convoys of carts loaded with bags of white flour, etc., daily passing through the streets of Petrograd. They go to the barracks. The soldiers are being highly fed on the best and in return attend no parades, but spend their time either at meetings or loafing about the streets. But the civil population in Petrograd cannot get any white flour." I discovered that my hosts of to-night had not seen white flour since Christmas till a week ago, when they had had the luck to procure a small bag, with the result that there was actually a small white loaf on the table and an open jam tart, a thing they had not had for seven or eight months.

An amusing incident anent this food question arose at our Embassy. The Provisional Government asked the Embassy, in view of the shortage of food which was anticipated, to let them have a monthly list of their requirements in fresh provisions, vegetables, eggs, butter, and so forth. Unfortunately, the ladies of the Embassy happened to be all away in the country. The men had therefore to put their heads together. They made a poor job of it by all accounts. One of them, an elderly man, when faced with the conundrum of the number of eggs his household would require monthly, wrote down fifty. His estimate, at the end of deep cogitation, was based on the following—

" Two boiled eggs at breakfast. That makes sixty a month. Won't do to ask for the whole amount. So write down fifty."

He was quite unaware that eggs are required for other purposes than for breakfast in the domestic economy of the household. He heard all about it, however, when his wife surveyed the first month's provision supply. He now thinks that he knows all about cooking because eggs are required in it. Also how to run the provisioning of the household. But his wife doesn't !

As showing what there is in the Russian character, this lady told me that her cook, a woman, owing to the milk difficulty, persisted, in spite of remonstrances, in getting up every morning at 3 a.m., and going to stand in a queue for four hours, so that her mistress might have milk every day with her breakfast. And she had done it in the bitter winter of Petrograd ! On the score of wages and food prices my hostess waxed eloquent. Before the war good cooks and table-maids were to be had for eleven roubles a month apiece. She now had to pay fifty and thirty-five roubles respectively. Food was five times as dear as it had been before the war. Eggs and fowls were almost unprocurable. When the meat scarcity made itself felt a year ago, they all lived on fowls in Petrograd. They eat fowls for months on end. But it was appallingly improvident, for the Russian chicken-owners, finding a high market, just sold off all their fowls, lock, stock and barrel, and the chicks with them, oblivious of the fact that they were literally selling the bird that laid the golden eggs. Consequently, no more fowls or eggs are procurable anywhere near Petrograd. In suburbs like Tsarskoe Selo and Pavlost, for instance, not only are milk, eggs and fowls almost unprocurable, but other food is difficult to obtain ; and, quite rightly, the authorities will not allow food to be taken out to them from the capital. The food trouble is aggravated in Petrograd by the fact that the population of the latter has increased by a million persons, refugees and others from the fighting areas, and by the large number of Red Cross hospitals in the town. The question of doctors has necessitated the concentration of the hospitals. Owing to the bad communications in the country districts it was not possible to establish, outside Petrograd, the large number of small institutions started by the big commercial companies and private individuals, numbers of whom instituted private hospitals in the first patriotic fervour which followed the outbreak of the war. These hospitals are attended by private practitioners who would not be able to give the time to long, difficult and uncertain journeys into the country districts. But the presence of the large number of hospitals is now a difficulty of the very gravest in connection with the food-supply question.

The latest report of the Ministry is Kerensky's resignation, which has thrown all parties into the greatest excitement. As he could not form a Cabinet he has given up his office. It is a good move on his part. We shall now see whether he is strong enough to maintain the position he has taken up.

August 5th.—Kerensky resigned yesterday at 7 p.m., both the Premiership and his membership of the Provisional Government, owing to the fact that his proposals for reconstructing the Ministry were opposed. The Cabinet declined to accept his resignation. Kerensky refused to withdraw it and left the Winter Palace. Others amongst the Ministers wished to follow their leader's example, but Nekrasoff remarked that if all the Ministers resigned there would be no Provisional Government left. A special sitting was convened for 10 p.m. Rodzianko asked Nekrasoff whether, before opening the debate, he could reassure the public on the grave news from the front. The latter replied that the Russian front had been broken, and that General Erdeli had probably been killed by the soldiers. Godneff said that union would not be restored in Russia until all the parties united, and gave up their own special programmes. Tereshchenko (Foreign Affairs) said, " We have just received a curt reply on the subject of the piercing of our front as if it was a habitual thing. We are being dragged into infamy. In spite of this we ought to be preparing for a winter campaign. No one speaks to-day of peace. Every one understands to-day that that is an impossibility. We are faced with bankruptcy. The Russian railways have never known such total disorganisation. Prikaz No. 1 was the greatest of crimes. I would not belittle the importance of the Council of Workmen and Soldiers, but the Provisional Government should derive its power from all sections of the community. A. F. Kerensky is the only one in the country in whom all have confidence." Tseretelli said they were living in revolutionary times, and there was no safety outside of the Revolution, meaning that the counter-revolutionists should be put down.   M. V. Lvoff, Procurator of the Holy Synod, said that the only hope for the people was the formation of a strong Government with Kerensky, that powerful figure thrown up by the waves of the Revolution, at its head.   Miliukoff replied for the Cadets.   That party, he said, had always been in favour of the strong Government which all were asking for to-day.   He agreed with Tereshchenko, but could not subscribe to the vague statements of Tseretelli, which were of quite a different nature.   He also pointed out how dangerous to the public welfare were the agrarian politics, or the division of all land, etc., of the Provisional Government and the local committees. He advised that Kerensky should be asked to form a new Government.   Up to now he had been knocking his head first against the Cadets, then against the Soviets.   He should now be left to choose his Ministers for himself and be supported.   Efremoff (Justice) : We have not yet found a Government capable of saving our country.   We have spent three weeks in this Ministerial crisis, each one has put his own party first : we have discussed important matters, but they will not save the country.   Tereshchenko interjected that none of the preceding orators had shown that they realised that Russia was standing face to face with her downfall.   Nekrasoff wound up the debate with a frank statement.   " The Generalissimo, Korniloff, has asked us to reply to his decision to take up the supreme command only on certain conditions.   What answer can a Government give who does not feel itself standing on firm ground ?   The last two weeks have been a period of constant suffering for the members of the Cabinet.   They have had to spend more time in prayers and adjurations to the Council of Workmen and Soldiers to allow them to work than in doing the actual work.   Fear of slipping on a piece of orange peel has taken all the nerve from the Government, because the fall of one meant the fall of all. The counter-revolution exists and grows stronger day by day. The Government only asks for one thing, the time and the power to work." At 7 a.m. it was decided to recall Kerensky and give him a free hand in forming a new Ministry. The Cadets said that though they would support the new Ministry they would not join it.

Korniloff's conditions of accepting the supreme command are an indication of the man. They are: (1) I will be responsible only to my conscience and the people. (2) I ask for absolute authority in all orders issued on operations, and in nominations to the High Command. (3) The extension of measures recently taken for introducing order at the front, and in all parts occupied by reserves behind the front. (4) The acceptance of my suggestions (referring to army dispositions) already telegraphed.

Some of the papers in commenting on the new advance of the Anglo-French Armies on the Western front point the reason of this advance. This was the second big attack made on the German trenches since the Revolution, in which the Western Allies were sacrificing thousands of their sons in order to give the Russian Revolution a breathing space. And yet, say these papers, whilst the Allies were thus saving the Revolution, the Socialists are decrying the " imperialism " of the Allies. From day to day with flaming eloquence these papers are discovering dark projects on the part of the Allies, and decrying " that band of pirates and militarists " who wished to swallow up Germany and grab at world power. When in fact the Russian Army had lost its fighting power, and was permitting Germany to transfer large quantities of troops to the Western front to hold up the Anglo-British advance. Forty divisions are said to have been so transferred, whilst Turkish divisions have been sent to Mesopotamia.

A big railway official, with whom I was discussing to-day the disorganisation, summarised the present industrial position as follows: The employees want to have (a) as much pay as possible, (b) as little work as possible, (c) all to have a voice in the management, (d) no one to take any

responsibility.   He added that in his opinion the position
would probably get much worse and famine would come
to Petrograd.   " And then one way or another outside
assistance will have to be asked for," he remarked.   This
is the opinion of many.   In fact many Russians ask why
this assistance has not already been sent here, to stop the
disintegration of the army, and checkmate the German
propaganda which is rife throughout the more densely
populated parts of the country.

August 9th.—Matters are not so rosy here in Petrograd
as the world or we at home are led to believe.   The police
have disappeared, and an untrained militia consisting of
men in soldier's uniform and armed with rifle and bayonet,
which they do not even know how to carry with safety,
either to themselves or the public, much less how to
use, have taken their place.   The state of the streets in
Petrograd to-day, is only explainable by the fact that
90 per cent. of the civil population are quite unaccustomed
to the use of firearms, and therefore blissfully unaware
of their danger.   Never in my life did I expect to find
myself so often and unwillingly looking down the muzzle
of a rifle, often as not loaded, as I have already done
here.   As no record is kept and life is cheap at present
in Russia, it is impossible to say how many " accidents "
occur daily from this cause.   Expert thieves from all
Europe and probably America are now congregated in the
city.   Their work is childishly easy.   A soldier in uniform
can go anywhere.   They have only to dress similarly,
therefore, and on the plea of a warrant to search on behalf
of the Government, pillage any house they like.   Three
nights ago, six men dressed as soldiers broke into one of
the Government offices, temporarily housed in a building
containing valuable *objets d'art*, and made off with many
carefully chosen articles of enormous value, including
some historic Peter the Great relics !

The Russian frontier at Tornea has been closed now
for a week.   It is thought to be due to the troubles with
Finland.   The Diet have apparently accepted the edict
proroguing them, but some trouble is expected from

Helsingfors.   The Senate only passed the Diet's acceptance of the edict by the casting vote of the Governor-General of Finland, a Russian.

Kerensky has at last formed a new Ministry in which Tchernoff, the Minister whose dismissal and prosecution for political activities against Russia the Cadets have been demanding, still retains the portfolio of Agriculture; though many say it will not be for long.   The Socialists demanded his inclusion in the Ministry and a promise that he would not be proceeded against.   Kerensky agreed. The basis of the Ministry is Kerensky (Premier and War and Marine);   Nekrasoff (Vice-President and   Finance); Avksentieff (Interior);   Tereshchenko (Foreign Affairs); Skobeleff (Works);   Peshekhonoff (Supplies);   Tchernoff (Agriculture);   Prokopovitch (Commerce and Industry); Nikitine (Post   and   Telegraphs);   Oldenburg (Justice). I see that Professor Bernatsky is appointed Assistant Finance Minister.   He is said to be one of the soundest financial experts in the country.   The Cadet party, in view of Kerensky's declaration that the members of the Ministry would only be responsible to the people and their own consciences, issued a statement saying that they had left it open to the members of their party to join the Ministry if they wished to do so.   Tseretelli, who took a great part in the formation of the new Ministry, remains outside it at his own desire, saying that he would be far more useful in the Soviet Councils which he could influence than in the Ministry.   This was agreed to.   Having discussed the new Ministry, the responsible papers with one accord are now exhorting the Ministers, and all competent, to take a hand in starting the work of reorganisation throughout the country.   To this end the first thing, however, is to get the soldiers once again in hand, and this the Council of Workmen and Soldiers do not want.   The return of discipline will be the end of them, and they know it.   As a general rule the Press does not expend much flattery on the new Ministry, and many openly give it two or three months at the most, if so long.

I have had several conversations with professors, leading

bankers and others on the subject now being discussed by all parties, of the economic development of Russia, and the necessity of restarting her industries. The bulk of the Socialists take up the attitude of " all for Russia." They have no knowledge of how commercial business is run, nor have they any idea apparently that capital is needed. Their idea is a try back to mediæval times, and go in for a kind of barter in piece goods and so get rid of the capitalist. This, I am assured, is only an example of the many extraordinary ideas they hold. The land question is aimed at the other class they wish to get rid of, the wealthy landed proprietors. It is admitted that land legislation is required to do away with gross abuses, which were rigorously maintained under the regime of the Czars; but in the face of the total want of education of the masses the disappearance of the educated landowner, to whom in the majority of cases the peasant has naturally turned in the past, would be a grave disaster for the country. I asked an official how far the new ideas had penetrated into the central Government offices in Petrograd, mentioning that I had seen a red flag hanging in the big entrance hall of the Department of Agriculture. " Oh, that is Tchernoff," was the reply. The civil servants, the subordinates at any rate, take their tone for the moment from the known opinions of the Minister in charge of the branch. " Yes, so it appeared to me," I replied; having in my mind's eye the striking contrast between some of our big offices in Whitehall, and the appearance and manners observable in the Ministry of Agriculture in Petrograd to-day.

Some amusing stories are current of the early revolutionary days, and the way in which the paid orators of the Nevski were sometimes drawn by their listeners. For months after March (it was only stopped late in July), at every street corner in Petrograd meetings were held throughout the day, mostly addressed by soldiers or sailors to soldiers, sailors, and any one else who cared to listen. The chief topic of the soldier orator was that the war was only being kept on by French and English capitalists, that it was being fought in their interests; that the war must cease at once. The hand of the German propagandist is easily seen here. These orators spoke bitterly in the most opprobrious terms of the French and English. Next to the Allies the *bourgeoisie* came in for their invective. A soldier orator was one day haranguing a small circle of mixed soldiers and civilians, declaiming against the *bourgeoisie*. After listening to him, a Russian civilian wearing a black coat went up and said : " You are a soldier, are you not ? " " Yes," said the orator, glowering at his interrogator. " And you call me a *bourgeois ?* " " Yes," with some quite uncalled-for abuse. " Where do you come from ? " inquired the civilian. " From —— village," replied the soldier surlily. " And I suppose you own a house in the village ? " " Of course." " And a horse ? " " Yes." " And a cow or two ? " " Yes." " And a field and piece of rough grazing ? " " Yes." " You tell me that you own all these things, a house, a horse, cows and fields, and yet you declaim against the *bourgeoisie*. Look at me. You call me a *bourgeois*. And yet I own nothing. I possess no house, horse, cows or fields. I have only my weekly salary to depend on to live and support my wife and children. Why, you and your like are the *bourgeoisie* who you are inveighing against—not we poor men." There was no reply. The soldier was far too taken aback at this novel view of the position, and some of the listeners laughed and openly sided with the civilian.

Another story is more amusing. A woman Socialist, well dressed, was holding forth on the equality of all men and women, that all wealth should be equally divided up amongst all, and so forth. We all know the kind of thing. One of her male listeners, after giving her careful attention went up and said : " You say we are all equal ? " " Yes," and she broke forth again into perfervid periods. Her interrogator waited patiently till breath failed the orator. " And you say we should divide all wealth equally ? " Again she agreed and started afresh. At the next enforced pause the man produced three roubles from his pocket. " I agree with you," he remarked; " you

F

have convinced me." Turning to a bystander, he asked him to change one of the roubles for him. He obtained two fifty-copeck notes. Facing the lady orator he said : " This is all the money I possess. I will halve it with you," and he held out the 1.50. She had to take it. She was about to commence her oration again when her questioner continued : " No, no. How much have you in your purse ? We must now divide that, since we are to share equally our wealth." Reluctantly she produced her purse. It was opened and found to contain forty roubles. The spectators were now thoroughly enjoying the lecture. The forty roubles were carefully counted and divided, twenty of them being given to the man who had shared his three. He pocketed them, thanked the orator for her interesting discourse, and departed.

The Leninite affair as they call it, in which Lenin, Trotsky, Parvies (Helfand) and other socialistic anarchists are implicated in the rising of 16th to 18th July last, is now before the courts. Charges have been formulated against this gang. They are accused of having in 1917, being Russian subjects, conspired with agents of the enemy States at war with Russia, in order to disorganise the Russian Army at the front and rear, and thus reduce its military value. With this object and with the aid of enemy money they organised a propaganda amongst the troops and the civil population, in order to force Russia to make an immediate peace. To this end they brought about the rising against the existing Government, accompanied by assassination and violence, and attempted arrests of some of the members of the Provisional Government, inciting certain regiments to disobey orders, and have thereby assisted the enemy. They have not yet laid hands on the whole of the ringleaders, however, who are under the protection of the Council of Workmen and Soldiers.

Petrograd is full of the latest rumour that Germany is going to invade Finland and capture Petrograd. On the whole, the concensus of opinion seems to be that the project is a doubtful possibility. For one thing, there is little food in Finland, and so the Germans would get nothing in that direction to help them.

August 10*th*.—The great three-day Liberty Loan came to an end this evening. Streets, shops and hotels have all been given over to it. Kiosks adorn all the streets, built in the graceful Russian style, and most deftly and tastefully decorated, and ornamented with flowers and branches of yew and other evergreens, and besprinkled with the red bunting of liberty and banners bearing inscriptions. There must be two score or more of these kiosks in the Nevski alone. Soldiers and girls arrayed in summer kit, for it has been intensely hot lately, have been hard at it, the former almost extorting money, the latter pleading for it. Bonds of all denominations down to five roubles were on sale, and the loan has, I believe, done well. I took a photograph of the boat kiosk at the corner of the Nevski and the Moika, and was nearly arrested by a wild-looking old and totally ignorant peasant in the uniform of the militia police. The man could not read my papers, nor did he recognise the Russian official stamp, but an officer came to my assistance and I was, reluctantly, allowed to go my way. It was a foolish risk to take, but the scene was so typical of the Petrograd of to-day. This boat kiosk had been erected during the Revolution, and it was from here that the sailor Batkine, who earned some notoriety for himself at that period, delivered fiery harangues to the excited crowds. Why the kiosk with its ugly memories has not been removed passes comprehension.[1]

I read some of the London telegrams in the papers to-day, and amongst them the amazing utterances of a few of our Members of Parliament on the subject of Russia, predicting that all will be well with her. Is this really believed at home ? If not, why so mislead the public ! If ever a country was on the brink of a total and appalling collapse, a collapse which must seriously interfere with the plan of campaign and calculations of the Allies, Russia

---

[1] It was taken down three days later.—E. P. S.

has reached that point to-day. Can the real position be understood at home ?

I had an interesting conversation with a Siberian Member of the Duma. He was enthusiastic over the immense wealth of Siberia, especially in timber, all easily accessible to rivers. He said that the Yenesei harbour was now open for two and a half months in the year, but with improvements such as had been introduced at Archangel in the way of big ice-breakers, electric light to enable work at night, etc., the harbour would be kept open longer and much more work be possible during that period. He said he thought there was a great future before the northern Siberian forests. That before the war the best timber was railed all the way to the Baltic ports, and paid even then. But with improvements on the Yenesei far more will be carried by sea. A Norwegian merchant has already a fine saw-mill plant on the Yenesei and is hard at work.

There seems to be a considerable opinion that the Cadet party have not put their best men in the new Cabinet, whilst the Council of Workmen and Soldiers, after agreeing to give their men who are Ministers a free hand, have now made reservations. The refusal of Tseretelli to enter the Cabinet is also regarded as meaning that he intends to prove a thorn in their flesh—in other words, he has placed party above country. All the men I have talked to are despairing of the situation. To aggravate the difficulties, the Ukraine and Finland questions are troublesome and anxious ones, both wishing to separate themselves from Russia.

General Korniloff appears to have obtained assent to most of his conditions. The general position at the end of five months of the Revolution is well summed up to-day : " The appeal of the new and fourth revolutionary Government is before the people. Russia, instead of lifting herself up after the fall of Czardom, is rushing downwards to the depths. Discontent with the Revolution and its results is increasing amongst the people day by day. Even those who have grasped the power are feeling it. Even the

Socialists are beginning to feel it. For a short time after the Revolution a real national Government was in power. But at the same time a second Government, the Council of Workmen and Soldiers, was making its voice heard— a Government which was not a national one. Having the army at its back it placed itself above the national Government, which retreated (oh, the pity of it!) before it. The Revolution was replaced by a counter-revolution, instead of liberty a Dictatorship of the armed people has appeared. Instead of fraternity, mortal hatred between the classes. This counter-revolution has achieved the work of the monarchy. It has brought Russia to a state of feebleness. Germany is invading her territory unopposed. The areas of land being cultivated diminish. Industry and the transport services are paralysed. The capital is feeling the first pangs of a severe famine. Has conscience begun to awaken amongst these counter-revolutionists? Will the fourth Government be given a chance? It may be so. But their actions are disquieting. The chiefs of the people are hurriedly visiting the Petrograd regiments. They have already extracted promises from these regiments, that the latter will recognise that the main power does not rest with the national Government, but with the committees of the parties. But one must still hope that the chiefs of the Soviets will at the last minute place the good of their country before their party."

It looks a very forlorn hope, though!

CHAPTER VI

PETROGRAD IN AUGUST 1917 (*continued*)

THE WOMEN SOLDIERS — THE UKRAINE AND FINNISH
QUESTIONS—THE STOCKHOLM CONFERENCE—THE SOU-
KHOMLINOFF TRIAL

August 13*th.*—The women soldiers are proving a source
of some interest to the town. I have been to watch them
at drill several times. These Women's Battalions have,
I believe, been embodied with the idea of shaming the
Russian soldiery back to discipline. The hope has been
disappointed so far. It is a pitiful thing to think that
these women are training to go out and take life, which
is so contrary to Nature's intention. But although
from this point of view inexpressibly sad, it is very
amusing to watch these girls and women all so keenly
anxious to learn their new job, decked out in the
uniform of men. The little tricks of looking, moving,
motions of the head, the raising and dropping of the
eyes—all the mannerisms so peculiarly female remain.
To watch a few of them in the dinner hour practising
amongst themselves the shoulder arms, present arms, and
coming down to the ready preparatory to the lunge
forward with the bayonet, and the peals of laughter
when a mistake was made in the movement or when
the recruit overbalanced herself — it was amusing but
sad for a man. Some of the girls are so small and
comparatively weak that even the light rifles (for they
are armed with a light pattern, topped with the long
vicious-looking bayonet), would pull them off their feet
when they lunged forward. What chance will they have
when up against a man seeing red in the real mêlée of

THE COMMANDANT OF THE WOMEN SOLDIERS BATTALION AND PART OF HER TROOPS

THE WOMEN SOLDIERS: A GROUP OF RECRUITS

battle! But now they are merry enough. They are a
mixed crowd. I watched a working party putting up a
wire fence. The N.C.O. was obviously a lady and a very
pretty girl too. She was most particular about the
alignment and so on. But women have not the strength,
or only in exceptional cases. The ground was hard.
When the posts were in a wire was bent on. The wire
was rotten and kept breaking, but they got it into its
place. Then one of them made some remark about the
posts. One of the girls—a very different type this from
the N.C.O., obviously a peasant woman, strongly built
and sturdy, with the broad pock-marked face, narrow eyes,
broad snub nose and high cheek-bones of the Mongol—
this girl went up to the posts and pulled each one clean
out of the ground, amidst joyous shrieks of laughter from
the recruits and to the amusement of the spectators.
The fence was to keep their transport ponies out of the
neighbouring canal. Therefore the hilarity. The good-
looking N.C.O. flushed red and bit her lip with vexation,
but some of her privates patted her on the shoulder in a
caressing manner. Beyond on the barrack square a
platoon was practising marching in fours with rifle and
bayonet at the slope. They were being drilled by a
regular male officer. At times they broke into a marching
battle song, and their marching to this in slow step was very
good. Other squads were in all stages of squad drill
and dressed in an extraordinary variety of garments.
Once enrolled, the recruit's ambition is to get into uniform.
The first article supplied is the cap, and this is worn over
flowing locks or otherwise. Then comes the blouse tunic
and belt, also immediately donned when served out.
Our woman recruit now has her upper portion clothed
as a soldier; skirt, etc., still remained. Khaki breeches,
buckling at the knee, forms the next garment, and the
recruit then considers herself fully equipped as a soldier;
she does not bother about the arrival of the putties and
boots. It does not inconvenience her in the slightest
that her kit from the knee downwards consists of thin
stockings and high-heeled shoes. But to the man accus-

tomed to the niceties of military dress it is sufficiently
astonishing to see a squad of recruits drilled by a corporal
with flowing tresses inadequately confined beneath her
cap, with legs clothed in openwork black silk stockings,
and feet shod in thin-soled, very high-heeled buckled shoes,
whilst her squad are variously attired, some even still
wearing the despised skirt. The last article to be served
out is the soldier's grey greatcoat with a narrow leather
waist-belt. The women are particular about the fit of
this article. They understand it better. I watched a
couple sitting under a tree yesterday, the one sewing
industriously. When ready it was tried on a third who
had come up. It was like being in a woman's tailoring
department. The wearer craned her head at all angles
to see the fit, the fitter patted and pinched and stuck pins
in at places where it was voted to hang badly. The wearer
was evidently not going to trust the regimental tailor
for the fit of this, the chief part of the kit. Soon after
I saw a slip of a girl, buttoned and belted in her brand-
new coat, walk up to a group of companions with a smile
on her face. She halted, saluted, and at the word about-
turned to be inspected. At some remark she craned and
twisted to see her back, exactly as if it had been the matter
of the hang of a skirt. There is a little corporal who is a
great joy to the onlookers. A most energetic little woman,
in full kit to her knees. She kicks out her legs in the most
approved German goose-step fashion, and is now endeavouring to make her wretched women recruits, still in skirts
many of them, do likewise. They were a hot, tousled, and
very ruffled crowd that squad, but she would not permit
any remarks.

One of these battalions has already been in the fighting.
It was not intended to use them, I believe, but there was
a withdrawal during an attack and the women were sent
up, fought like cats, losing heavily but taking a number
of prisoners. I wonder what those men thought when
they discovered the sex of their captors !

I have already alluded to the attitude and appearance
of the soldiery in Petrograd. It is amazing, and the

saluting of officers is more noticeable by its absence, to use an Irishism. The manner in which the sentries perform their duties is almost beyond belief. When on duty guarding important buildings and so on throughout the city, they are to be seen either standing in lazy attitudes, leaning up against a door or wall or lamp-post, or *sitting down*, and invariably smoking cigarettes; their rifle, with bayonet attached, is either propped up against a wall, in the corner of a doorway, or shoved away in a sentry box or any spot which first comes to hand—the main object being to get rid of it. The men are usually in conversation with one or two passers-by who have squatted down beside them for a talk—the eternal rouble, like the paisa in India, forming much of the conversation. This appalling want of discipline is typical of the greater part of the Russian Army of to-day behind the front. It is therefore useless to pin any faith to the possibility of this portion of the army being of any further use in this war, unless a strong, ruthless soldier seizes the Russian helm. He might bring the mass of reserves back to their senses. No civilian could.

Amongst other classes of workmen who " came out " after the Revolution were, of all people, the waiters and women servants of the hotels, etc., in Petrograd. They had the usual processions and banners inscribed—you will never guess the inscription—" No tips." It is a fact! Most travellers would have rejoiced to see it, though they would have deemed such an inscription incredible. But these people did not think so. They were demanding equality in the management of the hotels which, according to them, now belonged to the servants as much as to the proprietors. They demanded a share of the profits and no tips. Before this, in the large hotels at least, they depended for their wages on tips, as is customary. During the period the waiters were " out " the guests of the hotels had to make their own beds, so I was told, clean their own rooms, and downstairs, they had to fetch their own plates and other articles, and go to the kitchen to get their food, and, most objectionable task of all, clean their plates, etc., after the meal. An extraordinary time they must have all passed. I can picture some of my friends doing it. Or, rather, I cannot see them doing it; or I could not before the war. We are all learning such a lot now about the things we can do when we have to try—coping with that nauseous black bread I found the most difficult in Petrograd. The hotel proprietors had to give in. Now, therefore, as the waiter has no tips to expect he throws the things on the table; keeps you waiting whilst he reads or discusses with other waiters in the dining-room the latest news in the evening paper; brings all the courses of your dinner together and dumps them down, the later ones getting stone cold before you reach them; and is more interested in his watch, as the time draws near to closing the dining-room, than in attending to you. For the hour of his attendance at dinner is fixed, and he departs to the minute and the lights are turned out. There is no cleanliness, no real service, and no smiles or bows. There is one fat old man at the Europe, a waiter of long service, his nice old face deeply wrinkled and creased, wrinkles and creases formed by the constant and perennial smile his face had worn throughout long years. The wrinkles and creases are now all awry, for his old face is cast in gloom, an enforced gloom—not sullen as with the rest. Neither face nor heart would compass that. I have once surprised him into a smile, but it disappeared immediately and he looked furtively round. No one may smile at a guest. Sullen service, or what is meant for it, is all that may be given. I never thought to say it—but give me back the tip. How long will it last in Petrograd? Already before I left, now and then in a corner you might catch sight of an upturned palm pushed out behind the back of a man who had served you decently, according to his lights. I never failed to anoint that palm.

I had two interesting conversations to-day. The first with a doctor of science who has been in England and Scotland several times, and though not a timber merchant has considerable knowledge of that branch of Russian industry, and of several others as well, I discovered. On the subject of the possibilities open to Russia in the development of her forests he was informative. He said they had suffered terribly in the forest regions of the north-west, from which the Baltic ports were supplied before the war. He was of opinion that the Baltic export trade must decrease greatly in the future from this cause alone; and for another, he did not believe that Russia would encourage that trade, as they would require the forests left for rebuilding the devastated areas on their front. "The exports from Riga to England will be very greatly reduced, you will find, in the future," he remarked. "You might cut in the Murman railway forests to some extent. But the railway of the future will be the projected line from Archangel to the Ob river. We want capital to build this railway, which will open out a fine, rich, undeveloped country. Some felling has been started in the Pechora basin (N.E. Russia), where there is good forest, and timber has been floated out by the Pechora river into the Arctic Ocean." "There is no harbour there," I remarked. "No," he said, " the material was loaded into ships from barges." There are, however, nearer and finer areas of forest than the Pechora at present unworked.

The other man, a big banker, was of a different type. His sympathies, I had been told, were pro-German, as were a great part of his commercial interests. But he told me something about the German methods of trade. He was interested in cotton, and said they were hoping to make arrangements to grow and spin all the cotton they required at home. At present they imported large amounts of linen. Germany, he said, has been our *bête noire* in the past owing to the commercial agreement made at the time of the Russo-Japanese War. Germany, he informed me, had rows of cotton-mills on her frontier. She obtained the raw product from Russia, made it up in her frontier mills just over the border, and then re-exported the manufactured article to Russia at a large profit. I agreed that we all hoped the days of that kind of thing were over. We discussed the land question and the peasants' claim to all the land. "Surely," I said, " the peasants do not consider that they have any claim to the great State forests." "Oh, no," he replied, "nor to the extensive appanage forests. These, as you know, formerly belonged to the Imperial family, and were worked by their own servants. They now belong to the State and go to swell the State forest area." At the close of the interview the banker said : "We have lots of wealth, undeveloped wealth, in Russia. What we lack is capital and, to some extent, organisation. When the present troubles are mitigated, give us these and it will repay you at a higher rate than you will get in most parts of the world—even in your own Empire." He exhibited anxiety on the score of the tonnage question. Would there be British tonnage for Russian use after the war ? I concluded that that would depend entirely on Russia's own attitude and actions after the war. It did not appear probable that, as things were shaping, any nation would be ready to grant special facilities to other nations without a *quid pro quo*. It would not be either sound business or economically possible, owing to the depreciation of the world's stocks of almost all save armaments. "I see," he replied slowly; and then, "We shall have to get rid of the Germans." But did he mean it ?

That the question of Allied intervention in Russia is widely discussed and earnestly hoped for by probably the majority of the educated Russians who are not pro-German in sympathy, which usually means commercial interests, the following outburst of a Russian friend who is well behind the scenes is worthy of record. Mentioning the obvious advantages to Russia of a flow of capital into the country with the object of opening out the country and providing more work, a better wage, etc., for the masses, I happened to say, "If only the people would understand!" "Where are the people who can understand?" he warmly retorted. "There are probably not many more than a score or so of men in the country really capable of governing it, and these men are getting so played out, as a result of their unremitting patriotic work started with the outbreak of war, that they may break down at any moment. We have our professional classes and our commercial classes and our landed proprietor class, who may or may not be properly educated. Beyond this fraction of the population you have the great masses entirely uneducated for the most part, or with what is even more dangerous, a smattering of education. Take our Zemstvos Committees, for instance, which you English have lauded to the skies. We liked your praise and it was deserved, for they have done great things in the war. But oh, the difficulties! The men on the country town Zemstvos Committees are very good men and for the most part honest, but they are without education and simply cannot see beyond their own petty purely local affairs. And this state of affairs obtains throughout the whole country. And how can it be different when there is no education in Russia ? To our people the words ' affaires' and ' ruling' mean nothing, convey nothing. I'll give you an illustration," he went on. " A week or two after the Revolution, I was lounging up the Nevski one morning and stopped to listen to a soldier orator.

" ' We have done with Ministers. We must send them all off,' he shouted. ' But how, no Ministers, who will govern ? ' queried a bystander. ' We will govern,' said the soldier. ' Then you will be the Ministers,' said a second listener. ' No,' shouted this soldier statesman in embryo, ' we don't want any Ministers, I tell you. All the people will govern themselves with no Ministers.'

" There you have it," he said. " But," I ventured, " if they can credit this kind of thing, it ought to be possible for your educated classes to band together and lead the people with ease." " Yes. We know that. It ought to be possible and we all know it is—those of us who think about these matters and see truly the direction in which our country is drifting; but, well, we have not the initiative of you English. We are too ready to let things slide, and though we may start hot enough on a quest, we quickly cool and may not, often do not, attain our goal. We are not what you English call practical—not as a race. We are too dreamy. You can see it in the Provisional Governments

we have already had. We are now at the beginning
of the fourth since the Revolution. Look back on the
records of the other three. Am I not correct in what I
say of the Russian character? We all believed in Kerensky. Most, as you know, believe in him still. But he is
a true Russian in character with a soft spirit. I believe
that in the end the intervention of the Allies will be the
only possible way out if the Bismarkian policy of a dismembered Russia is not to be the end of this appalling
war. And that, of course, is the German object and that
of Austria. Has England realised that?" He had been
striding up and down excitedly, but suddenly halted and
threw out the query. "Well, it's pretty self-evident, is
it not?" I replied: "It will not be much good making
the eastern route to India safe if we are to have a dismembered Russia at the mercy of Germany, I imagine."
But pondering over this question since quitting my friend,
I am doubtful how far we have realised this danger. A dismembered Russia with a number of little States practically,
if not openly, under German protection along her eastern
frontier. What an opportunity for her should it materialise! And yet there are people who talk of no more wars.
Has the world ever before been brought face to face with
such a crop of difficulties—not European difficulties, or
Far Eastern difficulties, or New World difficulties, by themselves, we have seen all these before and pulled through
—have we ever had such a world-wide crop of burning
international difficulties on the subject of frontiers and
peoples to settle before? The answer is known to us all.
And the Russian imbroglio has added to these—unneces-
sarily added, I fear, unless the opinions of many men on
the spot here capable of forming an opinion are widely
astray.

Speaking of the disorganisation and the short hours
worked, my friend said: "I wonder any one works at all
since it is not necessary to do so. The workmen can now
draw their pay and do nothing for it. So evidently there
are some with a little conscience left." On the subject
of Russian apathy in trade he quoted some instances worth

chronicling.   In the Crimea before the war it used to
be possible to obtain plenty of fish.   This fish was caught
by Turkish fishermen chiefly, only a very few Russians
being engaged in this pursuit on their own coast, although
fish abounds in these waters.   Fish is now unobtainable
in the Crimea.   When the Turks joined the war the
Turkish fishermen, of course, disappeared, and the small
coterie of Russian fishermen gave up fishing, as they could
make more money on shore and do less work for it.   " In
connection with the Batoum oil trade," he said, " you
know that the oil and naphtha are put into iron drums, and
these drums are placed in wooden boxes.   The wood for
these boxes all came from the Austrian forests (in the
Bukovina mountains).   And yet we have great forests in
the neighbourhood of our own !   And then the match industry," he continued.   " We used to send large amounts
of matches to Persia.   The Japanese discovered this and
entered into competition with us, selling a more cheaply
made match, an inferior match, at the same price as we
received.   But they put a wrapper on their box displaying
a great lion and a rising sun on one side and a Persian
inscription on the other.   What was the result ?   The
Persians bought the Japanese match in preference to the
Russian.   Our Chamber of Commerce pointed this out, but
our match merchants refused to alter their boxes and thus
lost the trade.   I will give you another instance.   We used
to send soap wrapped in a white covering to Japan.   White
is the colour used for mourning in Japan.   Germany came
into this trade and wrapped her soap in beautiful rose,
yellow, blue and black coverings instead of white.   The
Japanese at once bought the German soap instead of the
Russian, as they said white was an unlucky colour.   ' It
will bring bad luck,' said the Japanese housewife, ' to
buy soap enveloped in white paper now that you can
obtain it in coloured paper.'   Our people would not change
the colour of their wrappers, so they lost this market.
And so on *ad nauseam*," he said wearily.   " And yet,"
turning to me, " there are people who say such things do
not matter.   The psychology of the markets is a very

important matter indeed. And the Germans and the Japanese have realised it. I don't think you English have, though," he remarked shrewdly. I made no reply. But I think we are just beginning to realise that we have not.

Most disquieting rumours are coming from Kieff and Odessa. There appear to have been outbreaks in both places and shooting, not that the latter is anything new in Russian towns by now. But thousands of people are said to be leaving both places in panic, fearing that they will otherwise be taken prisoners by the Germans.

In order to prevent further immigration into Petrograd the Government have issued an order forbidding persons to enter Petrograd with the object of remaining in the capital. They also intend to try and clear out a considerable proportion of the *emigrés* and some of the big Government offices, like education and so forth, whose work could be carried on quite as well outside the capital. This action is to be taken with the object of relieving the food pressure, which the Government freely admits is going to become far worse. Even when the harvest is got in it will take time, with the depreciated transport, to get it up to Petrograd. It is announced that several more railway lines, branch lines, will have to be closed down, and a strike on the railways is threatened. Most certainly the Revolution has made the proletariat mad.

A somewhat reassuring statement on the finances has been issued by Nekrasoff and Bernatsky, Minister and Assistant Minister of Finance, but all of it will not be pleasant reading to Russia's Allies. Especially the part of it alluding to the repudiation of the agreement arrived at at the Paris Economic Conference of last year.

Bernatsky in his statement of the case said that the Revolutionary Government did not hold themselves bound by the resolutions of this Conference, with which his Government could not agree. His department, he continued, must confine themselves to the question of re-establishing the finances of the country on a sound basis and to attracting foreign capital with the object of restarting their industries and opening out their great sources of undeveloped wealth. The future, he said, did not belong to the socialistic masses, but to properly controlled capital employed for the development of the country.

The disease in the army is being discussed. I have already alluded to the famous Prikaz No. 1 issued by the Council of Workmen and Soldiers during the Revolution. The general opinion now appears to be that, although this order most certainly started and hastened the rupture of all discipline, had it not appeared the subversal, though retarded, would have been inevitable from the moment when the Socialist propaganda, Russian and German, and German gold commenced to permeate in ever-increasing waves throughout the Russian Armies. That, in fact, the absence of all real check to this propaganda was in the end the chief cause of the present state of affairs. This had become evident even before Kerensky's meteoric advance which was followed by the disgraceful retreat. Many, it is said, have thought from day to day that the army would come to its senses and would then present a united front to the enemy instead of remaining an undisciplined, disobedient horde. But the reverse was to be expected. A network of German agents and spies is spread throughout the army and has made use of the favourable opportunity unchecked and with much cleverness. All these men had to do was to din into the soldiers' weak brains that the Revolution was threatened and that the Allies were going to force them back to the trenches again. " It is not difficult to foresee," says a Russian writer, " that it will require all the best skill of the Government to reinstate discipline in the army, without which it will be impossible to assure victory for the democratic hopes of Europe. For the moment," he adds, " amongst the Bolsheviks some are keeping quiet, others have changed their skin. But we need be under no misapprehension that they will continue their work, hidden amongst the masses of the people."

The Stockholm Conference appears likely to achieve fame and go down to history even if it should never

G

materialise. Its reception here naturally depends upon the party to which you belong, but there is evidently considerable doubt amongst some members of the Cabinet as to the advisability of holding such a Conference. To many the whole thing appears suicidal—to others a farce. Truly Germany is a past master in diplomacy or, shall we say, in diplomatic tricks engineered by questionable agents whose very nationality, not to speak of their baptismal names, are so shrouded in their mysterious pasts as to be almost untraceable. One of the papers commences a long leader on the Conference with the following opening paragraph : " It appears that the democracies of the Allies are beginning to realise the danger which lurks in an International Socialistic Conference. A conference of which the larger number of members will consist of spies and traitors led by Schneider & Co."

August 14th.—News comes from Kieff of a fracas between a newly raised Ukrainian regiment and Russian soldiers. The regiment was apparently entraining to leave for the front when the Russian troops guarding the station and railway line fired upon it. This is the Ukrainian version. The Russian one is that the Ukrainian soldiers first opened fire on the Russians. The incident has brought into prominence the threatened attempt to break up the Russian Empire into independent States as, *e. g.*, Finland, the Ukraine, Poland and, the latest candidate, the Mussulmans. The Mussulman Congress is now in session at Kazan. The Congress has decided to organise Mussulman regiments, and this they propose to do even if the Provisional Government veto it, which of course they will. It is fully expected that other parts of the Great Empire will follow suit. And yet it will be, economically at least, unsound, and especially for European Russia. The reason for the want of homogeneity in the component parts of the Russian Empire is due to the deliberate policy of the Czars, under which different nationalities were governed on totally opposed principles. The Finlanders, *e. g.*, were treated comparatively generously, though even here the

policy varied and concessions granted were arbitrarily
withdrawn at a moment's notice. But the Finns were
granted a political automony, were allowed their own
coinage, and were not required to serve in the army. In
Poland, on the contrary, the people were kept under a
reign of terror and oppression, as is well known. In the
Ukraine the separatist movement was never very strong,
since the politics of the Ukraine, which is interested in
the Mediterranean question, were in harmony with the
Imperial aims which demanded for Russia, and consequently for the Ukraine, access to the Mediterranean via
Constantinople. The new strength acquired by the
Ukraine separatist movement is attributed to the abandon-
ment by the Provisional Government of the Constantinople
and Mediterranean policy, aided by German money and
propaganda. But for these factors it is not considered
by experts here that the Ukraine question would have ever
cropped up.

The present attempts at separation are then primarily
due to the policy of successive Czars to prevent all fusion
of the different nationalities, fearing, doubtless, that such
a fusion would see the end of the purely autocratic rule
which they maintained as the only form of government
they understood or which fell in with their own inclina-
tions. But is the separatist movement now being attempted in European Russia in the interests of either
the different nationalities themselves or in those of the
Russian Empire? The answer appears to be over-
whelmingly in the negative. Finland is a forest and
maritime country similar to its neighbour Sweden, of
which it is a poor duplicate. Poland industrial, like its
neighbour Germany. The Ukraine, a great corn country,
similar to Hungary and Roumania, which are contiguous
to it. These, then, Finland, Poland and the Ukraine, are
all required by Russia for their several national pro-
ductions, and by remaining within the Russian Empire
they retain their markets. Separate from Russia they
would have to compete at a disadvantage with foreign
neighbours. Administrative autonomy, ethnological and

social, for her different nationalities would appear to be the solution to be aimed at by Russia, with the military and diplomatic services common to all, combined with a close economic union with customs, communications and coinage in common. Such a solution of the problem would be an essentially democratic one, and whilst strengthening Russia it would also strengthen the revolutionary democratic elements. Is it not because they recognised the democratic character of such a solution and the strong Russia which would be built up upon such a democratic basis, that the Central Powers have exerted all their strength and pressure, and will continue to do so, to make such a settlement an impossibility?

The American telegrams on the subject of Russia are amusing—rather like our own, in fact. The Americans have discovered that Russia is rich in undeveloped wealth and are lauding her to the skies. Senator Root, who was over here with a Commission, has returned to New York. He declares the position here to be astonishingly good and the progress wonderful. A Mr. Scott also talks in the same strain. On the subject of the army he says that it is several millions strong (which is true so far as numbers go), of which the greater part is very well trained. A part were once. Anyway they could fight. At the present moment, however, they are mostly a rabble, and Mr. Scott had he used his eyes could have seen this for himself. Such reports are so utterly misleading that it would be infinitely better if the Allies kept all mention of Russia out of the Press rather than throw dust into the eyes of their own people, which is bound to end in bitter disappointment. This is the general feeling here, at any rate.

It is the irony of fate that the more purely socialistic the Provisional Government has become the more drastic the restrictions they have had to issue in order to cope with the disorganisation which the acts of the visionary idealists of the Revolution have given rise to. During the first Provisional Government, which contained one Socialist, the republic lived through its golden days and was given all its free institutions. The second Provisional Government

had to bring in some restrictions in order to enforce
the hard truth that man cannot live by play and talk
alone. This Government contained five Socialists. And
now when the majority of the Provisional Government
are Socialists, even more drastic restrictions have to be
introduced and enforced. It is now beginning to be
realised that at the commencement the Russian people
obtained a liberty possessed by none of the nations of the
earth, a liberty which they thought themselves qualified
to teach to the older nations. That they were able to
impress some, who were purposely sent and who ought to
have been able to help to steady them, the Allies now
know to their cost.

The separatist movement is not only going to give
trouble to the rulers of Russia, but is bound to result in
anarchy at home. News comes from the Caucasus of an
appalling state of affairs in that distant country. The
whole of it is said to be in the hands of bands of pillaging
brigands who are reproducing the days of Ivan the Terrible
—burning villages, killing all the males and carrying off
the women. The Cossacks have petitioned the Government asking that no more men should be drafted to the
Cossack regiments, but should be raised and equipped
and left at home to fight the brigands. The Government
will require to be a strong one to cope with the present
position in Russia.

August 16th.—I had a most interesting talk with one
of the two Assistant Ministers in the Ministry of Trade and
Industries. This official, Prilejaeff by name, had been a
member of the Economic Conference which met in Paris
last year. He told me that it was more than doubtful
whether the Provisional Government would adhere to the
agreement then drawn up and accepted by members of
the congress. That so far as the timber part of the
arrangement was concerned he was President of the Committee appointed to deal with the matter. They would
be unable to supply the amounts promised to England and
France this year. Nor would they be able to do so next
year. About a third, or 300,000 standards (out of 1,000,000)

might be practicable, but not more.   The failure to keep to
the agreement is, of course, ascribed to the Revolution; the
fellings are much smaller and the requirements in wood
fuel of North Russia, Petrograd, etc., are far larger owing
to the dislocation in the transport services which has resulted and will continue to result in decreased arrivals of
oil and naphtha from the south.   He was interesting and
emphatic on one point in this connection.   " The war,"
he remarked, " and the Revolution will not disorganise
for so long the forest work, as the great forest tracts accessible to Europe lie, as you know, in the north-east in the
less densely populated parts of the country, and forest
labour in those parts has been much less disturbed by the
Revolution and will more quickly settle down.   If you get
up there you will be able to note that for yourself.   Consequently there will not be the same risk in putting capital
into timber concessions as there would be, for instance,
in those connected with mines and minerals and so forth;
in these latter, owing to the prevailing unrest and disorganisation amongst the industrial classes at the present
time, the investment of capital would obviously be more
risky since one cannot foretell at present when these
classes will settle to work again.   In reply to a remark
the Assistant Minister said : " Yes, other nations are also
wanting concessions in these northern forest areas.   Norway and Sweden are beginning to come to Russia.   And
we are drawing up a scheme for opening out these great
forests with the help of foreign capital, and the Provisional
Government is prepared to favour Russia's Allies against
the Central Powers.   But," he continued, " and you will
hear this from the Ministers, in future we wish to have
Russians connected with foreign companies working in
this country.   The Government and the Socialists are
very strong on this head."   " Yes, I have heard the same
thing from the mouths of several of your prominent
merchants and bankers," I replied.   " Well, you will
hear it equally from the Government.   We want foreign
capital and we wish to treat foreign capitalists well, but
we don't want to be exploited any more."   " That is right

enough," I remarked, " but it was not the English but the Germans who exploited you before the war." " Yes, the Germans. That is what we want to stop if we can. But the Allies will have to help us. It is not going to be easy for us. We don't want to export the raw product any more. We want to manufacture it in Russia and then export the manufactured article." " Yes, that is what we all want to do," I replied. " But your people, your Socialists, do not imagine that Germany is going to help you to do this or allow you to do it if they can help it, do they?" " We don't expect it," he replied emphatically. The following day I had a conversation with a member of this committee of which the Assistant Minister was president, and heard what may be termed the unofficial view of the matter. As regards the supply of timber to the Allies he was frankly pessimistic. " It will come to an end altogether," he stated, " unless I am much mistaken. We shall have as much as we can do to supply Petrograd, Moscow and the other towns, as also the railways in the north, with the wood they require. Work connected with the supply to the Allies is practically at a standstill, though I don't believe your people understand this." " No, they do not," I replied. " What is to be the outcome? We must know definitely what you can do." " I will arrange a small meeting of men interested in this question and we will have a discussion." I left it at that for the moment.

But, as a matter of fact, the whole of this timber question is in about as unsatisfactory a state as it could well be. For instance, there is a big firm at Reval who supply us with three-ply wood for aeroplanes. Of course, in common with every one else, they are having trouble with their labour. The firm also has contracts for this material to fulfil for France and Russia. Our Foreign Office is at present sending daily telegrams asking why British consignments are not being despatched. The Russians have a man on the spot, and I was given to understand that the French have sent one to Reval also. We are trying to work the business from Petrograd, and expect the head manager to visit us instead of sending our nominee to visit him—live in his office, if necessary, until he gets the job through. And our other competitors are getting the goods. If we propose to continue this method of transacting business in Russia we need not expect to be able to cope satisfactorily with more energetic and business-like foreigners. In this instance the manager of the firm asks : " How is it possible to satisfy all three Governments when they have no working arrangement amongst themselves ? And this at the end of three years' war ! "

Petrograd is full of officers of all grades out of a job—officers dismissed from their regiments, brigades, divisions, etc., by the privates of these units. Many, the majority I should think, have been decorated, many wearing several decorations gained in this war. A large number of these men have been wounded in the service of their country—a country they are no longer allowed to serve. And the war is still being fought ! What must be the feelings of these men ? Can we imagine the torture it must be to most ? It is most disheartening to see all this fine material eating its heart out here in idleness when it is so badly needed at the front. During the recent great retreat the officers of the retiring regiments formed themselves into battalions—Death Battalions they were called—and threw themselves into the breach in a useless endeavour to stem the tide and through emulation or shame bring the men to face the enemy once again. It was a futile waste of valuable material, and orders were issued forbidding it. No army in the world could stand such a useless waste of trained officers, and one was glad to hear that it had been stopped. Battalions were also formed of men who had won the Cross of St. George for valour, and hundreds of these brave men sacrificed their lives. Vain was the effort to stem that disgraceful rout. But not in vain for Russia was this heroic sacrifice, for it showed that Russia possessed sons who knew what disgrace was, and who were quite prepared to die to save their country, if possible, from that stain. When the history of the deplorable Tarnapol retreat comes to be written this will be one glorious page to read. Almost as grave and an infinitely sadder loss to Russia were the officers, and I believe they were numerous, who committed suicide in front of their regiments rather than live to see their honour disgraced when they realised that the latter were definitely bent on retreating, or, to use the more appropriate word, "bolting;" for this word " retreat " has a military significance and cannot be applied to the disorderly rout which took place from the Russian front. In writing this I am not painting the case a whit stronger, nor anything like as strong, as have the Russians themselves. I met an acquaintance, a British officer, who previously to the war had spent many years in Russia, and of course knows the country and language well. He tells me that the forces of the Central Powers were not in any numbers within thirty-five miles of the Russians when they opened their front. The Russians left all the fine new British guns with 2000 rounds of ammunition apiece behind them. The Central Powers have obtained so much booty that they cannot count it. And, in addition, all the cut corn, cut and stacked in shocks in the fields, was left *in situ*, the Russians not even delaying to set it on fire. It is said that this grain will feed the armies of the Central Powers on the eastern front for two months ! And added to this were the awful and horrible excesses committed by the fleeing soldiery on their own people. But I will not pursue that topic. We have already heard so much on that score in Petrograd that it will be difficult to forget the horrors during the rest of a lifetime.

There are rumours that the ex-Czar and family are to be transferred from Tsarskoe Selo to some place unspecified, the papers say Tobolsk, a one-horsed little town with a handful of houses and a small tumbledown Governor's residence, in Siberia. The matter has been kept secret, and it is as likely as not that the Royal family are already on their way there, as rumour has got hold of the news.

I suppose that no country—civilised country—has ever quite reproduced the state of affairs existing here at present. Hordes of useless, idle, extravagant soldiery drawing

7.50 roubles a week, instead of 80 copecks as before the Revolution, well fed on the best, loaf everywhere. The working classes are paid extortionate wages. I have been told, difficult as it is to credit it, that a bricklayer earns at the rate of 30,000 roubles a year ; a hotel waiter 80 roubles a day; a hotel boy 50 roubles, and so on—such wages as no country in the world could afford to pay, and doing only about four to six hours' work for it, and that work so badly performed as to be absolutely harmful. Witness the state of the rolling stock on the railways and the accidents now so numerous. Factory owners, and in fact employers of labour of all kinds, are at their wits' end to get work carried out and keep their businesses going. And with it all are told by the employees that the business belongs as much to the latter as the former, and that all profits should be equally shared. In fact, knowledge, skill, education and civilisation at a discount, and the owners of capital not knowing from day to day whether a total stoppage of their works will not involve them in financial ruin and with them the country. The same story is heard on all sides. The only rift in the clouds is that a considerable part of Russia, the major part, is not industrial, and all are unanimous in stating that these areas will be the first to settle down and commence the work of reconstruction.

The crisis in Finland has reached a grave stage. The Senate have resigned. A general strike has been proclaimed, and the Provisional Government have been asked— or rather ordered, for it amounts to that—to reassemble the Diet, dissolved a couple of weeks ago, without delay. This is going to be a bad business and an unprofitable one to boot. A general strike on the Russian railways is threatened unless the next instalment of rises in pay is at once granted, together with other concessions. A general strike will mean starvation in Petrograd and elsewhere within a very short time.

The Stockholm Conference continues to absorb our interest and is productive of an immense amount of talk. It is a pity that Henderson did not stay longer in Russia. It would have been to the advantage of both countries.

He does not realise that things have greatly changed here since his visit. The influence of the Council of Workmen and Soldiers is not what it was at first—for the moment it is on the wane. Whether it can be reduced to its proper position altogether will depend, all are agreed, on the Provisional Government and Kerensky in particular. If he coquets much longer with this Council it will mean his downfall. But even if this event occurs—not unexpected by many I have talked with—no one considers that the reign of the Bolsheviks will be very lengthy. They are far too ignorant and have not the faintest idea of what governing or national economics mean, to say nothing of the delicate nature of relations with foreign powers.

The Cossacks come in for a well-merited eulogy to-day. Alone of all the army (if we except the cavalry and artillery, who have to a great extent remained loyal so far) it is pointed out the Don Cossacks have remained faithful to their salt. The Bolshevik outbreak of July 16th to 18th was quelled by them. They have not put their country to shame nor committed treason. They joined with the people in aiding the Revolution in March, and have since been true to the Government in power. It is really wonderful that amidst the total disorganisation of the country the dreaded and hated Cossack, the former scourge of the people, should have remained so far the one dependable element of the Revolution, from which he himself had little to gain.

August 17th.—So serious is the position of Russia becoming that the possibility of having to make peace is being discussed here. In an article dealing with this question to-day it is pointed out that Russia has done a great deal for the Allies in the past three years by bearing the weight of attacks at critical moments. Can she with her small economic development be expected to carry on the war for more than three years? This theme is developed by a Russian writer and is well worthy of our careful consideration, though of course answers can be furnished to many statements. But their view is interesting : " Given the political and financial chaos which at present exists in Russia," says this writer, " isolation for us would be fraught with consequences compared with which the continuation of the war is the lesser evil. We can only extricate ourselves from our present position by developing our unexploited wealth. To do this will require foreign capital to obtain which necessitates our maintaining amicable relations with wealthy foreign nations. The political and financial isolation with which we are menaced leaves us face to face with financial and economic bankruptcy. This would leave us sooner or later a prey to the nations which triumph in the World War. For we should inevitably be reduced to economic and political slavery by the first strong and ruthless nation who wished to exploit us. This is what must follow a rupture with our Allies.

" This question must also be regarded from the viewpoint of our Allies. If we admit that the state of our army at the front and rear is so bad that we must frankly inform our Allies that we are unable to continue to fight, what then ? It is difficult to form an opinion as to the attitude of our Allies in face of such a revelation. Will they be able to realise that the conduct of such a long war presents much greater difficulties for us, with our undeveloped resources, than for any other European power ? Will they remember that we have done much more than could have been looked for from us, taking into consideration the political and economic situation of our country; that we saved the situation for our Allies in the west by a rapid mobilisation in 1914, by an advance into East Prussia; by our successful offensive in Galicia and by the defeat inflicted on the first Austro-German advance into Poland; that we drew upon ourselves the greater part of the German forces during the Austro-German offensive in the summer of 1915, in spite of the fact that our equipment was defective, due to the scandalous conduct of the old regime; that our soldiers had then to fight in the trenches with their hands, and that we lost in that struggle hundreds of thousands killed and hundreds of thousands wounded; that subsequently we never allowed the Germans to concentrate their forces on the western front, which it was extremely important that they should be able to do during the Verdun offensive and Champagne battles? In acting in this fashion we recognise that we did no more than our duty. But it has cost us dear. It has cost us the ruin of Poland and our western provinces, has reduced our slender financial resources to the lowest ebb, and has brought us to economic chaos. It would be unjust if the Allies were to forget all we have done in the common cause. Is it possible to think that the English have forgotten the troublous days of the birth of their Parliament, or the French the time passed during their Revolution and the events of 1849? We are passing through these stages, and what we require is a stronger link with the Allies—a strong moral backing and assistance which will prove so important in the future for us all—even if we now in our weakness have to cease from taking a further active part in the war. If the Allies, irritated or incensed at our inaction, abandon us now, they will commit the greatest error, not only from the standpoint of the development of the civilisation of the world, menaced by the ' mailed fist ' of Germany, but also from their own personal interests. Regarded from the practical point of view of self-interest, if the Allies abandon us either from irritation or disgust and withdraw their economic and financial assistance, they will throw us sooner or later into the arms of Germany."

August 19*th.*—Tereshchenko has issued a statement with reference to the attitude of the Provisional Government towards the Stockholm Conference. There has been considerable controversy in political circles on this matter. The statement also clears the fog which has enveloped Henderson's retirement, which has here been regarded as the outcome of the *bourgeois* attitude and the *bourgeois* Press in Europe. An idea had gained ground that Tereshchenko or Kerensky had written to Henderson stating that they did not approve of the Conference. The Foreign Minister gives an unqualified denial as to the existence of any letter written by

either of the Ministers. The attitude of the Government
has, he said, always been the same, and this attitude is
known to the Socialist members of the Government and
was also made clear to Thomas, Vandervelde and Henderson when they were here. The latter then entered into
discussions with the Socialist Revolutionary and Socialist
deputies, regarding these deputies as representing all the
Socialist parties of Russia. When the Executive Committee of the Council of Workmen and Soldiers Deputies
appointed delegates to go abroad to get into touch with
foreign Socialists in order to call this Conference, they
asked the Ministry of Foreign Affairs to assist the delegates in the arrangements for their journey abroad and
also to undertake to forward all their correspondence, a
request which was acceded to. This proves that the
Provisional Government never entertained a negative
attitude towards the Stockholm Conference. " But the
Government," continues the Foreign Secretary, " does not
consider it possible to express officially any particular
attitude towards this Conference; regarding it as a private
meeting of the parties taking part in it, whose decision
will not bind the Provisional Government. My telegram
to our London agent in this connection was as follows :
' The Government looks upon the Conference as a party
affair and its decision does not bind the Provisional
Government.' I now learn from the newspapers that
our agent in London, N. D. Nabokoff, had written a letter
on his own responsibility which is alluded to in the correspondence between Lloyd George and Henderson relative
to the latter's retirement. I have not seen this letter
and have telegraphed for the context.

" The remarks in opposition to the Conference attributed
to Kerensky are incorrect. In fact, both Kerensky and
myself have more than once pointed out to the representatives of the Allied Governments the desirability of
not creating any difficulties in the way of issuing passports
to the representatives of the Socialist parties of the Allied
Countries selected by the Workmen to attend the Stockholm Conference. We informed Henderson during his

stay here of our attitude in this respect and our attitude
has remained unchanged." In conclusion the Foreign
Minister said: " The Provisional Government presumes
that questions connected with the war will be officially
considered at the forthcoming Allied Peace Conference
between the Allied Governments. In this matter my
Government takes its stand on that part of the declaration of July 8th which touches on the question of peace
discussions, and which I drew up. This part of the declaration stated that in addition to purely diplomatic representatives there must also take part in the Conference
representatives of public opinion who will not express the
views of their Governments but will represent wide classes
of the democracy."

This Conference appears to contain all the elements of
a comedy in it, if only the various parties had eyes to see it.

General Vassilkoffsky now commands the Petrograd
military district, and is going ahead in proper fashion if
the pace can only be maintained. Last Thursday a new
move was sprung upon the public, the greater part of which
is still totally demoralised and under the impression that
it is its own master and able to loaf about in the fine hot
summer weather we are having and do nothing. The
Alexandroffsky Market was suddenly surrounded by a
body of Cossacks and other loyal soldiery, and all avenues
of escape barred. Every person inside was then examined.
As a result some 5000 individuals consisting of many
soldier deserters, thieves, receivers of stolen property,
etc., who were unable to produce their documents of
identity, were arrested and sent to jail. The same kind
of round-up took place in some of the shops on the ground
floor of this hotel (the Europe) a few days ago. I was
thankful I was not in the café which forms one of them
and which we frequent at times. We watched the proceedings from the balcony above, and it was amusing to
see indignant and very flustered ladies, let loose from the
net thus spread, issuing from the doorways and fluttering
off down the street through the crowd of interested and
remark-making sight-seers. A good haul was made on

that occasion, but nothing like on the same scale as the Alexandroffsky one. The latter market, having been cleared as above described, a search was made throughout the shops and booths it consists of, which resulted in the discovery of large quantities of military goods (sold by the soldiers) and also of stolen articles of other descriptions. In this latter connection Rodzianko has issued a notice stating that during the recent transfer of the Council of Workmen and Soldiers from the Tauridia Palace (which they had used for their deliberations since the Revolution, and from which they have at length been ejected by the Provisional Government) numbers of valuable and historical *objets d'art* have disappeared. This is the fashion in which the self-constituted people's representatives look after the national collections. The expert cracksmen of Europe must be having the time of their lives.

Vassilkoffsky gave out yesterday, on the subject of the defence of the northern front, that very strict measures will be taken to secure a high standard of discipline in the troops quartered in the Petrograd district. In order to make the northern army fit for war, soldiers found engaged in trade in the streets are to be arrested and sent to the front. The town was placarded with this order two days ago. Yesterday I saw a line of soldiers standing beneath a dozen notices of the new order affixed to a wall, selling matches, laces, newspapers and safety pins ! And the sentries, I note, still sit and smoke when on duty. Will the General be strong enough to enforce the order ? Not if the workmen and soldiers can stop him, it is opined.

As an indication of how the question of famine is impressing itself on people's minds here, the French colony in Petrograd are forming a co-operative society with the object of provisioning themselves daily as a society— not a bad idea when one comes to think of it, and so like the French.

The Ukrainian question is approaching a temporary settlement. Until the Constituent Assembly, that blessed Mecca to which all eyes are turned, meets and gives its decision on the newly formed Ukrainian Secretariat, the latter, which comprises Secretaries of the Interior, Finance, Agriculture, Education, Commerce and Industry, Labour and Questions of Nationality, is to be considered as the working Government of the Ukraine.   The Finland crisis, on the other hand, is assuming alarming proportions. The strike movement, led by the Social Democrats in close touch with the Bolsheviks who have escaped arrest here by bolting to Finland, is daily assuming wider dimensions. Started at first on economic grounds, it is now taking on a political character.   Workmen appeared in the new Socialistic Senate and demanded that the Diet should be reassembled.   They were referred to the Governor-General (Stakhovitch), who replied that he had not the power to carry out the demand.   The chief part in the strike movement in Helsingfors is being taken by the Municipal Guard who have replaced the militia.   This guard consists of Socialists and is terrorising the population of the capital, all the shops, factories and banks being closed.   The Governor-General has stated his intention to resort to force to quell disturbances; and also, probably a much stronger argument, to stop all supplies of food from Russia.   This threat should bring the strikers to their senses—for there is little food to be had in Finland short of importing it.

Petrograd is certainly a kaleidoscopic capital to live in at present.   One alone of the topics which afford us subject for conversation and inquiry daily would in peace time prove a nine days' wonder.   And certainly the trial which has just commenced of General Sukhomlinoff, former Minister of War under the Czar's Government, would prove sensational enough in peace times.   He is to appear along with his wife, also indicted, before the tribunal specially appointed to investigate offences committed against the State by high officials whilst holding office under the Czar.   There are numerous cases to come for trial, this being the first.   The indictment is weighty enough, and if proved the man should be shot, though this would be too good for such a criminal.   Briefly the whole state of the army, so far as its hopeless deficiency in

H

equipment and armaments went, is attributed to him—
not through sheer incompetency, it is said, but through
deliberate intention. Sheaves of telegrams from officers
commanding in the field, sent off during the actual fighting
and imploring the Minister to forward munitions, etc.,
telegrams to which a deaf ear was turned, are to be put
forward as evidence. The great retreat of the Russian
Army is said to be entirely due to his inactivity and the
intentional obstacles he placed in the way of supplying the
armies in the field. Many hundreds of thousands of men
were slaughtered owing to these deficiencies. If there can
be graver charges than these brought against a man they
are found here in the additional one that the War Minister
had personal relations with Miassoiedoff and other agents
of the German and Austrian Staffs; the former, though a
German spy, being given an appointment in the War
Department. The accused is said to have helped Miassoiedoff to obtain military secrets to be sold to the Central
Powers. Altogether a nauseating record, and almost too
bad to be credible.

Kerensky is jeopardising his Government again. At
least this is the opinion of many. He made his first
appearance for some time at the Committee of the Workmen
and Soldiers Council a couple of days ago. He was received
in a cold and deliberate silence. He made one of his
hypnotic speeches and was applauded vigorously. Avksentieff, received warmly, followed, and then Tseretelli
spoke and put a resolution to the effect that the Committee
were sure that the Provisional Government would fight
anarchy and the counter-revolution, etc., which was carried
unanimously. These resolutions, coming from this body,
who are now almost totally responsible for the continued
disorganisation in Russia, would be amusing were they
not so pitiable and so dark with the presage of a coming
Nemesis.

CHAPTER VII

PETROGRAD IN AUGUST 1917 (*continued*)

August 20th.—When we look back over the past half-century we are presented with some remarkable changes in front in European and Far Eastern political and diplomatic questions. And perhaps no *volte-face* has been so complete as our attitude towards Russia during the past decade. For very nearly half a century the Russian bugbear of a descent upon India through the northern passes formed one of the preoccupations of the British Foreign and India Offices, and lay heavily on the minds of successive Indian Viceroys and their Councils. Some years ago I had the opportunity of seeing a part of the defences of Quetta on the Afghan frontier, and other parts of that wild borderland which forms the northern marches of our great Indian Empire. It is perhaps not unnatural, therefore, that the Russian question always possessed a strong fascination for me, in common with many other Anglo-Indian officials. A shadow, which brought sharply to the memory those days out of the past, was thrown across my path to-day. I had gone to the Foreign Office, an imposing building situated in the square opposite to the Winter Palace, to keep an interview which the Foreign Minister had accorded me. I was shown into a great suite of reception-rooms, and waited in one of the larger ones—a magnificent room painted in white picked out with gold, with a fine hand-painted ceiling and deep freize. The furniture, covered in dust-cloths, was white and gold and ancient, much of it of beautiful design. Even the valuable pictures on the walls were covered with fine gauze screens, with the exception of the larger ones, obviously full-length portraits. These were now entirely veiled with white cloth. They were portraits of royalties, no longer in favour in Petrograd. The ones at either end of the room, of the Czar and Czarina, had smaller oval pictures, uncovered, hung against the cloth, as significant perhaps as anything could be of the times Russia is living through. It was easy, as one sat there, to recall the scenes these great rooms had witnessed, when all that was greatest and noblest and loveliest and cleverest in the Empire had thronged them at great official receptions—now a memory of the past. What will they witness in the future ? To me, waiting and musing there—and who could have stood in those rooms without peopling them with the ghosts of the past ?— there entered a small elderly man with a thin tanned face and pointed beard ; he was faultlessly dressed, and proved to be a senior secretary. Although he spoke English fluently, the language we used was the courtly language of old diplomacy—French. No other would have seemed fitting in those surroundings. We must have felt this instinctively, for no remark was made concerning the language we fell into. And this is when the shadow out of the past appeared to us both. We discussed the present position, which of course he considers hopeless (and equally of course, being an old official, he would—younger men with less deeply rooted convictions are required to tackle this world problem now) ; also, in connection with an inquiry of mine, the time it would take for Russia to get back to anything like normal again, owing to the want of education in the masses and their present attitude towards all authority ; this period, to him, appeared equally problematical. It then transpired that he had been in India. He had alluded to the fact that there was a great outcry and feeling in France, England, and above all in Italy, against Russia and her inaction. I replied : " In Italy there may be ; possibly in France also ; but not, I think, in England to anything

like the same extent." I said I thought we understood
Russia's difficulties better than that. That we had to
deal in our Empire with such a variety of different peoples
and races all over the world that we were in a better
position to appreciate the difficulties facing Russia, with
her large uneducated population. I quoted India as an
example, where we had been, and were now, confronted
with many problems not at all dissimilar to those which
Russia would have to face in the future, problems which
she would probably find it to her best interests to deal with
on similar lines to our own. " India ! " he exclaimed.
" Were you in India ? " " I spent sixteen years as an official
there, and saw most of the country," was my answer; and
it at once established a bond between us. Travellers all
know the feeling. " India," he said, " is a great country, a
magnificent country, and you understand it, you English. I
spent six years as Consul in Bombay between 1900 and 1906,
and I never had a better time—in spite of difficulties,"
he added, with a curious smile. " I suppose you were up in
Simla ? " I asked. " No," he replied, to my amazement;
" Lord Curzon would not let me go ! " An incredulous
ejaculation rose to my lips, but I shut my teeth on it in
time. " Were you ever in Central Asia ? " I asked carelessly,
remembering certain Russian friends who in the old days
poked about there " collecting " geological and zoological
specimens openly and industriously; and information and
topographical knowledge equally zealously but less ostenta-
tiously. " Yes," he replied, with a smile; " I had travelled
extensively in Central Asia before I took up my Consular
post in Bombay." It was now my turn to smile at that
word " Consular." This man a Consul ! and I contrasted
him with the type we usually put into the post. Seeing
the smile, he continued : " Yes, Lord Curzon (then Viceroy)
thought I was a spy." My smile broadened. " Oh, of
course it was natural," he went on. " In our case we should
not have permitted him to remain. But it was a nuisance
for me. Lord Curzon did not want me to remain in Bombay
and tried to get me removed. He had me shadowed everywhere the whole time." " Did you not see anything of

the historical places in India, then?" I asked. " I did
the tripper's round to Delhi, Agra, Lucknow, etc., once,
but the Viceroy did not like it, and would not let me repeat
it or go into the north at all again. I saw a lot of the
Madras Presidency, as Lord Curzon did not mind my going
there." Of course he did not ! The Russian shadow did
not loom from the south ! But what a comedy it was, a
minute curtain-raiser, played beneath the surface unbe-
known to all save the few participators in it. And how
like us to refuse to trust the man on the spot. For my
present acquaintance, now that that shadow has disappeared
into the limbo of the past, admitted in all but words the
real part he was destined to have played in Bombay, and
would have played but for the fortunate fact that we had a
Viceroy at the time who was well acquainted with the
Central Asian question. And this courteous, beautifully
mannered Russian now termed it a " nuisance " that he had
been foiled in the part he had then attempted to play, but
which now had lost all importance as a policy.

Amongst other information my new friend gave me, as
we sat in that splendid apartment looking out on to the
vast red façade of the Winter Palace, the following throws
into strong light the backwardness of Russia. We had
been discussing various aspects of this question. On the
subject of travelling he said : " There is no comfort to be
had in Russia, you know, and that is why we never travel
for pleasure in our country. I have never been in the north
and north-east of Russia in my life. I have never even
seen Archangel. Duty has never taken me there—curiosity
might have; but there is no comfort. I know the south
better. But in the past, well-to-do Russians always went
west for pleasure, to the European countries in that direction, as they could not get comfort for their money in Russia,
and spent less for it in Western Europe. Outside our few
really big towns there are no good hotels, no first-class
hotels as you understand them." As an illustration he
continued : " You know that we have mineral waters in
the Caucasus situated amidst magnificent scenery. The
waters are as good as anything abroad. But there is no

comfort to be had there. There are no good hotels. They
are very expensive and very uncomfortable. So we have
always gone abroad." But here the old Russian standpoint came up. His idea was mainly Government. " The
Government," he said, " should have improved these
places, but the old Government did nothing of this kind."
He did not appear to recognise that the Western nations
leave this kind of thing to private enterprise. But the
old regime did not believe in, or encourage, or foster, private
enterprise.

The Secretary told me one good story indicative of the
present outlook of probably the bulk of the ordinary civilian
lower classes in Petrograd. It was during the three days
of the Bolshevik outbreak last month, when there was
a good deal of promiscuous shooting in Petrograd. The
Cossacks, having obtained the upper hand, were engaged
in patrolling the streets. They were not using their
venomous-looking whips, so often brought into play on
the slightest provocation on the backs of the populace in
the days of the Czar, and had not done so since the first
outbreak of the Revolution. The ordinary civilian population of the town had by July begun to dimly realise that
matters were getting very bad, and that the Socialists
and agitators were bringing the country to ruin. Said
a man in the crowd to a Cossack riding slowly through
the throng (in spite of the danger of getting shot, the people
always crowded the streets during outbreaks and street
shooting) : " Comrade, you are not using your whip. Why
don't you use your whip as in the old days ? " " Ah, yes,"
answered the Cossack, " that is what you all understand
best, the whip. You don't understand anything else."
" And that Cossack soldier," said my friend, " has given
us the truest commentary on the outlook of the people
of the present day and our only way of dealing with them.
Until the new generations are educated it is only possible
to rule the present ones with the whip. You will see in
the future whether I am right or wrong. You Western
nations do not understand the psychology of the Russian
lower orders. Look back a couple of centuries or so and

see how you then ruled your lower orders. How they
acted in France and Italy, for instance." These two
remarks—the one made by the rude unlettered Cossack
soldier, the other by the highly trained and experienced old
official—at least indicate the extreme difficulty of the
present position, bound up as it is with the new socialistic
and equality ideas.

This conversation was brought to an end by the appearance of an under-secretary, announcing that the Foreign
Minister was ready to receive me.

Sir George Buchanan, our Ambassador, had arranged this
interview for me a day or two before. I was shocked, at
my first meeting with the Ambassador, to see how really
ill he looked. When one remembered the burden he was
carrying on his shoulders, once again the thought arose
whether we at home had given him during this trying time—
one of the most trying any Ambassador could have to pass
through—all the assistance within our power and had sent
him the right kind of assistance. Had the French done so
to their Embassy ? Have we since the Revolution looked
upon the Russian front as part of a whole or as a separate
entity by itself ? History will decide the point. But we
are not now concerned with history. We have set out to
clear up the mess the Germans have got the world into—
and our Ambassador has had to deal with no small part of
it. The Allied Governments have naturally the fullest
information procurable on which to make their decisions.
But from the reports on Russia which their censors allow
the Press to publish, and from the statements of some of
the Allied Ministers, it is difficult to believe that they are
aware of the true position. What the Embassies in Petrograd really think they keep to themselves. Expert opinion
of their compatriots well acquainted with Russia is practically unanimous in saying that all is not being done here that
might have been, or still can be, done. I leave it at that.

Russia's Foreign Minister speaks faultless English. My
object in asking for an interview was mainly economic, and
as Tereshchenko had been the first revolutionary Finance
Minister and occupied a prominent place in the Cabinet,

Sir George had advised me to see him. The future policy of the Russian Government with reference to exploiting the country's undeveloped wealth was our theme. The conversation which ensued ranged over the whole field of this subject, including references to the present state of the country, and veiled ones to the enormous loans we have made without guarantees to Russia—not that in a general way guarantees would have been of much use, considering the struggle we are all immersed in, and taking into account the present position of Russia as the result of the Revolution.

The chief and interesting point for the nations who have wealth to lay out in the future is that Russia will be dependent upon foreign capital to open out her as yet untapped resources. But the Russian Government have decided that no concessions of the old type will be permitted; that any concessions granted in the future will be to companies which are partly Russian in character. " There must be a combination of Russian and foreign capital," said the Foreign Minister. " The proportion of each is not so important as that there must be Russian representatives in the companies to advise on Russian methods of administration, law, and so on." " Anglo-Russian combines," I suggested. " Yes," he replied. " We have determined upon that." " Will that be for timber ? " " Yes, for timber." " How will the land question affect the State forests ? " I rejoined. " It should not affect them at all. The State and Appanage Forests belong to the Government of the country, and will continue to belong to them. As a matter of fact, as you doubtless know, only the Government could undertake felling work in the great forests of the north and north-east. There is only a sparse population in those regions. We recognise," continued the Foreign Minister, "that the timber matter is a very important one for Russia, for timber and corn will form the chief of our financial resources for some years to come, and the timber will be the first of the two. Therefore we have arranged to make a Government monopoly " (it was his word) " of timber, and we shall not allow it to be exported in the raw state. It will have to be fashioned in this country. We know that England, France and Italy will require large amounts of it. We propose to work our forests with foreign and Russian capital in this way. The material must be sawn up or made into pulp and the other forms for export in this country," he repeated emphatically. I pointed out that so far as England was concerned—and we took the largest amounts of timber, etc., from Russia before the war—practically the whole material had reached us in this form. " Your statistics, which I have been studying," I pointed out, " show that Germany is the country who has taken the bulk of her timber imports from you in the log form— cutting up the material in her own mills." " Yes," he replied, " that is so. I do not know to what extent, but I know that it is so. That is what we mean to put a stop to." " The figure is somewhere in the neighbourhood of 80 per cent," I answered. Other information I was given has no reference to this matter. But that these economic questions are receiving the serious consideration of the Provisional Government proves—and I have already seen it for myself in the course of visits and inquiries at several of the Secretariats, that serious reconstruction work is being mapped out, and will achieve results of value to the country; provided the Government can only deal firmly with the Council of Workmen and Soldiers, whose efforts are spent in thwarting all such reorganisation work.

August 23rd.—The Executive Committee of the Soviets has been in session, and Rozanoff has issued a report on the, to them, burning question of the hour, the Stockholm Conference; but the methods on which the report is drawn up are open to considerable question. Rozanoff is said by many to be an honest man but a dupe. The memorandum declares that the Russian delegates have achieved a complete victory; that the whole world wishes to participate in the Conference. The wish in this case is father to the thought. There appears to be no such general acceptance of the views of the Russian socialistic visionaries. The Belgian Socialists have refused to meet their enemies at a round table conference in spite of Vandevelde's heroics, paid for in German gold. The British national party of workmen have found themselves unable to attend, a result hailed here with gratification by all who see whither the socialistic efforts—they cannot be termed a programme—are leading Russia. The great Stockholm Conference, therefore, which according, as is openly said here, to the Russian Internationalists and the official German Social Democrats was to be of world-wide importance, is filtering out into a provincial meeting. The *coup de grâce* appears to have been given to this German plot, initiated in Petrograd and supported by German gold, when the reasons for the acceptance of the invitation by the British Labour party and French and Italian Socialists are examined. For their presence would not have aided the plans of the Russian and German Socialists (no annexations and so forth), but have smashed them—for disagreement was a certainty.

It must be confessed that here opinion is pretty well divided, opinion that is not rabidly biassed. But from what one can gather we are not alone in this respect, for public opinion in France, Italy and Britain is not at one over the matter.

It is difficult to say whether it would be the wiser course to give them all passports or refuse them to all and sundry. But how any one, be he Russian, French, Italian, Belgian or British, can wish for a moment to sit at a table with a German passes comprehension. Were the matter not so serious this Stockholm Conference would be the biggest world-comedy ever staged, and all the more so as so much heat has been engendered and ink spilt over it. The Germans as a nation are really to be commiserated, for they have put so many farces on to the world-stage during the past three years, and yet have been unable to see and appreciate the ludicrous side of even one of them—not even the few they have come out of successfully, much less the greater number which have gone against them.

The Ukrainian Rada are not apparently content with the terms yielded them by the Provisional Government. They are endeavouring to obtain the entire management of their own affairs by means of an Ukrainian Constitution, with the object of being able to present to the Constituent Assembly, when it meets, a *fait accompli*. The Ministers are being advised here to show a stiff upper lip to these demands, in which it is said they will be supported not only by the majority of the Russian people, but also by the bulk of the Ukrainians themselves (who, it is believed, are by no means in agreement as to the necessity or equity of the Rada's demands). Urkainian representatives are at present in Petrograd, and have now telegraphed to the Rada that in addition to the Ministers and the Petrograd public generally being against their demands, even Tseretelli and Avksentieff consider them excessive. The representatives therefore advise the acceptance of the Ministerial terms.

Matters in Finland are in an even worse case, and the basis of their efforts would seem to mean an entire separation from Russia. It is plaintively asked here why this should be so. That the Finns should have hated Russia under the old regime of the Czars in Finland was natural, it is said, but that this hate should be passed on to the Russian Revolution is incomprehensible to the Russians. The Finns have played a card which the Provisional Government is advised to resist to the death. Tokoi, who had formed the new Finnish Senate, has resigned, and there is now only one Socialist left in the Senate. If the Socialists refuse to reform the Senate the Governor-General will ask the members of the old Finnish party to come to his help, and it is thought they may succeed. Up to date this party has refused to work with the Socialists. The Socialist parties and Press here are evincing considerable perturbation at the conduct of their brethren in Finland. Although they insist on having their own way and in harassing and fighting the Ministers at every turn, they are dumbfounded to find that the Finnish Socialists wish to act in the same way in their own country; the Russians are adjuring them to respect the orders of the Provisional Government and to wait patiently for the meeting of the Constituent Assembly, who will settle their case fairly. But of course, they are told, they cannot be allowed to separate themselves from Russia.

Meanwhile the appearance of that great arbiter of the
fate of Russia from which so much is expected is to be
delayed. The elections for the Constituent Assembly are
to-day announced as postponed from October 1st to
November 12th, and the meeting to the 28th. The reason
for the postponement is said to be due to the fact that
the municipal and peasant organisations (Local Government
Boards), who are to have charge of the work of preparation
for the elections, are not all yet in existence.

The Russians are welcoming the advent of China into
the war. It shows, they say, that Germany is now the
outcast of the world. Also they point out that, however
matters turn out in Europe, whatever further trials Russia
may have in store for her, she will not now have to face
added troubles in the Far East on the Russo-Chinese
frontier.

The Moscow Conference is the next great event to be
staged, and it is accordingly assuming the chief place in
the wrangling and gossip of the capital. By some much is
expected of it—nothing short of a fusion of all the best in
the various parties in the interests of the country. Others
expect nothing but talk. The pessimists only look for harm
and worse discord as the result of this great Conference.
Its chief object is a free discussion of all the principal
points in dispute away from the unsettling atmosphere
of the capital, with the object of finding a common platform
to work upon. Perhaps the Government will remain in
Moscow and not return. To cut themselves adrift from
the headquarters of the Council of Soldiers and Workmen
and the undisciplined hordes of soldiers and workmen from
whom the latter derive their chief support would, in the
opinion of many, be a brilliant move. The turbulent
capital could then be left to look after itself and go its
own way.

In this connection it is pointed out that the Government
have pandered to the mob by convoking the Constituent
Assembly for October 1st (now postponed), countenancing
the demands of the workmen for their present enormous
wages, by the issue of (or failure to withdraw) Prikaz

No. 1, which led to the subversal of all discipline in the army, forbidding transactions in connection with the land, suppression of all local authorities, refusal to levy indirect taxes, and so forth. At first the Government feared the power of the *bourgeoisie,* but now they have a more deadly fear of the Council of Workmen and Soldiers.

The first meeting of the Moscow Conference is to be held on August 26th, the Conference lasting for four days. Several Ministers will be present, including Kerensky. The Minister for Posts and Telegraphs has charge of the arrangements. One thousand five hundred persons have been invited—representative of the provincial and municipal assemblies, the executive committees of the co-operative organisations, the central committees of the Soviets, commercial and industrial organisations, the professional, intellectual and scientific classes, the army, navy, and so forth. Past and present members of the Duma have a right to attend without special invitation. The Conference will be addressed by Kerensky and various other Ministers dealing with their own departments. There is to be a preparatory Conference on a small scale commencing on August 22nd. Rodzianko, Kropotkine, Miliukoff, Gutchkoff and General Brusiloff are to take part in the latter. Korniloff is to be at the main Conference. There will be some straight talk, therefore, but I fear the betting, from all one hears, is about 25 to 1 against anything coming of it.

The history of the transfer of the ci-devant Czar and the Imperial family from Tsarskoe Selo to Siberia has been divulged—rumour having become too strong for the Government to maintain secrecy any longer; for the most extraordinary stories were afloat in the capital and permeating the country.

The step was unexpected, although it is said to have been decided upon last month. The reasons given for the removal of the Romanoffs into the interior are the Russian retreat on the south-west front, rumours of an intended advance on Petrograd by the Germans, and the food difficulty, which will get worse. Neither transfer nor choice of place of residence—Tobolsk—should, say the partisans of the Government, be looked upon as an act of punishment on the Czar and his family. Their safety and the frustration of royalist plots which their near neighbourhood invited were the main reasons influencing the Government decision. As regards the place chosen. Tobolsk is nice and quiet and a long way away. It has about 25,000 inhabitants only, is situated in the heart of Siberia, on the Irtych, in the midst of dreary marshes and forests, and 200 miles from the railway. The late Emperor of all the Russias and his family arrived at this insalubrious spot at eleven o'clock at night last Saturday (August 18th), having left Tsarskoe Selo over a week ago. The Czar has two rooms, the family three, in the tumbledown residence which forms the quarters of the Governor of Tobolsk. From all accounts Kerensky appears to have made the departure and journey as easy as such a journey under the conditions could be, seeing to all details himself personally. Many hold that in sending the Czar to Siberia the Government have blundered; for they lay themselves open to the charge of continuing to maintain one of the worst forms of punishment of the old regime—banishment to Siberia.

A disgraceful incident has occurred in Petrograd. A secretary and attaché of the Roumanian Legation have been assaulted in a tram by a Russian officer. The assault was unprovoked, and has resulted in a wave of indignation passing over the capital. Kerensky, Tereshchenko and others have naturally hurried to the Legation in person to make Russia's apologies for so gross an act. The officer turns out to be a member of the Council of Workmen and Soldiers, and this has set that hive humming. Representatives were sent off hot haste to apologise, but the Council themselves considered that insufficient, and the officer, who pleaded that he was drunk (and drunkenness is on the increase in Petrograd, which means the reappearance of vodka), has been hurriedly evicted from the Council and also from the Officers' Corps. This incident does not stand alone, and the Bolsheviks are again implicated. On the second occasion it was the turn of the American Legation Consul at Odessa. A crowd of Bolsheviks were " manifesting," and ordered every one to uncover whilst they were passing. The American naturally refused. They knocked his hat off and surrounded and menaced him. The public took the Consul's part and rescued him, but failed to arrest the Bolsheviks. Another impending Bolshevik apology, as *Punch* would say.

Foreigners are even more suspected now than they were during the months after the war broke out. And who can be surprised, with all this German propaganda and gold undermining the whole nation ? I do not wonder at mistakes of the nature I am going to relate being made. It was hatred of the Germans in those early war days. Here are two incidents of those times recently told me. Two English ladies were talking in English in a tram. A Russian officer next to them curtly told them to stop speaking German. The lady he addressed knew no Russian, but her companion spoke it fluently. She answered that they were not conversing in German, and continued the conversation. The officer thereupon addressed them more roughly still, and ordered them to stop talking altogether. The lady who had a command of Russian turned and looked him full in the face, and then apparently let him have her full and unbiassed opinion of him as a man, officer, and gentleman, and that reduced him to silence. I do not know that I am convinced that the lady was right. After all, the officer thought she was a German, and to hate a German like poison was in his eyes highly patriotic. The other story also concerns two of my compatriots, both ladies. They were also sitting in a tram (every one travels in trams in Petrograd—when plentiful and in good order, they are rapid and cheap); the ladies were, of course, gossiping in their natal tongue. A General officer sitting close by sternly bade them desist talking German. Only one of the two ladies knew a little Russian, and she haltingly said in that language that they were speaking English and that the General ought to know the difference in sound between English and German. The General sprang to his feet, brought his hand to the salute, and said, " Vive l'Angle-terre ! "

I see Root has been saying in America that 100,000 locomotives sent to Russia at the present moment would be worth more than an army of several hundred thousand men sent to the western front; whilst another American says that American troops ought to be sent to Russia.

As regards the first contention, the head of the American Railway Mission here says that it is not rolling stock so much as better organisation in running the railways that is required; the mileage run by the engines having dropped by 40 to 50 per cent., whilst only half-loads are carried owing to the fuel difficulties. As for American troops, if these were sufficiently trained they would be better employed, one would imagine, in learning modern warfare on the western front. A small army of seasoned men from that front is what would be useful here, in the opinion of many, to hold up the eastern front and form a nucleus round which all the best of the Russian Army would very soon gather.

The chief sights to be seen in Petrograd nowadays, if we except the soldier hawkers of stolen articles and news-papers, who are to be found in hundreds, if not thousands, throughout the city, are the queues outside the tobacco-nists' and sweet shops. A most extraordinary mixture of classes is to be seen in these queues—for you have to take your place in them, or get some one else to do so, if you want sweets or a particular brand of cigarettes. Beautifully dressed ladies and men, artisans and servant girls, the poorest of the poor from the city slums, rough peasants, the workers of all degrees, and soldiers and sailors *ad lib*. These crowds stand patiently for hours, and the Russian can do this better than any other European I have acquaintance with. Russia must be the greatest cigarette-smoking country in the world. The people smoke at all hours of the day and night—eighty to one hundred cigarettes a day is quite normal—in and out of office, and so on. A subordinate will bring a file of papers into his superior's room, and whilst they are being discussed will light up a

I

cigarette in the official's presence as a matter of course. It is a national habit with them all. It is amusing to see how the venue of the queues changes in the Nevski. The shop on which there is a run for a particular brand of cigarette only opens for a few hours a day, but the queue, growing daily longer, maintains its position during the hours till the stock is exhausted, when it changes its ground to the next place known to contain the article. I have been ten days trying to get some cigars at a particular shop where I easily procured them soon after my arrival. But latterly whenever the place has been open there have been several hundred people in a queue stretching away from the door, and I have neither the time nor patience to wait hours. I did spend an hour one day just to watch the people. There is no shoving, no attempt to take another's place, not even by the soldiers. The Russian resembles the native of India in this respect. He just waits. And the queues at the tram halting-places are the same. For an hour in the middle of the day, the dinner hour, and two hours between four and six in the evening, when the work-people are going home, it is impossible to get a place in a tram unless you are prepared to wait. But there is none of our pushing and squeezing. Each one takes his place at the end of a queue—there is no police surveillance—and waits his turn. The sweet shops in the Nevski, big, very expensive places, are in the same state as regards queues. The price of sweets is absolutely prohibitive, but every one has plenty of paper roubles nowadays, and the common soldier can afford to buy the most expensive boxes, costing a large sum.

How far the Government are fighting against the increase in vodka drinking it is difficult to ascertain. But that it is on the increase there can be little doubt, and the Ministers are being earnestly exhorted to stamp it out. The prohibition of vodka by the Czar at the outbreak of war was a wise step. The experience of the Russo-Japanese War had taught the Russian rulers how impossible it was to fight a big campaign if the soldiers could get this stuff, as the Russian does not know when to stop in his cups. He apparently

A SOAP QUEUE IN PETROGRAD, AUGUST 1917

A DECORATED ARMORED CAR MANNED BY SOLDIERS AND GIRLS STARTING OUT TO COLLECT FOR A CHARITY IN THE CAPITAL.

has not the strength of mind to know when he has had enough, the Russian character and their climate being mainly responsible for this state of affairs. The recent excesses on the retreat from Tarnapol and Kalouch are attributed at least in part to the troops being vodka mad. If the Petrograd soldiers and workmen once get hold of vodka, the excesses and murders, in the present condition of affairs, will be worse than anything the capital has witnessed in the past.

An act which shows the way the wind is blowing, and which might be of assistance to the Provisional Government, is the announcement that the Council of the Astrakhan Cossack Troops has decided to recall their representatives from the Council of Workmen and Soldiers, as they regard the latter body " as assuming legislative functions without rightful authority."

The heated discussions over the Stockholm Conference have drawn an important statement from Kerensky addressed to the Council of Workmen and Soldiers. After denying that he was against the Conference or had had any communications with Korniloff on the subject, the Minister continued : " As regards the treaties Russia has signed with her Allies, I may say that the Provisional Government considers itself bound both by honour and conscience to respect those treaties as long as England and France remain our Allies. It is obvious that the decision of the Conference can have no decisive importance as regards our action towards those treaties."

August 24th.—The Nevski was a brilliant sight this morning. The street was given over for the nonce to a large force of soldiers and girls collecting for a military hospital. A long convoy of armoured cars without guns stretched away from the Hôtel Europe drawn up along the curb. The inhabitants of Petrograd have become accustomed to the sight of these cars under different and by no means so peaceful conditions. It is not uncommon to see an armoured car with the wicked-looking barrel of a machine-gun protruding from the casement fore and aft and a soldier standing at the ready at each, proceeding full tilt down the Nevski on occasions when rumour has it that a local outbreak is expected. As at such times the soldiers have a pretty wide commission with regard to loosing off, the wise people hastily dive for the nearest door or shop, a practice I invariably adopt. After all, one has not come to Petrograd to offer oneself as a target for the Russian soldier to keep his hand in upon. To-day, however, the errand of the cars was a peaceful one and they were hung with banners and tastefully decorated with drapery and cut branches of birch and evergreens. Big lorries were packed with soldiers, some dressed up as mountebanks, girls in flimsy dresses, for it was a brilliantly hot day, and Red Cross nurses. This incongruous horde of collectors armed with money-boxes, left the cars and distributed themselves over the side-walks vociferously demanding subscriptions, the soldiers thrusting their boxes under the noses of the passers-by and extorting money by veiled threats as much as anything else. In fact, I saw people pay several times over before they got out of the area in which the collecting was going on. It would have been a pretty sight under other conditions. In the present it was merely a glaring instance of the total absence of discipline in an army which could permit this sort of thing whilst the front is in such urgent need of drafts. Having exhausted the possibilities of the Nevski, which was rapidly emptying itself of its usual crowd of foot passengers, the cars separated and spread out through the capital to extort money from the suburban areas. It is difficult to say how long this state of affairs will be allowed in the army. It is rampant at present.

It is significant that a strong effort is being made to get Korniloff dismissed from the chief command. For the present the Cossacks have stopped it by informing the Provisional Government that, although they wish to remain loyal to Russia and the Government, they will withdraw their support if the Cossack General is deposed. The Committee of the Society of the Cross of St. George have also sent a similar notification. Of course it is the General's strong effort to reorganise the army which the Council of Workmen and Soldiers wish to put an end to.

In this connection several Ministers yesterday interviewed Korniloff, Kerensky being present. It was then agreed that the former should be present at the Moscow Conference. Further, it was decided that the General should lay before the Conference the measures he deemed necessary to re-establish discipline in the army and the steps to be taken for its reorganisation. As the Socialist Members of the Cabinet and the Soviet are already objecting to his proposals for reorganising the military revolutionary tribunals in the rear, the Moscow meeting is likely to prove a lively one. The Leninites or Bolsheviks have refused to attend the Moscow Conference, stating that it is a *bourgeois* movement. They are accusing the other Socialist parties of joining with the *bourgeoisie* to upset the Revolution.

Great things are expected from the first Polish Army Corps now in process of formation under General Dowbor-Musnicki. The regiments are being formed and trained under the most strict discipline on the French system, and it is hoped will soon give a good account of themselves on the Russian front, and perhaps inspire emulation in the Russian soldiers.

As an indication of the illiterate state of the masses in Russia, the following is of interest. There is a big bookshop near the Admiralty end of the Nevski. In one of the windows a great war map of Europe and Asia hangs. Over this map a giant spider's web has been drawn in ink, the centre of the web being Berlin, with a great black spider stationary over it. The fronts of the fighting forces are shown on the map, indicating the large stretch of country occupied by the forces of the Central Powers. Alongside is a second map showing the Russian front from Riga to Odessa, and the big gap in the line where the Russians broke and retreated at Tarnapol and Kalouch. Almost daily latterly at this part the red and black line of the front of the Central Powers is repainted on the map in advance of the position it previously occupied, numbers of big bold black arrows showing the position and direction of the striking forces. Five successive lines are now painted on that map depicting the Russian retreat. A child could understand the

meaning of these maps.   I have watched the faces of men
and women who have stopped to look at the second one.
The soldiery, for the most part, glance at it unwillingly,
as if it possessed a mesmeric fascination for them, forcing
their glance to it against their will.   Almost invariably
they pass on with a shamefaced leer.   The exceptions are
the soldier leaders who glare at it with lowered brow and
dogged obstinacy.   Younger soldiers or those wearing
the Cross of St. George are seen examining the map with
faces dark with anger and shame.   Well-dressed men and
women also wear this expression.   But saddest is it to
see the illiterate lowest classes examining the map with
puckered brow and a look which only half comprehends
and wonders what it all really means.   This class do not
understand the retreat in the least or the meaning of it.
They have been so often told that victory is crowning the
Russian arms, and that the Revolution has produced a
great and glorious free Russia.

The currency problem is naturally agitating commercial
people a great deal.   Discussing this matter to-day with a
banker, he said, " The Government will probably have to
fix the rouble at its present value (*i. e.* about 1*s.*) or at some
fixed standard.   This will not affect the country interiorly,
as wages for the most part are now fixed on that scale
for the rouble.   It is only the gold loans, foreign loans,
based on the gold rouble of 2*s.* which will be depreciated
by half.   How this problem is to be dealt with is a most
delicate matter.   It looks as if Russia would have to declare
herself a bankrupt or what would practically come to the
same thing.   This would mean that she would have difficulty in raising fresh loans.   It is a problem," said my
friend, " which bristles with difficulties.   In Russia prices
will be maintained at the higher level to correspond with
the depreciated rouble."   I tried to contrast the position
with that of the Indian rupee in the 'nineties of last century,
which gave plenty of trouble and resulted in great heart-
burning amongst salaried Anglo-Indian civil servants.
But unfortunately he had no acquaintance with the rupee
currency.   " This matter," he concluded significantly,

" is of some importance to us on account of the large loans we have made to Russia without security."

The possibilities of opening out the great forest tracts of north-east Russia formed the subject of an interesting discussion I had to-day with an old friend of mine in the Commerce and Industry Department. Both of us in our several ways had studied this problem from our own national view points. We had not corresponded during the war. To-day we found after an exhaustive examination of the question, that we had arrived at almost identical views in this important matter. And, what is more, that we were in agreement on the main points. The suggested method of procedure thus formulated was to parcel up the forest areas to be first dealt with into blocks of approximated 500,000 acres apiece, and offer them to capitalists who would provide the necessary capital to open them out and undertake the felling and extraction work. The capitalists would have to undertake to convert the material in Russia, erecting their own saw-mills, pulp-mills, etc., in that country, and only export material in a manufactured state, with, of course, the exception of pit wood, which would be exported as such. The broad outline of the scheme is therefore in existence, and now only requires the details to be filled in and the capital to work it. These details we now propose to go into more minutely.

One of the difficulties connected with the food question is the attitude of the peasants in holding up their grain and other food supplies—an attitude in which they are by no means alone; for other agrarian communities in the belligerent nations are addicted to much the same practices. The Russian peasant has his grievance. He is unable to obtain what to him are the necessaries of life, chiefly, cloth, iron, tea and sugar. He is ready to exchange the products he produces for the market in return for these commodities, but not for the paper rouble with which he is unable to purchase his requirements. Consequently not only will he not sell his grain, but he is refusing to plough his land. I have visited some of the districts to the south-west of Petrograd with a Russian companion.

On every side large areas of arable land were to be seen lying untilled. Small strips of crops in the vicinity of the villages, grown for the villagers' own consumption, comprised the only cultivation visible. The rest, good arable land, had been left uncultivated. My companion informed me that hundreds of thousands of acres were in this condition throughout the country. The peasants had stopped cultivation after the Revolution for two reasons : (1) they could not obtain their requirements in return for their grain; (2) they had been promised that all the land would be divided up amongst them, and they were awaiting the fruition of the promise, hoping to obtain more valuable areas. Socialistic propagandists, Russian and German, discoursed nightly on this theme at village meetings. Knowing the intellect of their hearers, all they attempted to do was to repeat over and over again a few phrases parrot-like. For instance, " The land for the people," repeated on end for five minutes, varied with, " We are all equal " (five minutes), followed by " Down with the proprietors " (five minutes), and then back to the land again, and so on. It paid, and this state of affairs, said my companion (as we watched the vacant faces of the village audience), will continue until a Government strong enough to enforce its orders arises.

The reason why the peasants cannot obtain their necessities—iron, cloth, etc.—lies, of course, in the fact that Russia has turned her very inadequate factories, etc., inadequate both in number and output, into works for the production of war material, as has been the case in other countries. Consequently the manufacture of agricultural implements, and so forth, has entirely ceased. America has apparently offered to help Russia out of this difficulty, and the matter is now being discussed here. America, with her huge industrial works and factories, could, it is admitted, easily aid Russia to surmount this difficulty. But the depreciated rouble comes in. Speculation would be rife and would, it is agreed, place an insupportable load on Russia if private enterprise in this direction were permitted. Even if the Government

were to take up the scheme it is pointed out that the
sellers sent from America would be strangers unable to
speak Russian and would, therefore, have to make use of
all sorts of intermediaries which would mean bribes, delays
and so forth. The following, in the opinion of financial
experts here, would be the best way of conducting this
matter—

(1) The Russian Government to obtain a certain amount
    of industrial articles as a loan.

(2) The Provisional Government to draw up a list of the
    essential articles required, such as nails, heavy
    boots, agricultural machinery, cheap clothing,
    cotton and woollen stuffs, leather, etc.

(3) The American Government to undertake to pur-
    chase these materials in America, paying for them
    through her own representatives. America to
    transport the goods to Russia at fixed prices, which
    will include the cost of freightage to the American
    Government.

(4) The price of the goods would represent a Russian
    debt to America, the payment of which would be
    settled in the customary manner of settling foreign
    debts.

(5) In this manner the Russian Government would have
    stocks of articles required by the peasants to sell
    in different parts of the country, and could arrange
    for their disposal according to local demands. By
    this means the Russian Government would receive
    a considerable sum of money which the Treasury
    badly needs, whilst the peasants would set free
    their stores of grain and other food-stuffs.

This settlement is sound enough from the Russian point
of view, provided honest men could be found to sell the
American goods to the peasants on behalf of the Russian
Government. It appears not a bad scheme for America,
as it would enable her to tap an enormous market in which
the Germans, up to the outbreak of war, pretty well reigned

supreme. I wonder what our manufacturers will think of it, though? There should be room for them in this market also.

The Ukrainian Rada has decreed for a struggle with the Provisional Government. An intimation has been received from Kieff that the Rada will not be represented at the Moscow Conference. At a recent meeting, after attacking the Provisional Government and Korniloff, the Rada decided to realise what are here termed its " separatist dreams " in a " revolutionary manner." They have determined to submit for the approval of the Ministers the nine General Secretaryships sanctioned by the Russian Cabinet, but to appoint on their own initiative the other five which have not been sanctioned and who are to administer the whole of the south-west and western regions of Russia, which the Provisional Government have excluded from their management. The Rada has also decided to make arrangements to convoke a Constituent Assembly for the Ukraine, who will decide the questions of political administration between the Ukraine and Russia.

There can be little doubt that the Rada, who maintain that they are voicing the wishes of thirty million people, include in their ranks some very able men who have already shown by their methods of dealing with their own problem that they know what they want and the means to take to attain their object. Moreover, they are not dogged and thwarted at every turn by the incubus of a powerful Council of Workmen and Soldiers. Many here think that the Government will have to put up a hard fight if the Rada is to be suppressed, and openly say that such a fight is an impossibility so long as the Government are ruled by the Council.

The latest comedy put on by the latter is a Conference on the subject of National Defence. The unanimous opinion arrived at appears to be that the National Defence can only be safely entrusted in the hands of the Soldiers and Workmen. A leading paper asks, " Who are these Workmen? The men who have decreased production to 10 per cent. of what it was in the days of the Czar. Who are these Soldiers? The soldiers who in hundreds of thousands fly before the German patrols and leave undefended the heart of Russia. Is it these workmen and soldiers who are called to save the universe and establish a reign of peace? "

A Mahomedan deputation recently appeared in Petrograd and were received by the Vice-President of the Council, Nekrasoff. The deputation presented three petitions dealing with the formation of a separate Mahomedan unit in the army; the abuses to which the Mahomedan population were subjected by the members of the local administration; and, thirdly, asking for an improvement in legal methods and in the sanitary conditions in the Caucasus. These grievances were promised attention. The position and well-being of the Mahomedans within the Russian Empire are of some interest and importance to the British.

CHAPTER VIII

PETROGRAD IN AUGUST 1917 (*continued*)

August 25th.—The much-talked-of Moscow Conference commences its sittings to-day. Moscow appears to be regaining something of its old importance as a national centre—a new phase of the revolution. During the first months after the upheaval the local Socialistic councils, blindly following the Petrograd Council of Workmen and Soldiers, dominated the city. But the rising in July injured Petrograd throughout the country, and restored the influence of Moscow, which has been selected as the centre for a series of conferences. A congress of merchants and manufacturers was held last week. The chairman in his opening speech drew a picture of the present position of labour in Russia, by which many industrial concerns were threatened with ruin owing to the excessive demands of the workmen. " The latter," he said, " do not seem to realise what a calamity the closing of industrial works would be to the country in its present condition, when most of the concerns are working solely to keep the army supplied with essentials." The Conference was summoned in order to create an organisation uniting the manufacturers of the whole country.

The business men's conference in its outcome did, in effect, amount to a political demonstration against the Workmen and Soldiers' Council and also against what was termed the lax and amateurish policy hitherto pursued by the Government.

This congress was followed by the conference representing the *bourgeoisie*, which has been sitting during

the last few days.   The big National Conference convened
by the Government commences to-day, and this will be
followed by a great Church Council.   The latter was
arranged for this date some months ago, and is to define
the status of the Orthodox Church, to liberate it from
political bondage and to elect a patriarch.   It is an elective
body, and will represent the Orthodox clergy and laity
from all parts of Russia.   Its deliberations will mark an
epoch in the history of the Eastern Church, but it is not
expected to have, save perhaps indirectly, any political
character.

The Conference of the *bourgeoisie*, whose sittings
finished yesterday, was settled upon during the July rising
in Petrograd, on the initiative of a private group in Moscow.
The decisions of this Conference have not yet been made
public, but it is hoped that the members may work out a
middle line of policy acceptable to both sides.   It will prove
difficult, however.   The Conference includes members of
the Duma, industrialists, bankers, co-operative societies,
representatives of the Peasants' Union, the Professional
Classes Union, and the leaders of the Cadet party.   Rodzianko presided over the meetings, and Generals Alexeieff,
Brusiloff, Yudenich and Kaledin attended.   The resolutions adopted are to be presented to the big Conference
meeting to-day, whose sittings will last four days.

The history of the Moscow Conference is of interest.   It
has been chequered owing to the vacillation of the Government, due chiefly to the opposition and efforts of the
Council of Workmen and Soldiers to prevent the Conference
being held.   It was first decided upon by the *interim*
Government in power immediately after the July crisis,
who had received news of the calling of the *bourgeoisie*
Conference.   They feared that the attitude and decisions
of this latter might be one-sided.   The idea of the Government was to call a National Conference and appeal to it
for support.   Subsequently, fearing that the Conference
might prove hostile to them, they abandoned the idea.
The present Cabinet, realising that the state of opinion
in the country was hopelessly confused and conflicting,

revived the project and decided to invite delegates from every organisation which could be considered representative throughout the country. The Conference is to be consultative in character, and the decisions will not be binding on the Government. But there is considerable distrust amongst the various parties, the socialists considering it a move in favour of the *bourgeoisie*, and the latter in favour of the former. Rumour says an open conflict is possible. Whatever the possibility of this latter, no one is bold enough to offer any forecast as to the outcome, save the pessimist, who simply says it will be *nil*. At the best it is hoped that it may serve as a temporary substitute for the postponed Constituent Assembly. The exhortations of all the influential and moderate papers to the Conference may be summed up in three words : " Think of Russia."

Some interesting figures have been issued with reference to the number of deputies the different governments and towns, etc., will send to the Constituent Assembly. The figures serve to illustrate the great variation in numbers of the population in different parts of the country. The Petrograd Government sends 7 deputies, Moscow 8, Petrograd city 11, and Moscow city 9. Transcaucasia will send 32. The most densely populated government, that of Kieff, will have 22 deputies; the least densely peopled Governments, those of Archangel and Olonets, only having two, although the area covered by these two governments amounts to 854,372 square versts (1 sq. verst = 255 acres).

Kameneff, who was arrested during the July rising, has been released, there being no evidence against him.

It is one of the minor drawbacks to Petrograd that one is not able to spend agreeably such spare hours as one has at one's disposal, especially in the evenings. August has been exceptionally hot in the capital—the men mostly donning thin tusser silk kit—with stifling nights. One's inclination naturally turned to open-air restaurants in various pleasant gardens of the capital. I had been, however, specially warned against such places on my arrival. In the present state of Petrograd they are not the safest of spots to have your dinner in, and, further, are now liable to

being rounded up during the drives instituted to capture
deserters, thieves and cut-throats. And such are by no
means unattended with shooting—atrociously bad shooting,
and therefore the more dangerous. For the whole military
population, and such of the workman as care to be,
are now armed to the teeth. There must be hundreds of
thousands of rifles and bayonets in the hands of the
population of Petrograd, not to speak of revolvers, long
knives and such-like. I witnessed to-day a nice little
incident at a restaurant where I was partaking of lunch.
A family party entered, consisting of the parents, elderly
lower middle-class Russians, the mother rather stout and
dressed in her best, followed by two lads of about seventeen
and sixteen years respectively, both cadets, the one wearing
the ordinary Russian private's uniform and the other that
of a sailor, a youngster of ten or so bringing up the rear.
The restaurant was crowded, and the party, rather out of
countenance, had to proceed the whole length of the large
room before they found a vacant table in a retired corner.
This they took possession of, the father and mother mop-
ping their brows after the trying ordeal to which they
had been subjected; for it was easy to read on their plain,
homely faces, that dining at a restaurant of this class was
not an everyday experience in their lives. Rather did it
appear to be a first attempt to show " life " to the lads.
These latter took the two seats against the wall, and
therefore facing the crowded room. Just as they were
about to sit down the elder, the soldier, touched the sailor
on the shoulder and whispered in his ear. They squeezed
their way out of the table, and, their faces growing more
fiery with embarrassment at each pace, advanced in single
file about a third of the way down the room to a table
occupied by an officer, which they had unwittingly passed
without noticing on their way up. Army etiquette pre-
scribes that an inferior should salute a superior officer when
meeting in a public place. The salute is performed by
advancing to within a pace of the superior and coming
smartly and stiffly to attention, clicking the heels together
and then, after a few moments, turning away. The young

soldier performed the feat successfully, though in the face of that crowded restaurant he had probably never done a more difficult action in his life. As he turned away the young sailor took his place and halted uncertainly. He obviously did not know what his salute to a military officer should be. He stared to the front for a few moments, bobbed his head, turned away and made hurriedly for the safety of his corner. Under ordinary circumstances the incident would have been scarcely noteworthy. With the almost total absence of discipline in the capital the action of these two youngsters stood out bright with hope; for it shows that Young Russia is still in good hands and unaffected by the appalling example of the older men.

I woke suddenly last night and thought for the moment I was back in the midst of last year's gallant work of the Serbians in the Macedonian Mountains. Rifle and machine-gun fire in dropping shots and bursts was coming from somewhere quite close. I went to the window. The street was brilliantly lit down below, and the sound came from a road on the far side of the square, two to three hundred yards away, I estimated. The firing lasted for a quarter of an hour or so, and then died down. Rounding up deserters, I imagined, but whatever it was I see no mention of it as yet in the papers. One can but hope to keep out of such a mêlée.

Yesterday afternoon, whilst walking up the Nevski, I heard the sharp, sudden sounds of what appeared to be big guns firing close to the Nicholas Station end, and suddenly the sky at that end was blotted out by vast black clouds of dense smoke. Further explosions took place at intervals. Having an engagement I was not able to go and investigate, but the cause could be guessed at and is confirmed to-day. A munition factory at O——, fuses apparently, caught fire or was purposely set on fire by workmen, quite a common proceeding of theirs nowadays, and has been burnt to the ground, together with nearly the whole of a neighbouring street. The scenes of panic were apparently appalling and quite beyond the powers of the militia, till largely reinforced, to deal with. Gangs of looters quickly appeared on the scene, and a good deal of free shooting was indulged in. This promiscuous shooting is a pretty safe pastime for the performers, as they are such bad shots. Passers-by and spectators are the sufferers.

The situation on the Great Russian front is being discussed here with considerable keenness by Russian and Allied military experts. They point out that the whole long front from Riga to the mouths of the Danube presents the same state. In place of definite objectives and determined advances on the part of the enemy, the only operations being undertaken are tentative and hesitating in character, subject to constant changes, which would seem to imply either disagreement or vacillation in the Councils of the Great General German-Austro Staff. The conclusions are drawn from the state of the Northern and Roumanian fronts. In the north the hesitation to advance on the part of the Germans is attributed to climatic conditions in the Dvina region. Within three or four weeks at most the autumn rains will commence, with a consequent rise in the level of the rivers and of the water-logged marshes which cover so much of that country. The roads, consequently, will be impassable until the frost comes to harden them. It is therefore regarded as in the highest degree improbable that the Germans are contemplating marching on Petrograd, or that they will be able to get further than Pskoff and Velikaia Rieka—even if they reach as far. The one possibility in the north is that the Germans may try and capture Riga before the inclement season sets in, so as to win a victory which may serve to brag about to neutrals. There have been plenty of rumours about this Riga offensive, which was expected to commence somewhere between August 20th and September 2nd, and the Russian Chief of the Staff and the Generals in command have been endeavouring to stiffen up the troops in this region for the expected attack. But the Germans have not yet moved. The Russian line has been pushed back slightly at Toukkoum at the extremity of the tongue of land they hold on the shores of the Gulf, but no importance is attributed to the movement, which is said to be one

K

of outposts only. The points of strategic importance are, firstly, Olai, half-way between Mitau and Riga; and secondly, the island of Dahlen, formed by the two branches of the western Dvina to the south-east of Riga. As long as these two positions remain unattacked Riga is not threatened. Riga is also, of course, protected from the attack of the German fleet owing to the Gulf being heavily mined. The *morale* of the Russian troops in this sector of the front is said to have gradually improved. Recently the revolutionary tribunal of one of the divisions, near Dvinsk, on its own initiative condemned to death a corporal convicted of fraternising with the enemy. The General commanding this army himself intervened and asked for a commutation of the sentence, which otherwise would have been immediately carried out. Knowing well the psychology of his own compatriots, this may have been a clever move on the part of the General. But the action of the tribunal is significant, if one is to believe all one hears, of the present condition of some considerable part of the front. The soldiers there are living in a soldiers' atmosphere facing their enemy. It would not take much even now to bring them up to fighting trim again : to a sufficient state of efficiency, at any rate, to hold the front even if they are not capable of an offensive. The danger still is not so much at the front as in the rear. We shall doubtless see the removal, at the order of the Council of Workmen. and Soldiers of Petrograd, of the members of the tribunal who condemned the corporal to death. And they will be lucky if they themselves do not mysteriously disappear. It is at the rear, and especially in Petrograd, where the moral and practical help of the Allies is so much required. The Russian Staff admits, as in fact all know, that the Germans are concentrating important forces round Mitau, and that considerable masses of heavy artillery and huge stocks of shells have been brought up. If, however, nothing happens within the next three weeks on the Dvina, this part of the front may be regarded as out of action until the December frosts set in, or even till the early summer of 1918.

Now to turn to the far south of the front. Here the Austro-Hungarian forces are very far from having carried out their promised blows and advances between the Dniester and the Pruth, on Bieltsi and Kichineff, and on Odessa. A fortnight ago Russian military experts were prophesying an invasion of Ukrainia and a march on Kieff and Odessa. It is true that climatic conditions do not play the same part as in the north, and that these will not delay any projected operations conceived by the Austro-German Staff. But up to the present the four Austro-German armies which surround the Moldavian positions, between the Dneiper and the estuary of the Danube, have accomplished none of the objects they were credited with. The big thrust from west to east in the direction of Okna is not making progress; the southern offensive, based on Fokshani, has only managed to gain a little ground in the direction of Marasheshki Pancin. In fact, only small strategic operations have so far been accomplished, in spite of Mackensen's great numerical superiority. Great admiration is expressed at the conduct of the Roumanians who, supported by the Russians, have for the last fortnight put up a fine fight and contested every foot of ground with magnificent bravery. Each village has been taken and retaken, the hand-to-hand fighting being of the bloodiest description. The King of Roumania is under fire with his troops, and shows himself determined to dispute every yard of his country with the enemy before he accepts the hospitality of Russian soil at Kherson, which has been chosen by the Russian Government as the headquarters of the Roumanian Court. Local Jewish societies and revolutionary bodies have objected strongly to this selection, but without success. The four armies on the Moldavian front are then more or less stationary, and the enemy, instead of fighting, is adopting measures for the spread of Austro-German propaganda. His airmen are constantly flying over the Roumanian lines dropping notices and proclamations advising the Roumanian soldiery to turn their fire upon the Russians, in return for which at the peace settlement Roumania would be given Bessarabia,

Podolia and Volhynia! The experts note with curiosity the obvious nervousness of the Germans in the neighbourhood of Brody, east of Lvow. They are maintaining a heavy artillery fire here, and appear to expect a Russian advance in this direction, and such an advance, it is maintained, if it were pushed home vigorously, would be the best way to draw off forces from the Roumanian front and reconcentrate the main weight of attack in Galicia. The Russian military experts do not fail to point out the reasons for the present comparative quiet on the great Russian front. "It is due," they say, "to the great Anglo-Franco-Italian attacks carried out simultaneously on the western front. These attacks have disconcerted Hindenburg, and have forced him to send his reserves to the front where his lines are bearing the main brunt of the assaults. This time, at least, the unity of the fronts has not remained an entirely dead letter. Our Allies, seeing the extreme peril of their eastern front, are hammering at the German and Austrian fortified defensive lines, and will continue to so hammer. This is the comforting position for us. Shall we not then pull ourselves together as soldiers, get back our discipline, and, following the example of our Allies, once again carry the army to victory and glory?" This is the expert opinion. Whether it is altogether correct in its assumptions is at least open to doubt. Obviously there is no cause for the Central Powers to sacrifice life, or rather (for sacrificing life does not worry them) needlessly waste men they cannot afford to lose, if their object can be achieved by keeping them in their trenches; whilst gold and propaganda work makes an end to the Russian Army. Advance at any given point or points will then be simple.

August 26th.—I spent the day, it is Sunday, at Pavlost, a suburb of Petrograd, lying out beyond Tsarskoe Selo. The day did not begin auspiciously. All I could obtain in the hotel was a glass of weak tea for breakfast. They had run out of everything else. I have not dealt much with the personal aspect of the food question here. It is at times, becoming increasingly frequent, sufficiently ludicrous—also exasperating. The Russian has no notion of what the Anglo-Indian terms "bundobast," a most comprehensive word in its way, as significant as the word "cushy" (also Anglo-Indian), which has come to stay with us, I suppose, as indicative of a soft (and safe) job. To return to Russian management. Take this hotel, for instance. When they have sugar, tea, coffee, etc., they are lavish with it. You can have as much sugar as you like, they do not attempt to ration you to a lump or two; and so with other things. You pass a few joyful fat days, and then come the lean ones, and on these there may be nothing; often there has not been anything for breakfast, save a glass of insipid tea. Of course, the guests can surmount the sugar difficulty by pocketing a few lumps during the time of plenty. But this does not apply to other articles; and sugar does not affect me particularly.

It was a pouring wet morning and not a drosky to be had, so the journey to the fine Tsarskoe Selo Station was a matter of some difficulty. The sixteen miles to Pavlost took fifty minutes at present-day rates of travelling, but it was enlivened by a well-dressed girl, who came in and played the zither beautifully and then collected money from us. She did not mention what it was for, but I meekly followed the example of my fellow-travellers and shelled out without inquiry. One has got so used to this collecting habit, with which all Europe has become afflicted. It is simpler to pay and look pleasant over it.

The railway terminus at Pavlost is more like a casino than a station, and answers the same purpose. The Government, in this instance, have become inoculated with western ideas. There is a large restaurant, concert hall, and well-laid-out gardens, all planned on the grand scale to attract Petrograders, much on the lines of the Londoner's White City, and similar places. Concerts and ballets are given throughout the season during the short summer weeks, now coming to an end. Hard by is a fine park belonging to one of the Russian Grand Dukes, a cousin of the ex-Czar's. This park is open to the public and is of interest since it was laid out about 150 years ago by a Scotsman.   It has much the appearance of the " policy " portion of a large Scotch estate, laid out on the monotonous level of the great Russian plain, which stretches away on all sides.   Pine and spruce woods, with large clumps consisting of hard woods interspersed with stretches of grass, spread away on all sides.   A small river meanders through the park, opening out into artificial lakes with rustic bridges, carrying the roads and paths over the river. The whole thing was admirably planned originally, and the subsequent growth has well justified the anticipations of that long-headed Scotsman of a far-off past, whose name I failed to ascertain.   Pavlost is a real suburb to all intents and purposes, similar to a London one, save that all the houses are detached, built of wood, and stand embosomed in trees, mostly pine, spruce and birch.   The majority of the villas are what they term " summer houses " with single windows, and only meant for summer residence. My friend, who resides here all the year, possessed one of the few more strongly built, and fitted with the double windows the rigour of the winter of northern Russia make essential.   In the vicinity of the place, lost amongst the trees, are some more pretentious summer houses inhabited by millionaire merchants of Petrograd.   In the erection and finishing of these money has obviously been no object, and I have rarely seen more luxurious nests, for their size, than these present.

The one drawback to Pavlost at the present time, in my friend's eyes, is that it is more or less on the direct line between Petrograd and the Army Headquarters in the field. Any advance against Petrograd would see Pavlost swarming with troops, and turn it into a far from desirable place for peacefully inclined folk.

I was given some interesting side-lights on the results of the Revolution from the view-point of a Russian Jew, who turned up at my friend's house in the afternoon.   He had spent several years in England and Scotland, and knew Edinburgh and Glasgow well.   He acknowledged the gravity of the present position in Russia, but maintained that the Revolution had already given them a great deal: the right to form societies and companies of their own without being subjected to the previous harassing restrictions; the right of free residence; free speech; a free press, and free education. " All these things," he said, " the Revolution gave us at a stroke of the pen. The trouble is, that the great bulk of the population are socialistic and uneducated and cannot understand the present danger. They are unable to realise that there are limits to the amount of pay they can be given. They were grossly underpaid before the Revolution, and now insist on getting too much. Of course," he continued, " the dearness of living will necessitate the maintenance of a high wage, not the present preposterous one. It is the ease with which the paper money can be printed and circulated that is to a great extent responsible for the present high wages. As it is only paper, no one attaches any value to it, and the workers do not see why they should not have as much as they can get." I made a remark about the apparent inaction of the *bourgeoisie*. " Yes," he replied, " the *bourgeoisie* are not really tackling this matter with any skill. We are, it is true, small numerically, and are fighting for our capital, and consequently our future means of livelihood. The commercial portion of the *bourgeoisie* are relatively so small in numbers that we have really no voice." " How about your Congress at Moscow the other day? Do you think it was wise to make such an open attack on the Council of Workmen and Soldiers?" " Oh, we were all talking, and got carried away a bit, doubtless," he replied. " But it is a duty of all the *bourgeois* parties to stand up against the attempts of the Council to grasp at the real power—to seize the Government. For should they do so it will mean the end of everything—the war, capital, domestic safety—everything. Don't you think so?" he said, turning to my friend. " Oh yes, of course, if they get out this Coalition Government it will be the end—for a time at least. They could not last long—that's a certainty." I could see, however, that the Jew thought that it might be long enough to bring about one of the dreaded pogroms. " You will doubtless have noticed," my friend said, " the crowd of men you see in the middle of the day several times during the week in the hall and lounge of your hotel. They use that place now-a-days as their stock exchange, the exchange being closed." " But what are the men in uniform doing? There are always a number of them. Are they combining speculation with their military duties?" " Oh, they are stockbrokers right enough, engaged on their business. That is the point. The commercial class is relatively so small that, although their representatives of military age had to get into uniform when the war broke out, they are useless for military purposes. They don't know any drill, and would not be able to exercise any command over the men. So they are put into some job with no work to do, and allowed to pursue their civil occupations. Their numbers are negligible, you see, so that they can be treated in this fashion without causing any jealousy." " How strong are the Cadets?" I inquired of our Jewish acquaintance. " Oh, they are pretty strong," he replied, " but the trouble is, that in their way they are almost as ignorant as the people; anyhow, the latter form the great mass of the population, and they really made the revolution and think they can run it. The peasants are another difficulty. They now consider that all the land belongs to them. The Bolsheviks have told them it does. In many parts they are, therefore, cutting down and burning the ripe crops of neighbouring landlords in order to prevent the latter realising their price. It will lessen the food supplies in the north, but they are so ignorant that they do not understand that. Nor are they concerned about the food supplies of the cities or industrial districts which do not personally affect them, save that they indirectly supply them. And at present they will not part with their grain for the paper money."

August 28*th*.—Roumania is endeavouring to stir up Russia to a remembrance that the latter is to a great extent responsible for her present deplorable position. A prominent Roumanian member of the Senate points out in a manifesto issued here that the Roumanians should be accorded at

least as much sympathy by the Allies as is evinced towards
Belgium and Serbia.   He points out that his country had
two whole years in which to watch the ruthless treatment
to which these two countries were subjected at the hands
of the Central Powers: that they realised the grave
danger to which they would expose themselves by entering
the war.   They hesitated a long time, because they well
knew the strength of the Central Powers and also their
own deficiencies.   But with a full knowledge of the risks
they came in.   They considered that their duty towards
their compatriots groaning under the Austrian yoke was
paramount, and outweighed the easy and luxurious life
they were leading and could continue to lead if they
remained neutral.   " With the Allied guarantee that at
the least we should be able to liberate our brothers from
Austria, we agreed to range ourselves on their side.   Also,"
he adds, as an *arrière pensée*, " the disgust with which we
witnessed the German crimes against humanity would alone
have brought us in against her.   In three months three-
quarters of our country was invaded and ruined, whereas
if one Russian army corps had been sent to Tjin or two
more divisions to the Dobrudja at the decisive moment,
we should have been able to stave off this disaster.   The
following winter was the coldest within the memory of
man; we spent it in retreating, with famine and epidemics
to contend with.   Then came the spring, and with it an
alleviation of our misery.   During the four following
months, under the supervision of the French military
mission headed by General Berthelot, the army was completely reorganised and the *morale* of the soldiers reached
a high point.   We felt we could beat back our enemies,
and get back into our beloved country once again."

By the way, in an interview here early in August,
General Berthelot spoke in the highest terms of the reformed
Roumanian Army, and said it was then as fine a fighting
machine as any which existed on any front.   As he had the
remodelling of it, allowance must be made for some national
gratification.   But it was doubtless true enough.   For the
French reorganised the Serbian Army after their great

retreat, and I saw for myself on the Macedonian front the magnificent way the Serbians fought to recapture Monastir. But the General, in his remarks, says that when Roumania entered the war, in August 1916, she was totally unprepared. She had, he says, no modern organisation, no guns, and very inferior equipment; that, in fact, she was quite unprepared to enter the struggle. Why, in God's name, then, was she allowed to come in? Surely at the end of two years. the Allies had learnt what modern warfare necessitated. I remember reading the eulogies and transports in the Salonika Press at the end of August 1916. One would have imagined that Roumania was going to finish the war on her own. There appears to have been *tête monté* somewhere. It is said that out of the 600,000 men with which she entered the war she lost last year 450,000 in killed, wounded and prisoners. The army reformed by Berthelot consisted of 250,000 rifles.

To return to the senator's review of the position : " A small offensive was commenced on July 25th last, which in a few days gave us 100 guns of all calibres and 10,000 prisoners, including a general, a number of officers and a large amount of booty. This was to have been followed by the big offensive along the whole Roumanian front, which had already been prepared by the necessary preparatory bombardment. As our soldiers were standing ready to leave the trenches mad with joy at the thought that they were about to advance, the order was received to stand fast. At the supreme moment, when they were assured that victory was in their hands, they had to stand inactive. The Russians had broken their front at Tarnapol and were in a disgraceful retreat. For the second time fate was against us. Will our tragic situation ever be really realised ? With a crushing superiority over the enemy in front of us, with success within our grasp, we had to stand fast; and then, more galling still, we had to draw back and yield up the last corner of our beloved country to the enemy and retire into Russia : and this at a moment when some of the Revolutionary leaders are really championing the cause of Austrian

Imperialism. These men, however, do not represent the true Russia, and the kindness and hospitality of the latter will compensate us for the acts of the Kaiser's Russian friends. Our soldiers on the Sereth front will continue to defend Bessarabia, Odessa, Kherson and the rich southern Russia which is so coveted by the Germans. Whilst the full measure of the bitter cup we have had to drink will never be understood, we may hope that when the Peace deliberations commence our great Allies will not forget Roumania and all she has suffered : and these last sufferings, perhaps the greatest of all."

Germany publishes the following figures with reference to the booty she secured in Galicia, Bukovina and Rumania as a direct result of the Tarnapol break in the Russian front : Prisoners captured, 655 officers and 41,300 soldiers ; 257 guns, 546 machine-guns and 50,000 rifles ; 25,000 gas-masks ; 14 armoured cars, 15 motor-trucks, 2 armoured trains, 6 goods-trains, 218 wagons and 26 locomotives—altogether a pretty haul to secure without having to fight for it.

The Moscow Bolsheviks tried to bring about a general strike in order to impede, if not prevent, the Conference, but beyond the fact that the tramways stopped running they have not been very successful. Things, so far, have gone quietly, but general disappointment is expressed that the Government decided not to make any fresh announcement of policy but to stand by their July declaration. The Soviets have issued earnest exhortations to the people not to cause disorder during the period the Conference lasts unless, presumably, they receive orders to the contrary from the former, *i.e.* the Council of Workmen and Soldiers. Considerable military precautions have been taken at Moscow to prevent outbreaks, the Bolshoy Theatre, where the Conference is taking place, being guarded by troops. The Bolsheviks are attending with the object of trying to promote disagreement. Kerensky's opening speech has disappointed most people. Instead of announcing a firm policy he confined himself to platitudes. The various parties were having separate conferences yesterday. To-day should be a great day, and some think the Government may go to pieces again under the attacks. Tchernoff will come in for a good deal.

A Japanese mission has arrived in New York, and rumour here has it that as a result of negotiations now in progress between the Japanese mission and representatives of the Allies and America, Japanese troops are to participate in military operations in the European theatre of war. Rumour says that that theatre will be the Russian front. Whether such a contingency is possible or not, only the statesman can say; but if there is anything in it, and there is any chance of the Russian Government agreeing to it, it is thought that Petrograd, Moscow, or some southern Russian town would have been a better meeting-place than the New World. The Allied Press are apparently welcoming the idea, but it is a pity that it was not mooted and settled two months ago. Here a partial demobilisation is being talked of, and there is no doubt that if it can be carried out it would be the best thing possible in the interests of that portion of the army which has not yet forgotten its duty to the country. It is pointed out that the great mass of the reserves are now nothing but an undisciplined horde. That amongst them there are hundreds of thousands of men who are totally untrained, who, in fact, do not know one end of a rifle from the other. Russia mobilised on far too large a scale at the beginning, and large numbers of these so-called soldiers are quite useless. Furthermore, the bulk of these men are so infected with socialistic ideas that they will never go to the front; in fact, drafts cannot be made up of them. It would be better, it is said, to keep the army at the front on a smaller scale, even if it cannot be supported by drafts, than to risk losing the whole army, which will be a certainty if matters are allowed to drift in their present condition. In all countries there is a limit to the number of effectives who can be supplied with equipment and trained, and beyond that limit a useless extra burden is placed on the State by mobilising men. A reduction of the army will enable the soldiers to be better trained, better

equipped, and better organised for their task. But will
the Council of Workmen and Soldiers permit this demobilisation of the reserves and consequent strengthening
of the army at the front ?

The Ukrainian Rada has passed a resolution protesting
against the Provisional Government's instructions to the
General Secretariat. These instructions are said to display
an imperialistic tendency towards the Ukraine on the part
of Russian capitalists and middle classes, and it is held
that they violate the agreement of July 14th arrived at
between the Rada and the Russian Government. The
instructions are also said to show distrust of the Ukrainian
people. The Secretariat had, in face of these instructions,
resigned, but this resignation was subsequently withdrawn.
The Central Rada have refused the invitation of the
Government to be present at the Moscow Conference.

In Finland the head of the militia at Helsingfors has
resigned, as he states that it is impossible to re-establish
order in the capital. The elections for the new Diet have
commenced. The *bourgeois* party has entered on a keen
struggle with the Socialist and Swedish parties. The old
Finnish party and the agrarians of Abo have formed a
bloc against the Socialists. This bloc entered into negotiations with the young Finns in an endeavour to obtain
their support. The negotiations were successful. These
parties do not believe that the old Diet can be reassembled.
But the Central Committee of the Finnish Socialists have
issued an appeal to the people, criticising the action of the
Provisional Government in dissolving the Diet as uncon-
stitutional. They announce that in spite of the Government's threat to use military force, the Diet will reassemble
on August 29th and continue its work. Nevertheless, the
Socialists are taking an active part in the new elections.
To-morrow (August 29th) is regarded as a critical day.

The Soukhomlinoff trial had a long and most interesting
sitting on its third day. General Ianushkevitch, formerly
Chief of the General Staff and Chief of G.H.Q. at the
front during the war, in giving evidence, said that he had
repeatedly asked the War Minister for shells, always

receiving promises but no shells. " You can imagine the condition we were in at the front," he said, " when having no shells we had to content ourselves with hearing the guns firing blank ammunition." The Germans were aware that we had no shells, and placed their guns within 2000 yards of our men, when the normal distance would have been three and a half to four miles. The offensive in eastern Prussia was only made to help England and France. We knew we were short of shells, but the Chief Director of Artillery did not anticipate a long war. The advance in the Carpathians was undertaken by General Ivanoff, who considered inaction in war dangerous, and hoped that shells would be sent to him. Some interesting information was forthcoming anent those fateful days of July and August 1914. The witness was asked if on the day of mobilisation the Czar had not telephoned to him to stop mobilising. " Yes, the Czar wished to only mobilise the four regions in the south-west.

" When matters between Austria and Serbia became alarming it was decided to mobilise four regions. But on July 31st, after receiving my report, the Czar signed the decree for a general mobilisation. Emphasising the urgent necessity for a general mobilisation, I pointed out to the Czar that the partial mobilisation undertaken to frighten Austria was insufficient, for behind Austria was Germany. We were fully aware that Germany ardently desired war, and that it was to her interests that this war should commence before we had completed our big programme of army reorganisation, which could not be before 1918. As soon as the decree for the general mobilisation had been signed, I went at once to the Council of Ministers at Peterhof. On that same day the Czar again rang me up on the telephone. He once more asked me whether it would not be possible to substitute the partial mobilisation against Austria-Hungary for the general mobilisation. I replied that the change would place the Empire in the most serious danger, and added that 400,000 men were already on the march. The Czar then said that he had received a telegram from the Emperor William II, in which the latter gave his word of honour that Germany would remain on friendly terms with Russia, if the latter restricted herself to a partial mobilisation." After this conversation General Ianushkevitch visited the Minister for Foreign Affairs, to endeavour to persuade him that the postponement of the general mobilisation was impossible. The next day another conference was held between the Foreign Minister, the War Minister (Soukhomlinoff) and General Ianushkevitch. In ten minutes it was decided that the postponement of the general mobilisation was impossible, and the Foreign Minister submitted a memorandum to this effect to the Czar. The resolution to proceed with the general mobilisation was definitely decided upon at five o'clock in the evening. The witness made it plain that the Czar only signed the decree for the general mobilisation because the Foreign Minister and the War Minister were both agreed that the measure was essential. " It is of interest to mention," he continued, " that the spy service of Germany was so efficient, that all my telephonic conversations with the Czar, and those of the Czar with me were known to the German Headquarters Staff." To prevent this leakage the witness had to have a private direct line installed.

The accused General Soukhomlinoff asked to be allowed to make a statement on the last witness's remarks in regard to the mobilisation. " During the night of July 31st the Czar rang me up on the telephone, and gave me the order that the general mobilisation was to be postponed. The order was formal and I could not object. I was aghast. It was a terrible position. The general mobilisation had already been made public. For technical reasons I knew it could not be postponed, that to interfere with it would result in calamity. I was at my wits' end. Half an hour later General Ianushkevitch rang me up and said that he had also received a similar formal order from the Czar. He asked for my orders. I told him the postponement was impossible, and that he should allow matters to proceed. The next day I saw the Emperor and lied to him. I said we were only carrying out the partial mobilisation. I was mad that day. I knew the general mobilisation was proceeding and that we could not stop it. Happily towards evening the Czar was persuaded to withdraw the order, and I subsequently received his thanks for the smoothness with which the general mobilisation had been carried out. Had the latter not been carried out I should have long ago been doing hard labour." As to the want of shells, the accused declared that that was due to the rudimentary condition of Russian industries. Germany had been preparing for this war for forty-eight years, and for that period she had been mobilising her industries with this end in view.

General Ianushkevitch added some interesting information on what took place on July 30th, the day before the general mobilisation, events which determined his action on the two following days : " On July 30th, after the general mobilisation had been decided upon, but before it had been made public, the Czar ordered me to inform Count Pourtales, the German Ambassador, that the Russian mobilisation was not intended as a hostile act against Germany, and that Russia wished to maintain good relations with her neighbour. I informed the Foreign Minister (Sassanoff) that I had undertaken this mission. The Foreign Minister did not hold a high opinion of our German Ambassador. He informed me that Count Pourtales would be likely to interpret what I had said in his own fashion, and that it would be better if I saw the German military attaché on the subject. The latter, Major N., visited the Headquarters of the General Staff at my request, but whereas formerly he always appeared in military attire, and spoke Russian, he was now in mufti, and spoke in French only. I gave him to understand that Russia had no plans of aggression against Germany. He replied : ' Unfortunately, the Russian mobilisation is reaching completion.' ' Not so,' I told him, ' it has not even commenced.' He contradicted me with the greatest *sang-froid*, and said he had more exact information. I then gave him my word of honour as Chief of the Staff that on that day, July 30th, at that moment, three o'clock in the afternoon, the general mobilisation of the Russian Army had not been ordered or announced. The Major would not believe me. I was ready to give him my statement in writing but he politely refused to accept it.

"From the attitude of the German military attaché, I understood that Germany had already made up her mind and that war was inevitable. I also understood, and later on I ascertained it for a fact, that the German mobilisation was already *un fait accompli*, and that she had been able to successfully accomplish it without the fact becoming previously known." The General, in conclusion, again reiterated that the first day of the Russian mobilisation was July 31st.

August 31*st.*—I had an interesting conversation with an old Government official to-day. He had passed long years under the old regime, and though fully aware of all its deficiencies, for which he maintained the German influence at the court was mainly responsible, he held that for years to come some form of more or less autocratic rule was the only possible way to govern Russia. "The people should be given their free institutions, their Dumas and Parliaments," he said. "If the Czar had given them their constitution all would have been well, and the present state of affairs would have been delayed for another thirty years—would, in fact, never have occurred—for by that time the masses would have been educated. It was Germany who kept us back, German intrigues and advice given with one object in view which prevented the Czar, unfortunately a very weak man, from putting into execution the reforms which he knew himself were necessary. The war did not stay these intrigues, as the world now knows. Had it done so the Czar would still be ruling Russia." On the subject of the present regime he was very bitter. "Russia can never be ruled without a strong man. The greater bulk of the more moderate Socialists realise this now. But the leaders were weak at the beginning, and they let these ignorant men on the Council of the Workmen and Soldiers get the upper hand. They, that *canaille*, are now our real rulers." "They say Lenin is

L

now in Berlin," I remarked. " Yes," he said with disgust, " receiving his orders from the Kaiser. But you will see, he will be back here. I know my countrymen. A few months more may see a clean sweep of all these ignorant men who are now trying to govern Russia, and their replacement by more experienced ones. The Cadet party," he said, " are bound to run things in the end. They have experienced men in their ranks." " How long do you think that will be ? " I queried. But my friend would fix no time-limit, nor would he venture to prophesy as to what would happen before that desirable outcome arrives. " The demand of the hot-headed Socialists for a peace which can never be a real peace, and the certainty of famine must lead," he said, " to outbreaks and massacres. Petrograd will see bloodier times this winter than she ever saw under the Czars; for once the undisciplined horde of soldiery and the starving workers commence food-hunting and massacring, they will be joined by every hooligan in the capital, and there will be no force strong enough to get them in hand again. I have witnessed bloody days in Petrograd in years past," he continued; " the Czars were merciless in stamping out uprisings of the people, but they were carried out on a carefully thought-out plan and under an iron discipline. They went a certain length and then ceased. God knows what we shall see." " But is there not a chance of a strong man coming to the front, one of the Grand Dukes ? " " The people will not have any member of the Romanoff family—or rather the Socialists will not. There is not a chance of it at present. A strong man's only hope would be to find support in the army. Without such a backing it would be useless for him to try. You may have heard it said," he went on, dropping his voice [we were sitting in a crowded restaurant], " that if Kerensky would join with one of the army leaders " [he mentioned no name, but I knew he meant Korniloff], " there might be a chance for the country. That between them they would be assured of a strong part of the army. But Kerensky is too vacillating a man, too hesitating. He can talk, but he is no use

for anything else. And now I fear it is too late." I had
naturally heard many rumours and veiled hints at such a
combination. One could not have lived all these weeks
in the capital in ignorance of this possibility. I had been
told that after the July advance it could have been done
with a certainty, but at that time Kerensky had still much
to learn. He still relied solely on his eloquence. In fact,
he does so now, as his recent opening speech at the Moscow
Conference, made without a note, well shows. " That
gives you the limits of the man," said my friend; " he
has no constructive policy—no policy really. He lives
from day to day with his gaze riveted on the Council of
Workmen and Soldiers. What has this Moscow Conference
done ? It has not come to open blows, as many expected
it would, but it has done nothing. There has been a lot
of talk. We had that before. Korniloff's oration was
practical and good, and moderate enough in all conscience.
He has the makings of a statesman in him, that man—
and I have seen many in my time. But the Socialists
will get him out and the Ministers will sacrifice him. Some
of the papers make a lot of the fact that the Socialist
Tseretelli has joined hands with Boublikoff, who represents
the big industrial interests. That may be of some future
importance, but the main thing was the Government;
that they should have obtained such a fusion of parties
as would have enabled them to suppress the Council of
Workmen and Soldiers. Until that is done nothing is of
any use. They are the real source of danger to Russia."
My friend the old official ended gravely : " Your Government and the French Government ought to come and help
us. I have lived a long life in the service of my country.
I know Russia and I know Petrograd. I can read the
signs of outbreaks. They have come before, and we then
had a Government to repress them. There is one coming
now, or I am very much mistaken, and Petrograd and
Russia will run with blood before it is over, for we have
no Government capable of repressing it. Perhaps in this
one I shall go too."

There is considerable discussion in the capital, and not

a little relief amongst thinking men, on the decision (tele-graphed here) of the Allied Socialist Conference held in London on the 28th, with reference to their participation in the Stockholm Conference. The Conference apparently failed to agree on the two main points, *i.e.* participation in negotiations with the Socialist representatives of enemy countries, and on the question of the war aims which should be put forward by the Allied Socialists in any such negotiations. As Henderson presided over the Conference, at which representatives of Great Britain, South Africa, France, Russia, Italy, Portugal, Belgium and Greece participated, the decision is regarded as having driven home the last nail in the coffin of the much-trumpeted Stockholm fiasco. It must have cost Germany a lot of gold—that is one comfort; and how much more she spends on giving the coffin a decent burial will not, I fancy, worry any of us. And the invitation of the Russo-Dutch-Scandinavian Committee of Stockholm to attend the Conference, which some at least of the members of the Allied Socialist Conference had in their pockets, becomes another scrap of German waste paper.

The latest rumour in the Petrograd restaurants and cafés is that General Alexeieff may again be reappointed Commander-in-Chief of the armies, the Provisional Government having become frightened at Korniloff's popularity. But Kerensky has publicly said that he fully agrees with all Korniloff's proposals for reorganising the army and carrying on the war. In this connection the Annual British Statistics of British exports are interesting. During the past year England sent to Russia 1,700,000 shells and fuses; 3000 odd hundredweights of gunpowder; 37 hundredweights of explosives; 47,000,000 cartridges; 1,400,000 detonators and 65 guns. I wonder how much of these the Germans have already got!

I see Lansing has issued the following statement in New York : " I do not think it is the general opinion here that Russia is on the eve of collapse. As a matter of fact she is stronger to-day than she was a month ago, both from the general governmental point of view and from the military standpoint." Here the announcement is regarded by some with amusement, by others with disgust.

Siberia is now proposing autonomy for itself. She is preparing to constitute herself into a Federal State, with legislative powers in the hands of the Siberian Duma, executive power in a Siberian Cabinet of Ministers, which is to be formed, and supreme judicial powers in the Siberian Senate. So this is the latest recruit in the dismemberment of Russia scheme.

The dispute between the Ukrainian Rada and the Provisional Government is now said to have been settled, and no further complications are expected. The Secretariat has been reconstituted, the old President Vinnichenko remaining in office.

The new Finnish Diet has assembled after all. They were not allowed to use their own building, which was occupied by troops, but the seventy-nine members (out of 200) who attended collected in the Provincial Deputies' building. Manner, the former talman of the old Diet, said that the latest order of the Provisional Government forbidding the new Diet to assemble was illegal. The Governor-General in an open letter to the talman, pointed out that as the old Diet had been dissolved the new one, under the Finnish Constitution, cannot reassemble without the Government's permission. That if, therefore, the new Diet meets without this permission, it would be tantamount to a meeting of the former members of the Diet which had been forbidden. As the Government proposed to use force to see their order carried out, the resultant bloodshed will be on the talman's head. On receipt of this letter, Manner went in person to the Governor-General, and protested that the order of the Provisional Government was illegal and asking that it should be withdrawn. The Governor-General promised to transmit the complaint to the Ministers. It was after this that the new Diet met. The Socialists are now calling for assistance to resist by force any efforts of the Government to suppress the new Diet. So far there has been no disorder. Colonel Hulenbegel, whom the Governor-General had ordered to dissolve the Diet, refused

to obey, resigning his commission rather than carry out
the order.

Owing to the extraordinary unsettled conditions we are
living amongst in Russia, that *cause célèbre* the Soukhomlinoff trial is not attracting the amount of attention
it undoubtedly deserves.   It is in fact historical, epoch-
making in itself.   For the first time in the history of Russian
jurisprudence a public jury is taking part in a political
trial.   This is the first instance since the great judicial
reform of half a century ago of a public jury being asked
to give a verdict in a case tried by a special sitting of the
Senate.   And more striking still, perhaps, is the fact
that the first case to come before such a court is no less a
one than the trial of a great Minister, the War Minister,
of the old regime.   Under that regime political offences
were given but a scant formality of a trial and no jury.

This great trial, therefore, deserves to receive more
prominence than is accorded to it.   The scene is set in the
Navy and Army Hall, never intended for such a purpose.
But the old Law Courts were destroyed by the populace
during the first days of the Revolution to get rid of a hateful
reminder of the past.   In this hall, on the wall behind the
chairman's seat, hangs a great picture covered with white
cloth—a portrait of the ex-Czar.   At the top of the frame
still remain traces of a broken crown which previously
surmounted it.   On the stage sit the two defendants—the
one an elderly bald-headed careworn general, the other a
youngish woman dressed in black.   No sign of guilt rests
on their faces.   The acts of which they are accused, even
if committed, were the ordinary commonplace acts which
were the order under the old regime.   So long as you were
fortunate enough to hold an office, even one of the highest,
more often than not you filled your pockets at the expense
of the State as a matter of course.   It had been done from
time immemorial.   That was the prerogative of office.

Many of the witnesses in this case belong to the old
administration and are themselves awaiting trial, being
brought under military guard to the court from their
places of detention.   Others are well-known leaders of

the Revolution such as Gutchkoff, first Revolutionary War Minister, Miliukoff, first Revolutionary Foreign Minister, besides several well-known generals and newspaper editors, such as Suvorin, Editor of the *Novoie Vrcmia*, and so forth.

During the fourth day's proceedings General Ivanoff commented upon the remarkable thoroughness of the German espionage system, saying that from the first days of the war scare Germany had known all their military secrets. It was impossible to speak over the telephone without Germany obtaining a full account of the whole conversation. At Kieff matters were not so bad, as they had their own spy preventive organisation better in hand. General Polivanoff, who had followed Soukhomlinoff as War Minister, gave evidence on the fifth day. The General did not actually accuse the defendant of neglect of duty. He decried the former system, which was a system of inaction, which in war-time meant defeat. He thought the deficiencies in supplies of all sorts, and in reserves was due to the authorities basing their reserves on the figures acquired during the Russo-Japanese War. Further, that former War Ministers had chiefly confined their attention to the Far East and principally Japan. It was only from 1910 onwards that they began to recognise the danger confronting them from the German-Austro Coalition; from that year work on other frontiers was put in hand. Count Kokovzoff followed, and with sheaves of figures in his hand he established that the blame for the insufficiency in military stores and equipment could not be laid at the door of the Finance Minister. The War Minister had always been given all the money he asked for, army expenditure increasing from two hundred million to one billion and a half roubles. Kokovzoff accused the defendant of never having attempted to produce and follow a clear-cut plan for the reorganisation of the army. Stolypine, said the witness, who was my predecessor, considered that the defendant was not an able enough man to retain the office of War Minister, and had intended asking the Czar to remove him.

At the sixth day's hearing General Vernander, the

Grand Duke Serge and Timacheff, formerly Minister of Commerce and Industry, gave evidence. Vernander was Assistant War Minister under Soukhomlinoff. He explained the deficit in shells, and so forth, to be due to the inadequacy of the national industrial concerns to produce them in the abundance demanded by the General Staff. The War Minister had also considered the demands of G.H.Q. absurdly large. General Ivanoff, who was present, was asked to express an opinion on this latter point. " No," he replied, " the demands for munitions transmitted to the War Minister were not absurdly high. It was only due to their absence that we were forced to retreat." The Grand Duke Serge, who had held the post of Inspector-General of Artillery from 1904 to 1914, in giving evidence, stated that the outbreak of the Russo-Japanese War caught Russia in the middle of the work of reorganising her armaments. " During that war we were only able to reorganise our field artillery. Afterwards we were engaged in re-arming the infantry. Owing to the extreme slowness with which we were able to put through this latter work, due to the dilatoriness of the Russian workmen and the small number of our factories, the outbreak of the war found us very deficient in artillery." The Grand Duke was interesting on the subject of the relations existing between the Director of Artillery and the General Staff, which were strained. He said that the Russian factories required six, nine, or twelve months to carry out military orders. The shortness of munitions in the first stages of the war was not confined to Russia, but had also occurred amongst her Allies and enemies. Germany had converted many of her factories to the out-turn of munitions before the war; France had succeeded in mobilising her industrial resources shortly after the outbreak; as for Russia, her private factories had never risen to the occasion or proved capable of fulfilling the requirements of the army. Timacheff, Minister of Commerce and Industry at the outbreak of war, then gave evidence. " Between the 25th July and 1st August, 1914, he said, when Austria delivered her ultimatum to Serbia, and whilst our Government were uneasy as to the outcome, Soukhomlinoff, in reply to my queries as to what assistance my department would be required to give, returned the invariable reply : ' We (*i. e.* the Ministry of War) are going to run this war.' It was only after the reverses during the month of August were experienced, that the War Minister asked my department to call a conference of our big industrials, in order that they might co-operate to supply the needs of the army. The conference was held. But our private industries, to which the War Minister had never appealed, and with which he had never placed orders in times of peace, were never able, from the start, to give us any real assistance owing to the absence of the necessary machinery in their factories."

At the seventh day's hearing evidence was given, that the War Minister placed orders for munitions of known defective patterns through personal friends of his own, whereby, from being a poor man he was now said to be a wealthy one.   These accusations the defendant indignantly denied, stating that all the orders he had placed had been in the interests of the army and his country, and accusing the Director of Artillery of conservatism and routine.

General Michelson, who was for six years military attaché at Berlin, was then called and declared that the Minister of War had been kept informed of all the German war preparations.   " I sent him complete reports," said the witness, " not only on technical subjects, but also on possible alliances between the Powers who meant war. In 1910 we already knew that Germany meant to declare war in 1913, and we even knew who would be her Allies."

Colonel Bazaroff confirmed the previous witness's evidence, having been for three years a military attaché in Berlin. He had transmitted confidential memoranda to the War Minister in which he had, if anything, exaggerated the numbers of the German military forces.   He admitted, however, that he, in common with the French and English military attachés, underestimated the German reserves of munitions.   " The superiority of the Germans in the manufacture of munitions." he continued. " is explained by the fact that before the war Germany supplied the whole world with shells. As soon as war was declared she mobilised all her industries for her own requirements and those of her Allies."

The most interesting of the evidence given at the eighth day's hearing was that of Colonel Toujan-Baranovsky on the subject of the formation and equipment of the reserves. " The Minister of War never expected to have to send up to the front so large a number of reserve battalions, and had not rifles to arm them with. Consequently, it became necessary to send up reinforcements to the fighting line consisting of battalions without rifles ! ''

From the above brief commentary, it is impossible to deal with the whole of the evidence, this trial bids fair to become an historical record of the conduct of State affairs by the Czar's Ministers, or some of them, during the last years before the fall of the Romanoffs.

It also discloses an extraordinary condition of affairs, as existing between the Minister of War and the Director of the Artillery branches.

Telegrams tell us that Salonika is in flames and almost completely destroyed. More of the " hidden hand," I suppose. But it is difficult to picture the beautiful town —for it is beautiful from the sea and elsewhere—which was so full of interest last year, in ruins. It will also prove a difficult matter to deal with, considering that it is now practically a vast war base to a considerable army.

The Ministers have now all returned from Moscow to Petrograd, so they have not thought fit to take the opportunity offered them of getting away from the capital.

CHAPTER IX

THE MOSCOW CONFERENCE

THE Moscow Conference was an attempt to give the Provisional Government a stability, based on a fusion of parties, which would enable it to carry through the necessary operations having for their object the reduction of the hopeless chaos into which the country had drifted, and thus to save Russia from falling into the abyss on the brink of which she was standing.

Such being the object sought, the Conference will obtain a niche in the history of these dark days Russia is passing through, I propose, therefore, to deal briefly in this chapter with some of the most notable of the addresses, and to endeavour to give a brief analysis of the position as it confronted Russia at the close of this event on which, at its inception, such high hopes were based.

The First Day.—Saturday, August 25th

The Conference was opened by Kerensky, who received a great ovation. The Chief Minister said : " In conformity with the Mission confided to me by the Provisional Government I declare open this State Conference, convoked by the Supreme Authority of the State under my Presidency as Head of the Provisional Government."

Kerensky then proceeded to give an oration which, fine as it was as an oratorical *tour de force*, for he had but a few notes of headings in his hand, was scarcely the kind of speech which had been anticipated.

" The Provisional Government," he said, " had invited them to be present to hear the exact truth about the position of their unhappy country, in order that in the future no one of them would be able to say that they had not realised the grave danger, and so justify acts which, by their continuance, would ruin free Russia. All who attempted to lift a hand against the popular Government in the future would be repressed by force, including those who thought they could make use of the undisciplined soldiery for the same purpose. (Bravos and applause.)

" The old regime placed its confidence in, and its power rested upon, armed force. We place our confidence in, and rest upon, the masses, including the Great Army of our brothers who are defending our frontiers, the country, and the Revolution. My Government is assured that each one will only remember their duty to their country and to the great conquests of the Revolution—liberty, equality and fraternity. (Applause.) We stand before you all, citizens, for the first time as a Provisional Government, fully conscious of our great and heavy responsibilities, responsibilities which we shall bear in spite of all attacks upon us. Only by killing us will it be possible to reach and destroy the body of the great Russian Democracy. (Applause.) Russia is in mortal danger, citizens. We must all feel it, but we have not had sufficient courage to control ourselves, to give up our private interests and class interests in order to combine and devote ourselves to the creation of a great free country." After glancing at the disorganisation and demoralisation in the transport services and industries of the country, the jealousies amongst parties, and the tendency of parts of the Empire to separate themselves, Kerensky alluded to the recent suggestion of the Pope for an armistice. " The Provisional Government," he said, " see in this an attempt to draw our Allies into a separate peace, which cannot and will not be successful." At this the whole audience rose and accorded a great ovation to the Allied Ambassadors. " Of all the countries," continued Kerensky, " which have suffered great trials, we must remember Roumania, and if, as a result of a common mischance and a common fault, the Roumanians have for a time to leave their own country, they will find a welcome and hospitality in Russia." Touching on the troubles in Finland, which he said had reached a most dangerous point, the Minister asserted that, resting on the Russian people, they would not hesitate to employ force in order to restore order. " Our army, on which our power rests, is infected with a leprosy which it inherited from the old regime; with defects due to ignorance and absence of education; and by the absence of that spirit of sacrifice which is lacking in all the Russian people. But before we throw a stone at the army at the front let us look at ourselves. Have we made any sacrifices, save in words, for our country? The anarchy of the Socialists, the Bolsheviks, call them by what name you will, will find in democratic Russia their enemy. When I tell you that the hour has come in which to save Russia and our liberty, no one should dare to oppose his personal wishes against the orders of the Government. As Minister of Justice I suppressed the death penalty. As Minister of War I proposed to partially re-establish it. (Prolonged applause.) How can you applaud when perhaps at this moment a human life is passing? But, if necessary, we will lose our souls, but we will save our country.

" The experience of the past months has shown us that we must thoroughly revise all the acts, regulations, and so forth, passed during the first months of the Revolution : some were the result of insufficient reflection, others more or less accidental in their origin : and give to them a definite place in the working of the State, both rights and duties.

" Many occurrences, now attributed to the Revolution, came about in reality as the outcome of a natural force devoid of any human reasoning, and were not the result of two opposing forces of the Revolution. This is proved by the fact that all the enactments which the actual regenerators of the army are most indignant about were done before my time and by themselves. Not only the heads of the army, with unlimited authority, should know their rights and duties, but also those they command. And the commissions, committees, and disciplinary tribunals will be maintained. The whole army, independent of grades, should be a model of discipline. The other members of the Government will give you a picture of the present disorganised state of the country. Russia, you will see, is menaced with famine.

" Since March 12th, when we took up our duties of governing the country, we do not consider it a fault if we have been too patient in the struggle we have had to conduct; and it has not been difficult owing to the absence of a conscience in the Russian people. On the contrary, it has been precisely because that conscience existed that we have been able to hold on our course each time a larger wave threatened to engulf the State.

" We call you to our aid. And wherever violence and anarchy shows its head, we have resolved to put it down by force in order to re-establish order and maintain the Revolution."

Kerensky's speech took two hours to deliver, and he was accorded a remarkable ovation at its termination, though at periods his remarks were listened to in cold silence when distasteful to one or other of the parties; and more especially by the Left, represented by the Council of Workmen and Soldiers and their supporters.

Several of the Ministers then made brief statements on the position of the country from the point of view of their departments.

Avksentieff, Minister of the Interior, appealed for the union of all parties with the object of placing the full power in the hands of the Provisional Government.

Prokopovitch (Commerce and Industry) said that the Government had three pieces of work to carry out: To put an end to the industrial disorder; prepare for the demobilisation in order that no industry should have to cease work whilst that delicate and difficult enterprise was being carried out; and to develop industrial organisation as soon as peace was declared.

No fundamental agrarian reform would be undertaken by the Provisional Government. Speaking on behalf of the Ministry of Works, the Minister said that the Government were in favour of State Control of productive enterprises. (Applause on the right—Cadets.)

Nekrasoff (Finance) said that, if the payments which had to be met by the Government were not reduced, bankruptcy was inevitable. Indirect taxation should be imposed, but in no case would private property be confiscated. (Applause from Cadets, etc.) The expenditure of the new Government was far greater than that of the old one. Economy must be practised.

Roudneff, the Mayor of Moscow, offered the salutations of the town to the members of the Conference, and said the population of the town was disgusted with the anarchical demonstrations of a portion of the Moscow workmen.

Kerensky wound up the day's proceedings saying that the Government awaited its critics and looked for a loyal debate.

The Second Day.—Sunday, August 26th

This day was devoted to private meetings of the various parties and groups, most of the meetings taking place in the halls of the University. The debates were in many cases very heated ones. The Socialists spoke of the necessity of breaking definitely with the *bourgeoisie* and *vice versa*. The conduct of Ministers, even that of Kerensky, was subjected to a strong criticism. But most of this ebullient effervescence disappeared when the various resolutions were put to the vote, these latter being generally conciliatory in tenor.

At the common sitting of the members of the four Dumas, Aleksinski (member of the 2nd Duma) said : " I should prefer a Government who was frankly in favour of a separate peace, whose neck we would break in a week, than this vacillating Government who declare against a separate peace, and yet whose members are engaged in a propaganda in favour of the Stockholm Conference and in *pourparlers* with the Germans."

Aladine (1st Duma) said : " Kerensky continually speaks of a full power, of the strength which the Provisional Government finds in him; he addresses menaces to the air; he cries out against unknown people; whereas the truth is that the Provisional Government has no real power and never will have, unless it rests on the confidence of the nation."

Anrep (4th Duma) maintained that the principle of the sacredness of private property should be safeguarded.

Efremoff (2nd Duma) and numbers of the peasant deputies protested against the desire of proprietors to deprive the peasants of the land.

At the meeting of the Cadet party two opposing tendencies showed themselves. The first, voiced by Teslenko, considered that the Provisional Government should cease making further concessions to the Socialists; the second, advocated by Adjemoff, Roditcheff and their adherents, maintained that the time had not yet come to break with the Socialists.

The parties of the Moderate Socialists were mostly in favour of compromise and union. Martoff said the internationalists wanted the suppression of the death penalty, an amicable settlement of the Ukrainian and Finnish difficulties and an international struggle for peace. Other spokesmen desired a fusion with the lower class *bourgeoisie*. The party represented by Mme. Bréchkovskaia declared for national defence and support of the Provisional Government, provided the latter would suppress the death penalty.

The Bolshevik meeting adopted a resolution stating that the Moscow Conference had a counter revolutionary character, and therefore did not represent the opinion of the country.

The meeting of the representatives of the Council of Workmen and Soldiers confined themselves to the army. They adopted a resolution expressing opposition to the campaign which was being carried on against the Soldiers' Committees. Recognising that it was impossible to change the whole of the Higher Command, the resolution declared that nevertheless it should be rejuvenated, and that all the counter revolutionary elements in it should be dismissed.

The Third Day.—*Monday, August* 27th

The most notable event of the third day of the Conference was the statesman-like speech of General Korniloff. The

General on arriving slipped into his seat without being noticed. He quitted the hall shortly afterwards, however, and proceeded to the room set apart for the Ministers. When he again entered and took his seat he was accorded a great ovation, the members standing. Only the ultra-Socialists (Left), including officers and soldiers, remained in their seats and silent. A second ovation greeted the appearance of Kerensky, this time by the Left, who shouted " Vive la Révolution ! Vive la République ! " the Right taking no part in the manifestation, but shouting " Vive le General Korniloff ! " Cries were set up of " Vive l'Armée ! " and this being joined in by both sides, harmony was restored.

Kerensky opened the day's proceedings. He exhorted all the members to think of Russia and her calamitous position, and to give a calm hearing to the spokesman of the various parties, even if they did not agree with the views expressed. " Let us commence by saluting in the person of its Commander-in-Chief our heroic army, which is fighting for liberty and for the country." The great audience rose and cheered vociferously.

Nabokoff (member of the 1st Duma) said they were all grateful to the Government for having convoked the Conference, which gave all the opportunity of fully understanding the present position of Russia and their responsibilities towards it. The dissensions which tore the country apart were the greatest danger which confronted it. Perhaps the time would come when they would compose these dissensions and get back that *élan* which was so conspicuous during the first days of the revolution. The members of the 1st Duma considered that if the country was to be saved and civil liberty to be safeguarded there should be one strong and independent Government, and that the defence of the country required the union of all classes, parties and nationalities. The chief commanders of the army should be independent, and all attempts to dismember the Empire should be considered as acts intended to help the enemy. The agrarian question and all social reforms should be left over to be decided by the Constituent

M

Assembly. " We want an honourable peace, and that cannot be a German peace. A German peace can only result from a German victory, whereas an honourable peace will mean a victory of Russia and our Allies. We believe that the Commander-in-Chief will give us an honourable peace." (A long ovation to General Korniloff.)

Séménoff (1st Duma) said the first object the Duma set itself was to safeguard the rights of the citizen. Its second object could be expressed in three words, " Russia and Liberty." The agrarian question could be settled at the Constituent Assembly, provided that private interests were not placed beneath general ones.

Golovine (President, 2nd Duma) : We should combine to place the full power in the hands of the Government. The Coalition Government must be strong throughout, and cannot be unless we give it full confidence.

Alexensky (2nd Duma) : The members of the 2nd Duma will support that Government which will carry out the following : (1) Continue the War in full accord with our Allies until the enemy have been cleared from Russian soil and from that of our Allies. (2) Form a Coalition Government for national defence to consist only of members who will make national defence their sole object. For economic, political and international reasons Russia cannot resign herself to defeat.

Roditcheff (3rd Duma) : Where is the strength of the Russian Armies ? We have all we require to organise victory, but the victory spirit is wanting. No people can ever be free who in the hour of danger do not know how to create national unity. The army is an army of meetings.

Kerensky then rose and said that the Provisional Government had thought it desirable to ask the Commander-in-Chief to be present in order that he might explain the situation at the front and the state of the army. (Prolonged applause on the General rising, except on the Left. Numbers of soldiers remained sitting and were greeted with cries of " Slaves ! " which gave rise to greater tumult.) Kerensky invited the Assembly to maintain a calm mien and to listen to the first soldier of the Provisional Government with the respect due to him and to the Government.

Korniloff then gave his noteworthy and soldier-like address. "The measures taken by the Government, after the receipt of my telegram of July 23rd, with reference to the re-establishment of the death penalty at the front, have strengthened to some slight extent the army, but the pernicious propaganda which is undermining it still continues." The General then read a list of the officers who had been killed by their own men during the present month. These assassinations had been committed by ignorant or dastardly soldiers who had completely lost their heads. "A few days ago, when the Germans commenced their offensive near Riga, the 56th Siberian Regiment, who had conducted itself with heroism in previous battles, abandoned its position, and throwing away arms and equipment took to flight, thoroughly demoralised. It was only on action being taken on a telegram I sent ordering the regiment to be exterminated that it returned to its positions." (" Very good !" Applause from the Right.)

Kerensky : I must beg the Assembly to listen to the passages in the speech which tell us of grave dangers to the country without emphasising them with undignified applause.

The General continued : " The anarchy in the army will be crushed. But we are menaced with new disasters; the loss of more territory and towns, and the capital is in danger. Owing to the situation at the front we have lost the whole of Galicia and the Bukovina and all the fruits of our last year's and of this year's victories. The enemy has crossed our frontier in several places, and now threatens our richest provinces in the south. The enemy is trying to annihilate the Roumanian Army and to wipe out Roumania as a member of the alliance. The enemy is knocking at the gates of Riga. If the state of our army does not permit us to maintain ourselves on the shores of the Gulf of Riga the road to Petrograd will lie open.

" Russia, it is true, inherited from the old regime an

army full of defects, but it was an heroic army and had a great fighting value. With the introduction by people unacquainted with the soul and the necessities of the army of a series of measures after the Revolution, the soldiers became a demented horde, putting their safety above everything. There have been cases of regiments who expressed a wish to make peace with the Germans and were ready to give up all the occupied territory to the enemy, and to pay the latter, in addition, a contribution of two hundred roubles per head. At whatever cost the *morale* of the army must be re-established, and to this end the measures recommended in my report to the Provisional Government must be put in force. This report was signed without reservations both by Savinkoff and the Commissioner Filonenko. Only an army welded by an iron discipline and led by the undivided will of its chiefs is either capable or worthy of achieving victory. And discipline must be reintroduced into the every-day work, the fatigues of the army; the officers and N.C.Os. must have the power to order the soldiers to feed and groom their horses, to clean the barracks and encampments, which are indescribably filthy and threaten the army with epidemics. Even if, to the everlasting disgrace of the country, peace were actually concluded, demobilisation could not be undertaken, and the undisciplined army would turn and ravage its own country. The prestige of the officers must be restored. I am not an enemy of the Committees, but these should not intervene either in strategical questions or in the election of the chiefs of the army. But all our efforts on the front will be in vain if the army does not receive a flow of drafts and of munitions, guns and equipment. The railways are in such a state of disorganisation that by November they will be no longer capable of providing the necessary service for the army. I have just received a telegram from the Commander of the Army on the south-west front announcing that at his part of the front there is no bread. The biscuit factories are no longer working, and for the first time since the outbreak of the war the stocks of biscuits are being used

A COMMON SIGHT AFTER THE REVOLUTION IN PETROGRAD

THE GREAT PINE FORESTS OF RUSSIA

for rationing the troops in the rear instead of those at the front. The output of our factories, who work in the interests of national defence, has diminished by sixty per cent. as compared with their out-turn for the period October 1916 to January 1917. If this state of affairs continues we shall soon find ourselves in a similar situation to that of the spring of 1915. We are not at present able to replace the losses in our air service. The output of our aeroplane factories has diminished by eighty per cent. All the measures I have proposed should be put in force without delay." (The General emphasised the words " without delay.") " If the measures put in force at the front to restore discipline are the result of the dishonouring disaster at Tarnapol, and of the losses of Galicia and the Bukovina, it cannot be intended that we should wait till we have lost Riga before restoring discipline at the rear, or that we should abandon Moldavia and Bessarabia before reorganising the railway system."

General Kaledin followed General Korniloff and spoke for the Cossacks. This General has had a distinguished career. He commanded one of the Russian armies during Brusiloff's offensive in 1916, and is popularly known as the " Hero of Lutsk." Since the outbreak of the revolution Kaledin has been prominent as the foremost leader of the Cossacks. He is a Cossack by birth, and when the Cossack armies after the Revolution re-established their former elective system, they chose Kaledin to be their Hetman or Commander-in-Chief. He was now supporting Korniloff at the Conference. He spoke as follows : The Cossacks denied being counter-revolutionists. He considered the following measures necessary if the country was to be saved—

1. The army should be entirely disassociated from politics and their meetings should be suppressed.

2. The Soviets and Committees should be suppressed.

3. The declaration of the rights of soldiers should be revised.

4. Discipline should be re-established at the front and rear.

To obtain these essentials the General appealed to the Government to give their whole-hearted and unbiased support to Korniloff in order to carry out his suggestions which they had accepted. (Applause and hisses. Violent commotion.)

Kerensky : I beg the Assembly not to abuse the speakers. The Provisional Government wish to hear all the different opinions of parties. The Government invited you to be present here, and it is not right that any one should take advantage of the invitation. (A voice : " It is the Government who are playing and we are the dancers.")

Tchkheidze, speaking in the name of several democratic organisations, declared that the democracy was ready to make the necessary sacrifices to save the country and the Revolution. The Government should take in hand more energetically the programme of July 22nd and depend, both at the front and rear, on the democratic organisations. The Government should fight against anarchy and the counter-revolutionists. The Constituent Assembly would decide the question of the Russian Democratic Republic, which had already been proclaimed by the people. (Prolonged applause.)

Ponomareff spoke for the peasants. All the land should be given to the working-classes, but the Constituent Assembly could only decide that question. Discipline should be re-established at the front and rear in order to end the war with a near and lasting peace.

Gutchkoff (President 3rd Duma) : The existing authority is not an authority; but it is pompous, it has the attributes, the terminology, the gestures of authority.

The speaker gave a brief history of the Revolution in order to show that one section alone of the democracy took the responsibility of directing the Revolution and acting as a despotic guardian over the official authority of the Provisional Government.

Choulguine enumerated a list of acts which in his opinion were errors on the part of the Government, and which were responsible for the change in the spirit of the people. " Some one," he said, " mentioned here the celebrated expression ' Stolypine.' Why was it mentioned here ? You will not frighten us. It was with this word that they used to frighten the 2nd Duma. Who do you wish to frighten here ? Why are we being exhorted to save the Revolution when nothing threatens it ? Five months ago any one who ventured to say anything against the Revolution would have been torn to pieces. I was one of those who voted for the suppression of the death penalty, and a portion of the responsibility of that mistake therefore falls upon me. I know all the sorrow and pain which is felt when one has to part with one's ideals. I understand what it meant to the soul of Kerensky when he had to re-establish the death penalty. And I, a confirmed monarch-ist, by what irony of fate was it that I should have had to assist at the overthrow of two emperors ? That is why I understand the pain felt at seeing all in which one had believed fall into the pit. The President of the Provisional Government says, ' I will lose my soul, but I will save the country.' But, gentlemen, the horror of it is that we may lose our souls and yet not save the country.''

Kerensky read a telegram sent by President Wilson to the State Conference expressing the latter's conviction in the final triumph of the democratic ideals in spite of all the opposition of internal and external enemies : and stating that the United States were ready to afford the Government moral and practical assistance in the common cause which united the two nations, in which neither pursued any private end. (Loud applause). Kerensky asked the Minister for Foreign Affairs to transmit to the American Ambassador the feelings of satisfaction ex-pressed by the Conference after hearing the telegram from the President of the friendly nation.

Maklakoff (4th Duma) : He had always been a supporter of union and against the struggles of the parties. Although the Government were armed with dictatorial power they were not sufficiently audacious. The public conscience, which wished to believe in the Provisional Government, was alarmed at seeing in its bosom the traitors of yesterday. (This was a hit at Tchernoff, Minister of Agriculture, and provoked cheers and counter-cheers. Kerensky begged the speaker not to abuse the privilege accorded him of addressing the Conference.)

Continuing, the speaker said it was ridiculous to talk about an honourable peace if no measures were taken to restore discipline. It was ridiculous to talk about plots so long as the revolution carried out its duties.

Tseretelli (2nd Duma, representing the Workmen and Soldiers' deputies, replied to Maklakoff) : " There is a price which cannot be paid in order to restore stability in the country. It is the price by which we should lose the faith of the people, of the popular forces of the democracy. If we paid that price the order in the country would not be order in a living organisation but, order in a cemetery.

" There are two kinds of patriotism. The one formulated by William, who has said that his desire is that all the world should fear his country as in old times the Huns were feared. But there is also the patriotism of the revolution. We love our country and we will defend it with the last drop of our blood. It is our great pride that we have lit throughout the world the torch of liberty, the torch of the right of all democracies to defend themselves. (Applause.)

" That is what we understand when we talk of fighting for a general peace. Only the Revolution can save the country. Democratic programmes and programmes for the salvation of the Revolution are really synonymous. Are the proprietary classes ready for sacrifices ? Let the Government ask for what it wants to save the country and we will support it. Long live the Democratic Revolutionary Coalition Government." (Prolonged applause.)

Rodzianko (President 4th Duma at the time of the Revolution) : It has often been asked why the Duma remained inactive after the Revolution, taking no part in the subsequent movement. After the abdication of Nicholas II the Duma, in agreement with the Soviets, transferred all authority to the Provisional Government. That authority was created by this Duma, and the tragedy of the present situation is that the authority then created

(Laughter from the Left and cries of " And the 16th July!")
has never been interfered with by the Duma. The Government has fallen owing to the clash of class interests.
(Cries.) That is the reason for the disorganisation. The
greatest chaos is in the army. (Rodzianko turned towards
Kerensky.) The Government had not the strength, and
if it had why did it not employ it, to put an end to the
criminal propaganda which has debauched the soldiery
and taken from it its fighting value. With reference to
the separation tendencies making themselves felt within
the Empire, the responsibility rests on those who did not
know how to nip them in the bud from the start. We shall
only find safety in the union of all the citizens. I now
propose to read the resolution come to by the Members of
the Duma. I think that even though the time allotted
to me has come to an end I shall be permitted to read the
resolution. (Cries : " Read !")

Kerensky : Your time has elapsed. (Disorder.) Although the time has expired I call upon the President
of the Duma to read the resolution.

Rodzianko : The President of the Duma will never be
one to disobey the law.

Miliukoff (4th Duma and First Revolutionary Foreign
Minister) : The Revolution owes its victory to the Duma.
Neither the *bourgeoisie* nor the revolutionary democracy
should be accorded special privileges. Russia is not composed only of Socialists. (Applause.) I speak in the name
of a party which already in 1916 had inscribed on its flag
" Liberty for the People." This party has the right to
consider the victories of the Revolution as its own victories.
(Commotion.)

Miliukoff reproached Kerensky with the fact that the
measures which had resulted in the disintegration of the
army had been introduced whilst the latter was Minister
of War; that the latter had signed the Soldiers' Charter,
and that he was thereby responsible for the consequences.
" In the future it will be difficult to believe that, in the
hour of our great difficulties, the Government had in its
bosom a Zimmerwaldist, the Minister of Agriculture. The

Minister-President wishes to obtain the support of the members of that Assembly, and he will probably secure it. We shall wait and see what use he makes of it. The measures proposed by Kerensky are insufficient. We must adopt without reservation the measures proposed by Korniloff."

The speaker accused the Coalition Cabinet of having capitulated to the utopian ideas of the working classes and nationalists. The Cadet party would support the Minister-President. It rested with the Government to make full use of this assistance.

Tseretelli replied to Miliukoff in the name of Executive Committee of the Soviets. " We are not opposed to discipline. An undisciplined army is a menace to the Revolution. An army who questions and disputes the orders issued to advance on the enemy is without sense. But in re-establishing discipline in the army the army chiefs should themselves set an example of discipline."

Roudneff, Mayor of Moscow, spoke in the name of the branches of Municipal Administration in Moscow, stating that the Government would have their whole-hearted support.

Captain Sparjinsky, in the name of the Knights of St. George, made a speech pitched on a note of the highest patriotism to their country.

The Fourth Day.—Tuesday, August 28th

The proceedings were opened by Grousinoff, President of the Zemstvos Council of Moscow. " Want of union," he said, " is everywhere, as much in the Provinces as here in the Conference. Numbers of employees in the municipalities, in the railways, factories, etc., have been driven from their work simply because they were classed as *bourgeoisie*. The group he represented associated itself with the terms of the resolution of the fourth Duma, which Rodzianko had not time to read yesterday." The speaker commenced to read the resolution, but his time for speaking elapsed before he had completed it. The resolution declared that the chief aim at present was to save Russia from the enemy.

To attain this object the fighting force of the army must be re-established with the minimum of delay, by eliminating all politics from the army excepting only the campaign for the election to the Constituent Assembly. In matters connected with the war the Government should not be guided by the voices of the Internationalist Socialists, but only by the interests of Russia. In matters of internal politics the Government should retain an impartial attitude towards the resolutions adopted by committees, councils, and other organisations which did not represent the wishes of the whole nation.

Salaskine, President of the Chamber of Commerce of Nijni Novgorod and representing fifteen municipalities, said they did not agree with the resolution of the 4th Duma, but associated themselves with the Socialist organisation for which Tchkheidze spoke yesterday. You cannot separate the safety of the Revolution from the safety of the country. If the Revolution perishes the country will perish.

Toptchibache (1st Duma, representing the Mahomedans) : Although the Mussulmans of the Russian Empire have up to now remained quiet, their silence has spoken for them, and now they wish to be heard. From the first days of the Revolution they have rallied to the ranks of the defenders of the Revolution and the Provisional Government. They have decided to support the Government in all its enterprises and follow the road to liberty hand in hand with the revolutionary democracy.

Froloff (Engineer, representing the Union of the Mechanicians and Engineers) pointed out that if the present amount of work which obtained in the railway service continued, the transport service would cease to operate by November, a state of affairs full of menace. (Warm applause.) The danger would not only be to the towns, which would be condemned to famine and cold, but also to the front. The railways, as also the whole of Russia, were sick because ideal aims had been replaced by egotistical ones. Russia was fired upon by successive parties. First the army, then the land, then the industries, and now it was the turn of the railways. (Applause.) Commanders-in-Chief cannot be changed as you change gloves. (Applause from the Right.) Discipline under the railway chiefs, supported by the Government, must be re-established; acts of violence against the railway administration, passengers and employees, must be put an end to and the output must be enhanced. (Applause.)

Grousenberg (Jews Democratic Union): The Jews, like other nationalities, are divided up into numbers of social classes, but one and all are filled with devotion for the country and would support the conquests of the democracy. (Applause.) The Jews are ready to give their all, including their young men, in order to defend the country. (Applause.)

General Alexeieff gave a brief historical review of the war. " The anniversary of those days of 1914 approaches when the victorious Russian Army advanced over the battle-fields of Galicia. Lvow was taken September 2nd; on September 12th the entire Austrian Army, beaten, without munitions or artillery, defiled across the Carpathians. Only the fatigue of our magnificent soldiers and the great expenditure of munitions prevented us from taking Premysl. The terrible experiences of 1915 then came upon us. The army, without munitions, had to retire before a force stronger in men and munitions. But it only retired foot by foot, watering with its blood each corner of ground it gave up, and covered with honour. The army suffered much, but it maintained the grand Russian fighting spirit. The proof came on June 4th, 1916, when it commenced to turn those glorious pages, which were due to the victorious march of 1914. We met with reverses, it is true, in the north, where we encountered so well-equipped a force that we had nothing to put up against it, and we committed faults for which we had to pay. And·to these faults are explainable our reverses of October 1916 and January 1917, when we endeavoured to break the enemy front near Mitau and failed. Two and a half years of war give us the right to balance accounts. Russia possessed a strong and reliable army, but weak in technique and in artillery. The soldiers were magnificent when led by their officers. They preserved discipline, courage and *élan*. Deserters there were and poltroons who fled in the face of the enemy. Every army of size has such. But there was complete accord between officers and soldiers. The army passed quietly through the revolution and to the new regime; and it passed quietly because the officers in high command, animated by the sentiment that it was their duty to their country, passed along with it. But unfortunately a powerful and disciplined army appeared to some to be a danger to the Revolution. It must be weakened, and the first poison with which it was inoculated was the Prikaz No. 1. Prikaz No. 1 disorganised our fighting machine, setting the soldiers against the officers. In the future, history will decide whether this was an error of the Government or a crime against the State. The German spies, either with or without passports and papers, spread throughout the army, inciting it by pernicious propaganda. And those of our people who were chiefly responsible looked on with a fiendish pleasure whilst these orders of the German High Command were executed by their representatives, in whose pockets chinked German gold. In the eyes of the private the officer is now an enemy. The officer has lived the same life with the soldier, eaten the same food in the trenches, marched in front in battle, but he is now looked upon as an enemy. Formerly we have had instances where the soldiers, knowing they could not win without the officer to lead them, have made a rampart of their bodies to protect their chief; now, often, the soldier puts a bullet into the back of his officer marching in front. (Shame.) The Army Committees have done much harm, and the declaration of the rights of the soldier (*i. e.* Soldiers' Charter) introduced politics into the army." He advocated the acceptance without reservation of the Korniloff programme.

Koutchine (officer of 12th Army representing the Army Committees—received with great applause by the Left): The Army Committees have fought against disorganisation

and against fraternisation with the enemy. Repressive
measures in the army must be introduced in agreement
with the military organisations which cannot be reduced
or their powers diminished. They accepted the programme
of July 24th, which is the programme of all the democracy.

Madame Brechko-Bréchkovskaia, the Mother of the
Revolution, made an impassioned speech, much applauded,
in which she besought all classes and parties, workers and
proprietary classes alike, to unite and think of and work
for Russia alone.

Kropotkine : " Let us break once and for all with Zim-
mervaldism and close up to save the country and the
Revolution. The last few months have shown that the
question as to who is to be the victor in this World-War
is in course of being settled. If the Germans were to prove
victors the results for us would be so terrible that it is
better not to talk about them. If the Russian people
allow themselves to become war-worn how will it all finish ?
Poland, Lithuania and Courland will be taken by the
Germans. What will become of them ? Riga will become
a fortress like Kovno, not to protect Germany, but from
which Petrograd and Moscow can be threatened. (Voice :
" That is true.") I will not allude to what would happen
if Odessa was taken from us and perhaps Kieff; but what
is certain is, that Germany would saddle us with a war
indemnity which would take us twenty-five to thirty years
to pay off, as in the case of France after 1871. But there
is something, comrades, worse than this. I allude to the
psychology of a conquered country. I saw this psychology
in France. I am not French, but I have lived intimately
with the French, and my heart bled to see France bow
before Alexander and Nicholas II. The French Republic
bent the knee because she felt herself beaten, and had to
go anywhere for help to escape from the situation she
found herself in. Shall we be subjected to such an indig-
nity ? Never. (Applause throughout the whole hall.)
War is one thing, work behind the front is another, equally
important. But you will not do anything by repressive
measures. What is demanded is, that the whole Russian

people should realise each one for himself that a new era
is opening to them, an era which will make it a possibility
for them to educate themselves.

" I could give you instances of the incredible devotion
of the French and English women of all classes, from the
working classes to those of the richest, in undertaking the
work of organisation of the life of the country on the new
principles. It appears to me that this Assembly should
express its ardent desire to see Russia openly become a
declared republic." (The entire audience rose and cheered
the speaker.)

Boublikoff (representing the big industries) in a speech
received with acclamation, said they wished to conduct
their business in a democratic spirit with the aid of the
workmen and hoped that they would have the support
of the democratic revolutionaries, whom Tseretelli represented here, in this endeavour. Amidst great applause
Tseretelli accepted the hand thus extended.

Plehanoff : It is both true and false that the Duma
made the Revolution. A tempest burst over us, and the
Duma upheld it. If all parties commit faults their merit
is that they are in existence. The industrial classes should
endeavour to find a road of approach to the proletariat.
There can be no greater danger for the working classes
than to grasp at the supreme power, as Lenin recommended
them to do, without possessing the necessary education and
training which would enable them to carry the burden.

Kerensky closed the Conference. " The Government
Conference is at an end. The Provisional Government,
in spite of the fears expressed by many, does not regret
having called it. I think we have arrived at a better understanding of each other. The Government have, as it were,
been able to take an instantaneous photograph of the spirit
of the country. The Government have enunciated here
the formula of ' order, sacrifice, work ! ' The Conference
has replied, ' We will sacrifice ourselves, we will work,
order is necessary.' We are told here, I particularly am
told, ' You have already sold yourselves to the *bourgeoisie*.'
But those who say it are not those who are gathered here,

but those whom we forced to keep quiet on the 16th to the 18th July last. We are also told that we are guided by obscure forces and that we are incapable of initiative action. We declare that the Government is not guided by any outside influences, but only by the popular will. It is with that will that you must count. (Loud applause.) I declare that everything that is not in the interests of the State, all proposals made whose effect is contrary to the safety of Russia will be opposed by us, if necessary, by force. Various measures, with which we have been accused, were brought in by the first Provisional Government which represented the whole democracy. We must find the road to the salvation of Russia. Stolypine was mentioned here. But Stolypine crushed liberty by force. We are only defending the necessities of Russia and removing those who wish to repress liberty. The Government are of opinion that the placing of the army, finances, and the general situation of the country on a sound basis are the fundamental questions before it. We will do all that requires to be done. I promise that we will take every effective measure to restore the fighting force of the army. I hear that many of the military chiefs are taking measures to establish a form of discipline which is inadvisable. In these cases I shall take opposite measures. We take up to-morrow our heavy load, but allow me to say that we will never forsake liberty."

Perhaps one of the best brief commentaries on the Conference was that of Tseretelli, representing the great bulk of the more moderate Socialists, who are gradually separating from the more rabid members of the Workmen and Soldiers' Council, the Bolsheviks. Expressing his opinion of the Conference he said, " The bridge between the democracy and the *bourgeoisie* has been built."

I have necessarily only given a *résumé* of some of the more important or remarkable of the speeches out of the large number delivered at the Conference. A rigid time-limit had been fixed for each speaker, and this was adhered to with remarkable unanimity, orators breaking off in the middle of a phrase and sitting down, on a motion from the President that they had reached the allotted period. Generally speaking the meeting was also remarkably orderly, considering the great divergence of opinion existing amongst the parties present, and the firm conviction of one set of opinion that their opponents were bent on wrecking the Revolution, and of another that the country was being led to ruin by the Bolsheviks. That such a spirit should have been exhibited is partially due to what I heard called the " Russian calm "—to the Russian patience and the stoical nature of their character. There was undoubted relief, and not in ministerial circles only, when the Conference came to an end without open acts of hostility having either taken place or been threatened. In their absence the Government were certainly justified, and may congratulate themselves on their astuteness, in assembling the Conference.

Kerensky's opening speech is admittedly a disappointment. It was a fine effort from the orator's point of view. But it was entirely lacking in statesmanship, and in an exposition of a constructive policy which had been looked for from the Head of the Government. The *Novoie Vremia* has the following comment : " Kerensky's faults and mistakes, which were so clearly depicted at to-day's Conference, are directly attributable to his oratorical talent. When we journalists asked if we could be given advance copies of the Minister's speech we learnt to our great astonishment that there was no written speech, and that even his colleagues in the Cabinet were only aware of a few of the chief points of the speech he was to deliver. The shape they were to take would be given them during the delivery of the speech. And he actually improvised his speech from a few written notes ! Can such a thing be really possible ? Is such an action not above human powers ? Action taken at such a moment, at a State Conference of so great an importance, and remembering the great and responsible position the speaker occupies ! The whole thing improvised on the spur of the moment ! Is it the faith of a Titan who knows and has confidence in

N

his own ability ? or is it only a blind confidence in self ?
That was the painful reflection in the mind of many who sat
to-day in the great theatre."

By the concession of all shades of opinion Korniloff's
speech stands out as the one statesmanlike declaration of
this historic event. At what is considered to be the
psychological moment he had had the soldier's courage
and the statesman's clearness of vision to give the country
the truth in simple and direct phrases which all can understand without possibility of misconception. Since last
Monday (27th) we all know that the front cannot be treated
differently from the rear—that the same treatment is
necessary amongst the reserves, in the workshops, etc.;
that in the most democratic armies, as in France, England
and elsewhere, discipline exists and is essential. The
death penalty should, it is said, be re-established in the
rear just as it has been at the front : in fact, Korniloff's recommendations should be enforced throughout the
country. Kerensky understands this well enough, the
influential Press says : it is being said by all who have their
country's real welfare at heart. But will he have the
courage to cut himself adrift from the rabid Socialist
parties and carry out the only sane national policy the
times and conditions of the country impose ? This is the
question being asked. Of Korniloff no doubts are expressed.
The manner in which he and his policy are being openly
reviled in the organs of the Council of Workmen and
Soldiers, and to a lesser extent in those of the more moderate
Socialists, indicates the impression his speech has made
upon them and the fear in which they hold him. This is
undoubtedly the great danger of the situation, unless the
Government turns over a new leaf. As regards the chief
of the speeches, Kerensky's, after further examination, is
being received with coolness : by one side as saying nothing
at all, and thereby indicating that he has no firm policy ;
by the other as saying too much by threatening the use
of force against outbreaks or attempts to obstruct the
Government, taken rightly or wrongly to refer to such
attempts as that of the Bolsheviks last month. If we

except the organs of the Bolsheviks—which maintain that the Conference has been a great victory for themselves and the Council of Workmen and Soldiers, to which they claim all parties to a great extent deferred, thus recognising them as the real leaders—and the organs which, pessimistic before, are more sunk in pessimism over the results, the Moderate Press of all parties appear to consider that the Conference suddenly divided itself into two camps between which appeared a deep ditch. This ditch separated the utopian party from the men without party who placed the State first. The first stood for treason. The other for reaction and an attempt to restore the country. The most significant act of the Conference, they maintain, was the approachment between Boublikoff representing industry and Tseretelli, chief of the Revolutionary Democracy. Only the Internationalists, *i. e.* the Bolsheviks, witnessed this reconciliation without pleasure. Tseretelli by this act is showing that he is a real leader, for it proves that he is cutting adrift from the Bolsheviks. It may be a great factor in the future.

CHAPTER X

PETROGRAD IN SEPTEMBER

RETIREMENT OF RUSSIANS ON ROUMANIAN FRONT—KOR-
NILOFF AND THE GOVERNMENT—THE GERMANS AND
RIGA—GERMAN PROPAGANDA

September 1st.—Whilst Korniloff at the Moscow Conference was making his statement of the present position
of the army at the front, a portion of that army on the
Roumanian front was preparing to quit their trenches,
abandon their positions, and retire to the rear, thus
leaving the neighbouring Roumanian units in the air. On
August 28th and 29th this disgraceful movement was
carried out, whole divisions breaking and fleeing. Korniloff
returned to army headquarters at Mohileff immediately
after delivering his speech at the Conference, and at
once telegraphed to Kerensky (on August 29th, the last
day of the Conference), asking him explicitly, in view of
the retirement now in progress, to introduce all the measures he (the General) had proposed at the Conference. An
urgent Conference is to take place at field headquarters
on September 4th, under the chairmanship of General
Commissary Filonenko. It will include representatives
from the front, army committees, commissaries, and representatives of the Staff. This Conference is to work
out a disciplinary code. Disputes have already arisen.
The executive committee of the south-western division
complains that it has not been notified of the Conference and that the delegates to the latter have been
appointed by the Commanding Staff, the Soldiers'
Committees being ignored. If Korniloff is to succeed
in his object of re-establishing discipline, it appears fairly
obvious that these committees will have to be ignored,

or have their powers greatly curtailed, if they cannot
be got rid of altogether. But they maintain that the
procedure adopted is against the spirit of self-government, and insist that the elective bodies must have their
voice in measures affecting the army.

The chief importance of both retirement and dispute
resides in the fact that it places the Provisional Government, and Kerensky in particular, in a position in which
there now appears to be no longer a chance of hesitancy
or equivocation. All are aware that it is the Council of
Workmen and Soldiers who are exerting all their influence
against Korniloff's proposals. The Provisional Government will now have to make up their minds definitely
with which side they will throw in their lot. There are
plenty here who think that even yet they might find
sufficient support in the country to stand up against the
Council, which has lost the larger number of adherents
it possessed when in the heyday of its influence for good
during the first few weeks of the Revolution. But the
Government are well aware that, although the support of
all the better influences in the country is no longer given
to the Council, the latter has gained immensely in strength
by attaching to itself the great masses of undisciplined
soldiers and workmen. It is these masses that give the
Council its dread power at which all now look askance,
asking what is to be the end. And it must be confessed
that those who ridicule the idea of the Provisional Government ever proving itself strong enough to fight the Council,
in spite of the fine speaking at the Conference, have strong
arguments on their side. If this turns out to be the case,
Korniloff will be beaten, and it is difficult to foresee what
will happen then. His retirement will not help matters.
On this head Savinkoff, Assistant War Minister, has issued
the following statement to the Press : " Amongst the
measures which will be shortly introduced by the Minister
of War is the regularisation of the rear. The rumours of
changes in the War Department are false. The Commissaries, including the Chief Commissary, will remain at their
posts. The rumours that the power and competence of

the Soldiers' Committees will be limited are equally false. With reference to these latter a new plan will be energetically introduced, a plan which has been prepared by the Committees themselves in agreement with the Commissioner of the Council of Workmen and Soldiers at the front." This does not look like supporting Korniloff.

German activity is increasing both in the Gulfs of Finland and Riga, and this is regarded as a prelude to the pressing home of the effort to capture Riga. But Petrograd just now is more interested in the struggle between Korniloff and the Government and in the interminable articles in the papers over the real reading of the ": Moscow Conference riddle," as one journal calls it. In this connection there are two articles worth summarising.

A new journal entitled *The Proletariat* (the central organ of the Social Democratic party of Russian workmen, as it describes itself, which apparently replaces the *Pravda*, for the moment suppressed) concludes its leading article as follows : " Who has won ? you ask. Have the capitalists won ? For the Government engaged itself at the Conference ' not to allow the workmen to intervene in the management of industrial enterprises.'

" Have the territorial proprietors won ? For the Government gave an engagement ' that they would not undertake any radical reforms in the land question.'

" Have the counter-revolutionary Generals won ? ' The Government approved of the death penalty at the Conference.'

" Who has won you ask ? Have the counter-revolutionists won ? They have at their disposal the so-called ' revolutionary democracy ' as a convenient buffer against the popular indignation. The counter-revolutionists are not now isolated. They have the ' revolutionary democracy ' to work for them. Now that they have ' public opinion ' and the ' land ' at their disposition what will these people do ? The crowning of the counter-revolutionists — that is what the Moscow Conference has brought about ! But will this Counter-Revolutionary ' Coalition ' last ? The near future will show us."

The other article is of greater interest.

" There were two parties only which received the most attentive hearing. They formed the wheels of the Conference, but they were not connected by the axle. That was elsewhere. These parties were the Cadets on the one side, on the other the democracy of the Soviets. The Cadets, who included the agrarians and the big *bourgeoisie*, took part in the Conference in full review order, and exhibited great talent and *savoir-faire ;* but one felt that they lacked the living force they were trying to reach. What they wanted to achieve was not so much the power as to guide the governing power. For this they have a ripe experience, a large choice of good men and great talent. But they lack the one vitalising factor—the confidence of the masses. They are at present generals and officers without rank and file. The support of agrarians, *bourgeoisie*, and generals without commands, such as Rodziazko, Alexeieff, etc., cannot replace the support of the people.

" In the other party, the democracy of the Soviets, the tragedy is of a different kind. In their ranks they have an enormous mass of rank and file, but they want officers. The support and confidence of the masses made useless by the absence of men, of leaders, capable of utilising this faith, and by means of the enormous force and power it gives them guiding these masses into the road of safety. This absence of intellectual leaders at times forces the Soviets to leave undone work they know to be essential, or, worse still, to call in the aid of people wholly unworthy to be included in even the lowest ranks of this democracy. The leaders of this democracy are well aware of their weakness, and their declarations at the Conference, whilst showing that they realised to the full the great power of their following, also displayed anxiety as to the future. For without the support of an organised democracy no real reconstruction work can be undertaken. And the power of this democracy, owing to the absence of sufficient leaders, is weakening.

" The unorganised groups of the democracy, who were

grouped at the Conference under the title ' *Intelligensia du travail* ' (co-operative societies of all kinds, social organisations, professional classes, etc.), may be termed the smaller *bourgeoisie*. These groups united, but made no pompous declaration of policy. At times they supported the Soviets, at others the Cadets, the two wheels, but usually, and, above all, the Government. It is these groups, which attracted no great attention, that formed the axle of the Conference. But this group, this axle, is not sufficiently organised, although it made its influence felt at the Conference. The more highly it organises itself in the future the greater will be the part it will play."

It will be interesting to watch whether the axle joins the wheels together to enable them to fulfil their proper function.

A terrible fire has taken place at the old town of Kazan on the Volga. It startéd on August 27th at a railway station about five versts from the town. A truck loaded with shells suddenly burst into flames and exploded, setting fire to a larger store of shells close to the station. These exploded, many of the shells flying over the town, whilst others burst in the streets, setting fire to the houses. The inhabitants fled in panic to the neighbouring villages. The soldiers quartered in the town, throwing away their equipment, for the most part followed the former's example. Bands, however, reinforced by hooligans, set to work to pillage the houses. Munition works caught fire and explosions continued throughout the day and night and through part of the following day. A number of large tanks containing naphtha belonging to the Artillery Department, each holding about 2,000,000 poods (1 pood = 36 lbs.), also caught fire and caused further explosions. The post and telegraph building has had to be evacuated owing to its dangerous proximity to the burning areas, the service thus being suspended. The looting has been reduced by surrounding the town with cadets from the military schools. Steamers were sent up and down the Volga to warn incoming vessels not to approach the burning town, and a fleet of these latter are now in the vicinity awaiting the dying down of the flames to enable them to land their passengers and freight. The extent of the damage done has not yet been ascertained.

The Socialists of the Finnish Diet have given up their project for a plenary sitting of the Diet, owing to the absence of the other parties. On the subject of Finland Nekrasoff has issued to the Press the following : " The Provisional Government will firmly abide by its decision that the Finland question must be decided by the Constituent Assembly, and no interference with the sovereign rights of Russia will be tolerated." In the same statement on the subject of the Ukranians, he remarks : " The Provisional Government have prepared instructions for the General Secretariat of the Ukraine, and now awaits the official communication from the Rada. It is probable that a list of the Senators will shortly be submitted for the Government's sanction. The fact that Dorochenko is likely to head this list enables us to hope that there will be no further complications. Dorochenko was the Government's Commissioner in Galicia and the Bukovina, and is known to the Government as a loyal and tactful man. Members of the Rada will visit Petrograd, and, in consultation with the Government, will definitely fix the limits of their functions; the latter considers its instructions to be final and will make no further concessions. In these matters the Government considers it its duty to maintain intact the sovereign rights of Russia until the Constituent Assembly is convened." Nekrasoff concluded : " Both the army, through the Soldiers' Committees, and the Navy, through its central Committee, entirely uphold the Provisional Government and are ready to carry out its orders." But one is permitted to wonder—for how long ?

Lenin is said to be in Switzerland, from whence he is shortly to visit the Emperor William at Berlin. But, as likely as not, he is in hiding here amongst us in Petrograd, spending German gold on his propaganda and biding his time for his next effort against the Government.

September 2nd.—German propaganda is nothing if not thorough. And it must be admitted that they have a diabolical knowledge of the psychology of the uneducated Russian masses they are working amongst. It is well known here that an attack is preparing on Riga, and there are few who do not think that it must be successful in spite of the fact that the 12th Army are holding a very strong position which their General maintains to be impregnable. It is the disaffection amongst the troops which constitutes the danger. The following leaflet has just been received by a correspondent in Petrograd—

Translation of a poem which appeared in the paper " Jaunais Laiks," Saturday, 4th August, 1917.

" THE SONG OF PEACE IN WAR-TIME

BY LIHWU JURKAS

" Down with War.   Poetry is more powerful than powder.

" By Heaven, I assure you that the Germans do not like War, they much prefer poetry.   Come then, Comrades, let us sing together : ' A gay melody will be sung by us.'

" The German is our brother, he brings us his Kultur. This is well known amongst those in Courland.   That is why we will go to meet him with cries of ' Long Life ! Hurrah ! '

" Why should we allow ourselves to be killed ?   Why breathe the poisonous gas and suffocate ?   Even stones would refuse.   Why smell the smoke of the powder ?   Why allow the tear shells to close our eyes ?   Away with it all. William is coming to us as the God of Peace.   Kiss the weapons which threaten his life.   Throw up your hands and open the front, and sing ' Die Wacht am Rhein ! ' ' Come, dear William, Come hither.'

" Then he will come joyfully, and we shall all cry, ' Welcome, hip, hip, hip, hurrah ! '   He will dictate peace to us all in Russia and anoint our limbs with his ointment. Oh, what a joy it will be to all the Bolsheviks after their ' fight.'   We shall no longer have to sing the Marseillaise and all will be glad.   The new National Hymn will commence ' Heil dir, heil dir im Seigerkranz.' "

Another poem in the same style follows, and then come the words, " Authorised by the Russian Military Authorities, 4th August, 1917."

Stuff of this kind is swallowed by the masses of illiterate soldiers as sober truth; for it is read from a printed sheet, and what is printed is always taken as gospel truth by the ignorant. Moreover, it is authorised apparently by their military superiors. Why have the Allies allowed this kind of thing to go unanswered ? The above is the most crude and arrant nonsense, but it will do the mischief and fulfil its object for all that—in fact, because of it.

Undoubtedly we should have made an effort to fight Germany with all her weapons and answered leaflet with leaflet and propaganda with propaganda.

President Wilson's reply to the Pope's Memorandum on Peace is received here with that divergence of opinion which was to be expected. Acclaimed by the moderate Press as a crushing criticism delicately administered, it is treated very differently by the more rabid of the Socialistic organs. Here is a specimen : The condition of Greece, Ireland, India, Morocco, Albania, Mesopotamia, Syria, Dalmatia is apparently reconciled with the humanitarian ideal of re-establishing the sovereignty of the weak on a par with the strong. When Wilson speaks in the name of the Russian Revolution, as if he were its guiding hand, he is an impostor.

And yet it is these people who are endeavouring to grasp the supreme power here !

A big railway strike is threatened, and this is the more alarming on account of the breadless state of the south-west front alluded to by Korniloff at the Moscow Conference. The latest news from that direction states that the train-loads of flour have entirely ceased arriving, with the result that in a few days a million soldiers will be without bread, a material which forms a very considerable factor in the men's dietary, as is common with these Eastern European races. The peasants and shopkeepers are all holding up food. The situation is so dangerous that the High Military Command have been authorised to requisition flour wherever procurable, if necessary by force.

Kerensky, as Minister of War, will shortly issue a statement on the situation at the front and indicate the measures which he considers urgent to re-establish the fighting and disciplinary value of the army. These measures will be applicable to the front and rear.

Meanwhile the Council of Workmen and Soldiers have voted against the order re-establishing the death penalty. Tseretelli said it was necessary to support the order so as to consolidate the Revolution, and voted against the motion.

He is then definitely splitting with the Council, which is all to the interests of his country.

The Kazan fire is attributed to German agents, and it is said that further fires of a similar nature are to be expected. A Russian produces the following evidence : " In November 1916 and in January 1917 I received the following information from a Swedish source. In November 1916 a former Austrian military attaché came to Luleo. He had an interview with two Finns, who were charged with the commission to blow up military factories at Petrograd and Moscow. In January and March 1917 I was informed that one, Lotar Anders, had been sent from Berlin to Russia to blow up the works of Meister Lucius Brunning and those of Friedrick Bayer & Co., both working for the Artillery Department, and also some of the munition factories at Kazan. I immediately communicated this information to the military and naval authorities. The latter at once took steps to safeguard the works they were interested in. I do not think the military authorities acted on my information."

The Soukhomlinoff trial is proceeding. Further evidence was given by General Petrovsky, on the eighth day, on the orders for shells given to Giraud. The accused insisted on the contract being rapidly carried out. This order was given at the expense of Russian factories, the order to the Obankhovsky works being reduced. But the witness said that the Giraud factory was not capable of completing the large commission given to it. Colonel Bussoff said that the Ministry of Commerce placed obstacles in the way of the foreign orders given by the accused, probably with the object of developing the national industry. Soukhomlinoff explained that the Director of Artillery was chiefly responsible for the want of development of the national industry. " The question of aiding the national industry in this direction had already come to the front after the war with Turkey, and again after the Russo-Japanese War. When I became Minister of War I wished to develop this industry, but I did not receive the support of the Artillery Department. I have been reproached with not being interested in this department and with visiting it but rarely. But each time I went there they regaled me with wicked stories which caused me to lose my temper. The Finance Minister even declared when I toured in the Provinces that I wished to make money out of travelling. If I could have foreseen that we should be at war with Germany I should have taken the necessary steps to reorganise this department, from which I never received any support."

Colonel Botninkine, Chief of one of the Divisions of the Artillery Department, gave evidence that at the General's insistence a part of the order for machine-guns, in spite of the wishes of the Artillery Department, was given to the English firm of " Vickers." The witness was the more surprised at this order when he discovered, in ordering a machine-gun at Toula, that it only cost 900 roubles, whereas Vickers charged 2000 roubles. It is, however, somewhat difficult for a Britisher to credit the witness's further statement that the Vickers guns were proved defective and had to be sent to Toula to have these defects remedied. Doubtless there was some difference in adjustment which would not have been understood by the Russian soldier, but the evidence says nothing on this head.

General Velitchko, who was the next to appear in the witness box, made some scathing criticisms on the defendant's administration as War Minister. " Russia's military troubles are mainly due to the way Soukhomlinoff has managed affairs at the Ministry." General Velitchko is a great authority on military matters, being Professor of Fortifications at the Petrograd Military Academy, and in his evidence he gave a complete sketch of the present war. The witness related how Soukhomlinoff one by one abolished all the consultary chambers dealing with special aspects of warfare in existence at the War Ministry.

Immediately after Soukhomlinoff was appointed to the War Ministry he began to abolish these councils, which were composed of experts in all branches of military knowledge, and thus he attained the control of the whole management of the War Ministry in his own hands. This gave him a free hand to carry out his designs.

Witness further related how Soukhomlinoff completed his plan of abolishing a whole series of fortresses in the west of Russia, mainly in Poland. These fortresses were always considered the chief means of defence that Russia possessed against foreign invasion. They had been erected in the course of many years and had cost huge amounts of money. The defendant, however, on his appointment to the Ministry, immediately began to dismantle these fortresses one by one.

After General Velitchko's evidence, Soukhomlinoff desired to make some explanations. He said, with regard to the abolition of the fortresses, that he differed with General Velitchko as to the importance of the fortresses in question. The accused attaches greater importance to field defence and thinks that the western fortified district was simply a trap for the Russian Army. The shortcomings in supplies were due to no fault of his, as the Russian industry was unable to deal with all the requirements, and, moreover, the financial means had always been very scanty.

The evidence on the ninth day was confined to witnesses representative of Russian munition factories.

A director of the big Maltz munition factory said : " My first offers for manufacturing shrapnel made in October 1914 were refused by the Director of Artillery. On February 13, 1915, I again visited the Department and made further offers. General Smyslovsky did not even trouble to see me. He kept me waiting all day, and then wrote in pencil on my visiting card : " No further orders for shrapnel are under consideration."

A director of the Parviairn Factory said : " This factory has a capital of 10,000,000 roubles and employed 1500 workmen working for the Ministry of Marine before the war. On the day following the Declaration of War we offered to make shells. The Director of Artillery replied that the Russian Army had all it required."

The engineer Balinsky was next heard. He was said to be a great friend of the accused, and, consequently, was given some very big orders for his works. In this connection General Lonkomsky was heard. The witness said that the whole history of the orders given to the Balinsky works was a pure adventure, and the orders thus secured and the big payments made did not result in obtaining the materials paid for. The General gave some details on the private life of the accused couple. Madame Soukhomlinoff was very extravagant, and the General, in order to be able to provide for the caprices of his wife, led a very simple life himself. When Madame Soukhomlinoff went abroad to take the waters the General only spent 150 roubles a month on himself, sending the rest of his emoluments to his wife. The witness said that he had a talk with the accused General on the day the latter resigned, when he said : " Anyway it is fortunate that I have been able to save 500,000 roubles."

Grigorovitch, ex-Minister of Marine, said he had warned the accused of the rumours which were pervading Petrograd concerning Altchiller. Soukhomlinoff replied that Altchiller was an old friend of his. The latter was subsequently condemned as an Austrian spy.

Ledygensky, *chargé d'affaires* at the Council of Ministers, said that the accused had submitted a proposal to the Czar concerning the founding of an arms factory in Russia. The Council of Ministers had pronounced in favour of this project without, however, giving any definite decision. The accused and Balinsky, however, let the matter drop.

CHAPTER XI

ARCHANGEL AND THE NORTHERN DVINA

ONE of my reasons for going to Russia was to visit, if feasible, a part of the north-east region and study the conditions as affected by the revolution of this great forest tract of country. This region is almost unknown to us in this country—in fact, save to an exceptional few, quite unknown. Its importance as a great timber reservoir for the northern markets of Western Europe, not to mention other valuable economic resources, is very great. It has become imperative, therefore, that we should become better acquainted with it.

The north-east of European Russia, comprising the Governments of Archangel and Vologda (with Viatka and Perm to their south), is covered with fine virgin forests, chiefly of Scots pine, spruce and birch, some 80 per cent. of the Governments being afforested. The area covered by these forests is enormous, one district alone in the Vologda Government, that of Ust Sisolsk, is as large as Germany.

The journey from Petrograd to Archangel via the interesting ancient town of Vologda with its numerous old churches proved uneventful, though extremely tedious. The railways were rapidly deteriorating, and few luxuries were to be had whilst travelling in Russia. To procure a ticket in the sleeping-cars was a matter of considerable difficulty. The dining-car was not put on till we reached Vologda, where we connected with the train from Moscow, so for the first twenty-four hours of the journey we had to pick up food at railway buffets, greasy expensive messes. The distance from Petrograd to Archangel is some 700 miles, and we took about forty hours to accomplish it. Forest, and yet more forest, is the memory remaining with me as a result of that journey, practically all young growth up to fifty years of age, for in the neighbourhood of the railway all the old woods have long been cut out and utilised. The past two or three years have been very hard on this forest; fires originating from the railway swept through it unchecked, and the past year, a very dry one, was particularly bad in this respect. Miles of burning forest were passed *en route*, which, owing to the prevailing disorganisation brought about by the Revolution, were left to burn themselves out.

Archangel is one of the most surprising outcomes of the war. From an inconsiderable lifeless township before the war she has sprung into a thriving busy place with a celerity only comparable with that of the mushroom growths the New World has produced. One half, perhaps more, of the town is new, and there is an. offshoot on the opposite or railway side of the river which, in the form of new timber houses with plank roads carried on logs placed at intervals crosswise, stretches for several miles from the railway terminus on the river bank. That the town and railway should be on opposite banks of the river is a serious drawback necessitating transhipment of passengers, baggage and merchandise. The railway terminus was greatly enlarged to enable it to handle the enormous quantities of material it had to deal with, for the bulk of the guns, equipment, etc., supplied by the Allies to Russia has come through here; the station building has been doubled, and has now a large restaurant dining-room added to it, the building painted in the favourite Russian green and white and surmounted with domes and cupolas reminiscent of a mosque. Seen from the river it is a most imposing structure.

Archangel town is built of wood, with plank side-walks in the main street, which is cobbled with a vile *pavé*. The other streets have merely a central plank alley-way which is the only safe place to walk on. The fine Government House building, the picturesque cathedral and several other mosque-like churches form the chief, if not the only,

o

architectural features of the town. The shops vary from an inferior variety of the plate-glass window type to the open windowless bazaar-like structure one meets in the East, these latter occupying the narrow lanes running to the river and quays. Half an hour in Archangel will make you realise two things. First that you are very far north among a population which has a whiff of the Arctic Seas— a hard-looking people accustomed to leading a hard life, much of it spent warring with a harsh, inhospitable, uncomfortable climate; the second that the bulk of the population are concerned mainly with two occupations, the one of the sea and the commerce of the sea, the other of the forest and all that the forest can be made to produce when converted to man's use.

The greatest development of Archangel is on its river frontage, along both shores. Here numerous new jetties, strongly built of stout wooden piles, with broad timberways, stretch out into the river, and new wooden quays line the banks. A host of craft, ocean steamers of considerable size, and a large number of smaller vessels of all degrees, steam, motor-engined and sail, tied up and discharged their cargoes whilst others discharged out in the stream. In this direction the old and new Archangel were unrecognisable as the same place. The largest icebreakers in the world were employed in keeping the channel open, and work proceeded for nearly nine months, instead of five, as formerly. Big floating docks lay out in the river, and an enormous crane was brought out from Great Britain, arriving in August last. British and French Admiralty staffs were present until recently in the port, and worked harmoniously with the Russians.

Whatever the outcome of the present—I think a passing —phase in Russian politics, this great North Russian port has a big future, for the war has made Archangel an important northern mart, one which, far from dropping out when the war ceases, as will Harparanda and Tornea for instance, whose recent importance was entirely due to the closure of the other continental routes to northern Russia, will be likely to increase in prosperity. True, the new Murman railway is now in existence, with the ice-free port of Alexandrovsk at the head of the Kola Peninsula, but this railway, which runs through the Olenets Government on the west, is entirely independent of the Archangel–Petrograd railway, and separated from it by hundreds of miles of the desolate tundra country, consisting of boggy mosses and marsh. There is no connection between the two, and never likely to be for many years to come. The Murman railway, I may add, was working during the past summer. Gaps there were in it still where transhipment had to take place owing to the sleepers and rails having been laid on blocks of ice, that had the appearance of solid ground, but disclosed their true nature when the trains began to run over them. The Austrian prisoners, who were at one time employed on the construction, were accused of having done this intentionally. All I can say in favour of the Austrians is, go and have a look at the country and experience the freezing cold of it and realise the extraordinary difficulty of laying sleepers on such terrain. The task was one for giants, and they required to have a constitution impervious to an Arctic climate. Archangel, then, does not rely for its future on the prolongation of the war. A considerable proportion of the timber from the great virgin forests I am going to allude to will find its way to the northern timber markets of Western Europe from this port, and this is one of the first directions in which Russia may seek, must seek to rehabilitate her finances. Not timber only, but valuable minerals exist in this area, only waiting the capital to develop them. Besides the two northern railways I have mentioned, Archangel is also linked up with Central Russia via the northern Dvina river by a railway running from Kotlas, at the head of this river, due south to Viatka, which is in connection with the Siberian railway. These form the existing railway system of the northern Governments of Olenets, Archangel, Vologda, Viatka and Perm. To increase this system a line is projected from Archangel east to the Ob river via Soroka, Kotlas and Tomsk, crossing the Pechora at Ust Tsuilma, which will open out a far wider tract of country than is as yet accessible from the port. The northern Dvina starts at Kotlas, a town some 600 versts to the south-east of Archangel, where it is formed by the junction of two tributaries, the chief one being the Vichegda, which, starting in the north, soon turns and has a general westerly direction to Kotlas; the other tributary, coming from the south, is known as " the Little Dvina," formed by three tributaries having their sources in the south and south-east of the Vologda Government. My objective was the town of Ust Sisolsk, something over half-way up the Vichegda, which, higher up, is joined by a tributary known as the North Kiltma, which comes from the south; the upper Vichegda joining it here from the north. This river system is of interest, since the northern Kiltma and the southern Kiltma are joined by canal, thus connecting the river systems of the Vologda and Archangel Governments with the Government of Perm. The wonderful development of the Russian waterway system for transport purposes by means of canals linking up the great rivers and their tributaries, is but little appreciated in this country. It is due to their efficient use of this system that Russia has been able to get on with so inadequate a railway system.

Our first quest (I had a companion with me on this trip) on reaching Archangel was the river steamship office, where we learnt that a boat was leaving in the evening for Kotlas. Archangel, we heard, was crowded, not a room to be had for love or money, and we found this to be literally the truth on the way back. The river steamers, two and three deckers, which ply on the bigger of the Russian rivers, are well, almost luxuriously, fitted up with first-class accommodation on the upper deck; but you must take your own bedding. The steamer we joined at Archangel for Kotlas was a two-decker. There was not enough water in the river to run the larger boats, and this year they had been taken off very soon after the river opened to navigation in May, to prevent further harm to them. For with the new revolutionary ideas in the country, and the soldiery travelling free and

THE WOODEN JETTIES IN ARCHANGEL.

UNLOADING FUEL AT A DEPOT ON THE NORTHERN DVINA RIVER

occupying the first-class accommodation, the fittings of the boats had suffered seriously.

The saw-mills of Archangel now number some fifty concerns, most of them erected below the town. Some are well fitted with up-to-date frame saws and turn out work of a high grade—others are not so developed. Owing to the dilatoriness of the Russian workmen none of them turned out more than 60–70 per cent. of their possible output before the war. The soft woods, of which we use such quantities in Western Europe—pine and spruce— are the chief materials dealt with, brought down from the forests to the west and south-west of Archangel. This industry, which had its first beginnings in the latter half of last century, had made some considerable progress by 1914, but it did not then hold out a high prospect of successfully competing for many years to come with the timber exports and interests of the Baltic ports, Petrograd, Cronstadt, Riga, Libau and Windau. Over 48 per cent. of Russia's timber exports went from these ports. Some of the material for the two former came from north and north-east Russia; the other Baltic ports were supplied from the forests in the basins of the western Dvina, upper and lower Dneiper and Lithuania.

The war has put a different complexion on the position. This area will no longer be of great importance in the future. For one thing some 16,000,000 acres are in the fighting zone and have been ruined. For another, the Russians will want, when they get back these provinces from the Germans, as we hope they will, to keep the wood of this area to rebuild their devastated buildings in the regions destroyed. The demands of Western Europe will therefore be increasingly supplied from the forests of north-east Russia, and Archangel will be the main port of export for these materials. Flax and timber were her chief exports in the past. Of these, timber must of necessity occupy a far more prominent position in the future, owing to the enormous demands for the soft woods which will exist after the war. Bearing these points in mind, I think you will find something of interest in accompanying me up the northern Dvina and the Vichegda.

At Archangel I ate white bread and butter, the first I had seen for some weeks. I had hoped for a continuance of this luxury on my journey. But though butter was always present we dropped back to the black bread, though of far better quality than the nauseous Petrograd stuff. Generally speaking, in comparison with the food supplied in the capital, the meals served throughout the period spent on the river were good and became more plentiful, of better quality and cheaper the further we got from civilisation. Up the Vichegda we fed (almost) like fighting cocks.

Those who have seen and travelled on some of the larger rivers of the world will doubtless have noticed a great similarity between them in their lower reaches. A great broad stream of varying colour, the Dvina is brownish yellow when angry, and has low 8 to 12 feet cliffs on one side or the other. The shores are cultivated and dotted with villages, with a town here and there, the former either scattered and isolated or gathered together in clusters. The villages are unprepossessing, the houses black owing to their weathered, unpainted timbers, the whole having a squalid, depressing, funereal appearance. It is difficult to understand how the Russian peasant passes through the rigorous winter experienced in these inadequate houses, and one has but to see them to understand his addiction to vodka. But if the villages themselves are ugly and dispiriting, the churches, usually several in each village, are for the most part beautiful, with some form of a square tower carrying a steeple and painted white, with perhaps a gilded dome or minaret, or a yellow dome spotted with golden stars. The monasteries are even more imposing edifices, standing boldly up on some high bluff with a backing of dark pines and spruces, begirt with gardens, and surmounted with numerous golden domes, cupolas and minarets. The architects who planned these buildings were no mean men at their craft. In some of the bigger villages on the lower reaches of the Dvina, boat-building is practised on a considerable scale, the larger type of river and perhaps smaller coasting and fishing craft being built. I saw several hulls in various stages of construction on slips. Apart from this, fishing is one of the chief occupations of the riverain population on these lower reaches.

Some sixty miles or so up the river the real forest commences to make its appearance, and from here up-stream the forest belt is practically continuous; now approaching the river bank, at other times receding to a distance of 5 to 10 miles, the intervening space being cultivated. We saw a few examples of the old type of primeval forest of the river region. In one of the most beautiful reaches, a mile or two in length, the river runs through low cliffs of a dazzling white limestone, the summits clothed with thick old forest of larch, spruce, pine and birch; and in other places there were magnificent pieces of old Scots pine, the trees of great girth and running up to 45 feet without a branch. These were merely survivals, probably privately owned, of the old forest which has long since been cut for milling in Archangel. For the greater part the existing forest consists of young natural growth of varying age up to fifty years or thereabouts.

The riverain forests contain much birch which is cut for fuel, and the Steamship Company has dépôts all up the river, as the river boats and tugs all burn wood only. The engines on the Petrograd-Archangel railway also burn wood. The felling, cutting and transport of firewood billets gives work to a considerable population in northern Russia. On the Dvina the fuel is brought to the river bank in springless country carts of primitive type, drawn by shaggy, disreputable, but very hard-working ponies who possess as phlegmatic a disposition as the Russian peasant himself. Men and women unload the carts and pile the fuel in which long practice has made them adepts; for the stacks are packed with a deftness and closeness that would defy the non-expert to emulate. Fuel dépôts of varying size exist all up the river. Every village in the middle and upper reaches appears to be more or less connected with this fuel business. Where the bank is flat and shelving the wood is tumbled out of the carts in great heaps which are subsequently loaded into the capacious interiors of the great shallow draught barges. Where the bank is steep and cliff-like there will be several dry-earth slides cut in it. The fuel billets are shot down these slides to the beach below and then laden into the barges alongshore. I must have seen hundreds of these dry slides. In Great Britain in the past we have been extraordinarily backward in matters connected with the extraction of timber. To the Russian peasant in the forests the business is second nature and carried out cheaply, absurdly cheaply in comparison with our methods. In wood-craft, from felling the tree, converting it and getting it to the river bank, the inhabitants of this great forest region have little to learn.

In common with the other rivers of Russia, the Dvina forms one of the main lines of transport in this region. Amongst other things produce from Siberia finds its way down this river to Archangel. The chief forms of transport in use are the flat-sided barges some 80 to 100 feet in length, of very shallow draught, but capable of holding a large bulk of produce. These are towed to the number of three or more by small river tugs. Cattle are transported in this fashion, the barge being planked over and given a temporary roofing. The illustration shows a herd of Siberian cattle being towed down to Archangel, there to be converted into beef for the army. We passed numerous convoys of this description. The big rafts built higher up the river, and containing 4000 to 5000 logs apiece, are towed down to Archangel in the same way during the rafting season.

We had a very mixed crowd of passengers on board. With the new equality ideas prevalent, the whole ship was considered free to all, although the bulk of the passengers had only third-class tickets. Only the saloon and first-class cabins, which were kept locked, were regarded as private to first-class passengers, though this was only a recent improvement in the general situation. The whole

BARGE LOADED WITH SIBERIAN CATTLE PROCEEDING DOWN THE
NORTHERN DVINA TO ARCHANGEL, SEPTEMBER, 1917

TUG TOWING A RAFT DOWN AN UPPER REACH OF THE NORTHERN
DVINA. THE FOREST BELT IS SEEN BEHIND

FISHING VILLAGE AND APPARATUS ON THE NORTHERN DVINA RIVER

THE CHURCH AT KOTLAS, NORTHERN DVINA

of the deck space, including seats, was occupied by the
soldiery, amongst whom were many deserters, who had
no tickets, and rough peasantry who followed the soldiers,
and were probably unaware that they were not allowed
on the upper deck. The ship's officers took no notice,
experience having taught them that it was useless to do
so. One had, therefore, considerable opportunities of
studying the Russian peasant, as one saw a variety of
types, and marvelled at his wonderful patience. Hour
after hour he would sit with scarce a movement, absolutely
dumb and with totally expressionless face, the true type
of North Russia. The races met up the Vichegda were
very different, as we shall see.

The journey up the river was not all plain sailing.
The water was abnormally low, lower than had been
known for years, owing to the very hot, dry summer
northern Russia experienced last year. Sandbanks were
numerous, old ones daily becoming larger and new ones
drying off. We were hung up by river fogs at night and
navigation was tricky to a degree, strong head winds
making it even more difficult. Some of the passages
through the sands were so narrow and winding, that
only one vessel could pass at a time. Luckily we were
carrying the mails and so had precedence in this respect,
but even so we were held up in several difficult spots—in
one case for a couple of hours by a convoy of barges towed
by two tugs, who got into a winding channel ahead of us.
The fogs at night necessitated tying up. Our village
passengers often found the narrowing channel discon-
certing. The usual method of disembarking passengers
at the small towns and larger villages is by means of a
house-boat moored to the bank. Passengers for the
smaller villages are dumped out on the shore, the steamer
running her nose into the bank, a plank being thrust
over, and the passengers disembarked thereby. In many
cases voyagers to the more important townships had to
walk the plank in this ignominious fashion, their baggage
being incontinently deposited on the sands, where they
were left to fend for themselves, the house-boat being

anything from a quarter to a mile away over dry sands. This drying up of a wide river into a narrow stream is of course a common event in hot countries, such as India, during the cold and hot weather months of the year. The difference in the case of the northern Dvina—a marked difference—is that the river for the most part preserves its noble appearance, even when the water is as low as was the case this year. Most of the smaller tributaries dry up entirely; they are used for timber-floating in the season May and June, but after this run dry. But it was exceptional to see more sand than water between the two distant banks of the Dvina. For the greater length the water spread from shore to shore, only broken here and there with long humps of sand. The navigation buoys and booms, however, showed how much of this water was deceptive, consisting of great stretches of shallows which even the small-draught river steamers could not venture to go near.

This brings me to the buoying of the river for navigation. In view of the great disorganisation which existed elsewhere in Russia, this work was little short of marvellous. That the pilot service was most efficient to have enabled navigation to be carried on at all, was evident, as also was the fact that these men had stuck to their work. Buoys and booms dried off and lay exposed to view in countless numbers all up the Dvina and Vichegda as far as I went; but others always marked the channel, the boom being to starboard and the buoy to port, going up-stream. Moreover, the buoys were lighted every evening with an oil lantern apiece inserted in a small socket at the top, the lanterns being taken away to be trimmed and filled every morning. In their place the top of a young spruce is inserted to enable the steersman to pick up the buoy on a sunlit expanse of water. This work was performed by the villagers up and down the length of the rivers, each village having a stretch to look after, and the work appeared to be chiefly done by women and children, so many men being away. They came off in a cockleshell of a boat filled with the lamps, and had them all in position before the red flame of the sunset—we had wonderful sunsets almost every night of the trip—had died out of the sky. Not once had we to tie up or anchor owing to the absence of a lighted buoy. This was an amazing thing to witness after seeing so much of the dislocation and upheaval in Petrograd and the districts round it. Up here the Revolution in that respect had left the people untouched. The navigation is also assisted by high white posts driven into the bank at varying intervals, the position depending on the variations in the channel. The course is laid directly on these posts in succession. It is only at intricate places during the low-water periods that the posts become functionless and the buoys the sole guiding-marks for the steersman. With the state of feeling in the country and the low water, much latitude was accorded the captain in the matter of running to scheduled time. It says much for the type of men in command of these boats that their timing had been very good on the whole.

We ourselves had examples of a weak timorous man who tied up at the slightest contretemps and preferred his warm bunk to running at night; and of the converse, a man who considered it the greatest slur on his navigating powers to be late. I spent several hours one night watching with admiration this man's work. It was a dark night with banks of mist at dangerous bends; but he held on through it all, even negotiating some shoals at hairpin bends where there would have been every excuse for tying up. We were only one hour late in covering 400 miles under his command.

On the upper reaches of the Dvina they practise various forms of bank-fishing with nets. A common one is to suspend a square drop-net from a small wooden post erection built on the shore edge and let the net down when the conditions are favourable to a catch. Another method is to build a short length of wooden jetty out into the stream and net from the end of it. Both methods are common. They also have seine nets, and for these use a small canoe-like boat pointed at both ends, of great beam and very buoyant. This was the only village type of craft I saw on these rivers, pulled with two light spars to the end of which a narrow square of wood was nailed.

We reached Kotlas, 400 miles from Archangel, at the head of the north Dvina, on Thursday at 4 a.m., having left Archangel on the Monday at 5 p.m. We were called at dawn and told that the boat for Ust Sisolsk was leaving within the hour and that it was moored alongside of us. The manager of the company at Archangel had sent an order to the representative here that my journey was to be facilitated in every way, and I received the greatest courtesy and kindness from all—a point worth mentioning now. Kotlas as we saw it in the early light of a rainy morning was not imposing. Dull-looking, dirty wharves and jetties, with a line of dark-coloured slate-roofed houses on a low ridge, were relieved only by the white church. We spent a day there on the return journey, a bitterly cold wet day, and were not enamoured by its beauty. Kotlas has, however, undoubted possibilities before it as a commercial centre. It is linked up with Central Russia and the Trans-Siberian railway by the line to Viatka. It will also be an important centre on the projected Arch-angel–Ob railway. It was startling to see a long coal siding here on the river bank with a track running to the railway station and long mounds of coal—British coal, landed at Archangel and brought up the river in barges to Kotlas, whence it is sent by rail to Viatka and Central Russia. The railway station here is a large ugly structure, several tracks of rails in front of it, and a filthy fly-blown restaurant in which we had to have our meals amongst soldiery who eyed us with no friendly glance, and numerous train-bound civilians, chiefly women and children. There were numbers of Austrian prisoners up here employed on the railway who were comparatively free; the only escort I saw was an ancient soldier armed with a prehistoric musket which would certainly have burst had he tried to let it off. After all, these prisoners were safe enough there—distant some 2000 miles or so from the eastern front. Down near the wharves was the usual double row of bazaar-like shops kept mostly by Jews, squalid places with absolutely nothing of value in them. There was a long bread queue waiting for the bread shop to open, mostly Russian and Austrian soldiers and civilian men. We made an examination of the rest of the booths. The furs were of inferior quality, moth-eaten and of patterns worn by the peasantry only; the sweets, ever present in a Russian shop quarter, nasty looking and very expensive. No curios of any kind. In one shop only did I see anything I coveted, and this was a fine piece of bacon weighing five to six pounds. We had been feeding well up the Vichegda, and the shortness of the rations down the river had dimmed in my memory. I did not purchase the bacon, and lived to bitterly regret it. It was all sold within half an hour.

Kotlas is the up-river headquarters of the Steamer Company, and they had quite a fleet of river steamers, tugs and so on moored up the river. They have an alternative route to Kotlas from Kadnikoa on the upper waters of the Sukhona river close to Vologda. By September the water is usually too low to permit the running of their large boats, but they run them from Kadnikoa to Archangel via Kotlas, from the time the rivers open in May to about mid-August. Last year, owing to the exceptional lowness of the water, this route had become impracticable by September, and we heard that boats were aground on sandbanks all the way down the Sukhona from Kadnikoa. I had very nearly attempted the river myself.

The first news we received on reaching Kotlas was disheartening. The Germans had captured Riga.

CHAPTER XII

UP THE VICHEGDA—A GREAT FOREST TRACT

I NOW set out on not the least interesting part of my journey, proceeding up the Vichegda river. In its lower reaches, and in fact nearly up to Yarmuk, the river is of considerable size and volume, with a ribbon of cultivation on either side some two to six miles in breadth, beyond which stretches the primeval forest belt. The inhabitants of this region differ from the ordinary Russian, their origin and characteristics being of considerable interest. The greater bulk of the inhabitants of the Vichegda basin are known as Ziryanims, speaking a language or dialect of the same name, which is a mixture of Samoyede, to which I shall refer, and Russian. These Ziryanims are probably the descendants of the first Russian settlers in these parts who intermarried with the local tribe of Samoyedes, and gradually ousted the latter. The people and language are quite distinct. This language is not spoken to any extent round Kotlas and on the lowermost reaches of the Vichegda. The middle reaches of the river, with Ust Sisolsk as centre, appear to be almost entirely inhabited by the Ziryanims. They are a light-hearted, singing and dancing people, fond of bright colours in dress, and very different in temperament from the dull, stolid, expression-less North Russian peasant, and far easier to deal with. They are expert woodmen. Those we met appeared to speak Russian as well as their own language, but this may not be so in the upper limits of their region.

In addition to the Ziryanims there is the original local tribe proper of this region—the Samoyedes. These people are now confined to the more northern districts. The Samoyedes are Mongols, and extend, though now in much reduced numbers, from the White Sea to the Ob river and, under different names, as far east as the Yenesei and Lena rivers, and from there on to the borders of China. With the varying conditions in climate and other local factors, the habits and modes of life of these different branches naturally vary. They are all nomads, speak the Samoyede language, and support themselves by means of their reindeer, horses or dogs, according to the parts of the country they live in. All the Samoyede tribes have probably a common origin. The Tungusi on the Yenesei are Manchus proper. They split up into two tribes in the seventeenth century and, nomadic and illiterate though they are, they gave an emperor to the throne of China whose descendant was the last Chinese Emperor. The true origin of the Samoyedes and the Siberian tribes appears to be lost in the shades of antiquity. They live a primitive life, have, of course, no literature, and it is difficult to conceive of their ever having led a different life or having descended from a cultured race. Following on the dispersal of the existing races of the earth from Lower Asia, these people may have gradually worked their way through Central Asia to the Altai Mountains, and thence moved northwards and spread along the shores of the Polar Sea. Here through centuries they have lived a precarious existence and managed to persist. That in contact with the Russians they are dying out seems beyond a doubt. The Samoyedes appear to worship idols and spirits; even that portion of the tribe who live most in contact with the Russians are said to only possess the most rudimentary ideas of Christianity.

The scenery of the lower Vichegda is different from that of the middle and upper Dvina. The sparseness of the population in this great forest area of north-east Russia is evidenced by its tendency to cling to the river bank. A ribbon of cultivation a few versts only in breadth on either bank holds the greater bulk of the population and their villages. Behind this belt stretches the illimitable forest, 95 per cent. of which is owned by the Government. In the cultivated belt on the lower reaches of the river the forest is restricted to small patches, mostly young, the sandy banks and islands being covered with willow and to a lesser extent alder copses. The Vichegda is of historical interest. About an hour's run up-stream from Kotlas you arrive at the small township of Solvichigodska, which has a population of 1500 persons and twelve churches, many of them beautiful structures. This town is famous, for hence some two hundred years ago the great leader Yerma set forth to conquer Siberia.

It was already noticeable up here that the effects of the Revolution were dying out. In fact, save in the higher food prices and wages, neither war nor revolution have had much effect on the scanty population of these parts. And timber managers told me that the wages asked were falling. For these country people were beginning to think about the winter, and the necessity of either obtaining work in the forests or starving. They are a semi-forest population, agriculture only affording them employment for a few months in the year. They look to the forest to afford them and their ponies work, and consequently food throughout the winter, for the forest labourers are paid partly in food and are thus freed from all responsibility in commissariat. In the great forest area there are practically no villages or shops, and all supplies for the gangs of woodmen have to be taken up by those engaging them. This combination of forestry with agriculture is on the lines we may look to see in Great Britain some day, especially in the more hilly districts and Highland glens, where the small crofter will look to the forest to provide him with work and thus the means of subsistence throughout the winter months.

The boat into which we had exchanged was a small one and packed, unpleasantly packed, with soldiery, a lawless crowd of deserters for the most part; and of far better behaved peasantry. The soldiers looked at my companion and myself with suspicion and dislike. They were totally without discipline, and spent the time playing concertinas out of tune, chewing the seeds of the *Pinus cembra*, a habit as common among certain classes of Russians as it is amongst Punjabis and frontier tribes in India—the seed in the latter case being that of the *Pinus Gerardiana;* and in unlimited tea-drinking, cigarette-smoking and card-playing. Their spirit was very bad. The peasantry exhibited quite a different character, and there was plenty of evidence that the returning soldiery, who were of the same origin, once away from bad example and a full stomach obtained without labour since the Revolution, would soon return to sanity. There could be no doubt that their relations and friends up here would not provide them with free food or countenance their idleness. As they did not want to fight any more, the free food would not tempt them back to the risks of the army. I may give, as evidence of the army spirit, two instances witnessed up here. We went into the bank on which clustered a tiny village. A young soldier landed. As he put his foot on the shore he flung his knapsack up the bank with an oath, an act loudly applauded by many companions on the boat. He had done with the army if he could escape being taken back. The other incident was next evening. A small group of people stood on the bank as we put in. A smart young sergeant of cavalry jumped ashore with a bag in his hand. He advanced to the group and was clasped against the breast of a sturdy, bearded old man, typically clad in the Russian peasant's astrakhan cap, rough blouse belted at the waist, and trousers tucked into long black boots. Three times the father kissed his son on either cheek whilst tears rolled down his cheeks. Then after a few words he picked up the heavy bag, and refusing to allow his son to carry it, tramped sturdily down the well-known winding foot-path which led from the river to a small cot embosomed in trees. That is the other side of the spirit of Russia, and I am of those who believe that it is the more general spirit of the country. That father would rather have seen his son dead than a traitor to Russia.

The only town of any importance on this river below Ust Sisolsk is Yarmuk, which contains 15,000 inhabitants, many churches, and is a verst from the river bank. We arrived here much behind time owing to a river mist which

P

held us up at night for several hours, and the following morning a thick fog due to the smoke of a great forest fire which was raging in the pine forest to the south. This fire must have stretched over many square miles, for the sun, shining in a clear sky, was blotted out all the morning, and the whole countryside was filled with smoke and the acrid smell of burning wood.

We were now right up in the district of Ust Sisolsk, which has an area of 148,000 square versts (102 desyatines = 1 square verst, or 255 acres), of which 14,000,000 desyatines (35,000,000 acres) are forest. Already about 500,000 logs are floated down the river yearly from Ust Sisolsk, in addition to those brought down the tributaries below that town. A small stream, little more than a ditch, runs through Yarmuk into the Vichegda. From 40,000 to 60,000 logs are sent down this small stream in the floating season. It looked incredible. Felling is done in the winter, the logs being drawn out over the frozen track to the river edge. They are here made up into rafts and towed down by tugs to Kotlas, and from there to Archangel. Above Ust Sisolsk, small rafts only are made and floated down the river to that place. They are then built into the bigger rafts for the tugs. On the smaller tributaries the logs are floated down singly to the larger river before being made up into rafts. Floating operations begin as soon as the ice melts and the rivers open for traffic in May. The chief rafting month is June from Usk Sisolsk downwards, but continues through July and to a smaller extent in August. Ust Sisolsk district has a population of 116,000, or 1 per square verst (255 acres). In addition to its timber wealth the district contains copper, iron, naphtha, coal, mercury, lead and traces of gold. The lead is plentiful; coal has been worked to a small extent and is of good quality. Capital is required to exploit these minerals and to open out the big forests, which have as yet been scarcely touched.

Here we got into touch with the real primeval forest, which comes down in places to the river bank. The country becomes undulating, a pleasing contrast to the dull

ZARYANINS AND THEIR BOATS ON THE VICHEGDA RIVER, N.E. RUSSIA

CHURCH AND SCENERY ON THE NUSHAGA RIVER

uniformity we had seen so far, and is backed by range on range of low hills to the east, the foothills of the Urals, the bigger ranges being dimly seen on the sky-line some hundred miles or so distant. The whole countryside is clothed with one great, almost pathless, virgin forest of pine, spruce and birch—a forest as yet practically untouched by the hand of man, a storehouse from which Western Europe must for many years to come draw a considerable proportion of her requirements in these soft woods. It was what I had come to see. We were now in the middle of September, and already up here autumn had well set in, and the tints on the birch, willow, alder and poplar were beautiful. It was very cold, and the river was full of wild-fowl, duck, teal and geese. On our last day's run up the river there was not a breath of air, the surface was like glass in which the brilliant foliage-tints, the reds and browns of the banks, and yellow of the sand were mirrored so sharply that it was difficult to perceive where reality ended and reflection began.

I will conclude this chapter with a few brief remarks on the objects of my visit to the region I have just described. One does not travel for pleasure nowadays. I was not sightseeing. This region has a direct importance to ourselves. We are all aware of the present timber shortage—of the difficulty experienced in supplying our armies in the field. Wood of all kinds is almost unobtainable for the ordinary requirements of the country. It is all needed for the war. We are felling at a real sacrifice the woods of Great Britain. They must go if the war is to be won. But we shall only realise what a sacrifice it is, we shall only begin to feel our loss when the war is over. All over Europe the same sort of thing is going on, and in addition we have to add the enormous devastation of woods within the fighting zones. I have referred to the 16,000,000 acres of forest destroyed on the eastern front in the basins of the western Dvina, lower and northern Dneiper and Lithuania. The demand for timber at the peace will be enormous. A considerable part of our pre-war supplies came from Russia. It is absolutely certain that a portion at least of our needs in this respect during the next forty to fifty years must come from this north-eastern forest region of Russia. Capital will be required to develop this region, capital which Russia does not possess. Of all Russia's great economic resources, her timber will be the easiest to convert into cash with which to commence her rehabilitation. The unrest up here is, or was, not so serious, the dislocation nothing like so great as in the densely populated industrial regions. The Provisional Government, as I have shown, were alive to this fact, and a good deal of preparatory work was being undertaken in the Ministries with this end in view. Labour to carry out the schemes contemplated will be available in abundance when the country becomes more settled. Now, we can obtain this timber in the future in two ways—

1. By coming to a direct arrangement with the Russian Government, when a stable government in some form or other is in power, or

2. By buying from foreign middlemen, who will themselves come to an arrangement of this kind.

In the first case we shall be more or less assuring a portion of our timber supplies at a comparatively cheap rate during the next forty to fifty years. Under the new conditions which will exist after the war, we shall have, in common with others, to work on new lines, to throw over the old routine and the old ideas of trade and trading methods. In the second case we shall have to pay a higher price in all probability, as we should have no influence on the timber markets and should, at the same time, be at the mercy of the foreign timber merchant.

I am not advocating here the expenditure of public funds on this matter, the hypothecating of the national income. It should not be necessary. I have little doubt that the necessary capital will be forthcoming from the capitalists of the country; for it will be an investment yielding a good return. But the arrangements by which we secured an area or areas of forest in Russia of sufficient size and value to enable us to assure a portion of our timber requirements for the period I have mentioned would require to be made between the respective Governments, for reasons which need not be specified, but which are the outcome of the Revolution, and in order that the capital invested might be given that guarantee which the magnitude of the project would demand.

Up to the outbreak of the war we were entirely dependent on foreign timber imports. The war has shown what that meant. In this suggested scheme, which in effect would be a big British combine, my idea is to remedy for a period of years this entire dependence, during which the woods, which we hope to plant, would be maturing, or at least reaching pit wood and perhaps pulp size. We should have under British control a portion at least of our requirements of those soft woods—pine and spruce—of which we use such large amounts. We shall have to get the material across the sea, but this will be our position for a good many years to come in any event; and Archangel is nearer than the countries of the New World. A part of our soft wood requirements will come from north-east Russia—of that we may be sure. The point is, how are we going to obtain them? Shall we do it ourselves, or are we going to let the foreigner do it?—not the Russian, he has not the capital—be dependent upon the foreigner and pay him his price!

CHAPTER XIII

RETURN TO ARCHANGEL AND PETROGRAD

WE arrived at the wharf at Archangel just before seven o'clock in the evening, having something over an hour to catch the mail to Petrograd.

The first piece of news we heard on landing was that Korniloff was marching at the head of an army on the capital in order to put an end to the Provisional Government, and that the British Ambassador had telegraphed requesting persons of British nationality not to come to Petrograd except in cases of urgent necessity. Even in this land of surprises it was most startling news. My companion was staying on in Archangel for a day or two with friends, but I had arranged to catch the eight-o'clock train. In view of the unknown conditions in the south he urged me to remain here and return home direct from Archangel. But it was imperative that I should return to Petrograd in any event, and even had that not been the case I was naturally keen on seeing what the new development would result in. For the news appeared to be incredible from one point of view, coming so soon after the Moscow Conference. From the other, with such a weak vacillating body as the Provisional Government had shown itself to be, it was easily understandable that a soldier of Korniloff's calibre should wish to cut the Gordian knot. My companion, finding me adamant, offered to accompany me to the station on the other side of the river. No drosky being available, a small urchin whom we picked up carried my bag and took us to the wharf from which the ferry steamers leave. We were in luck, as one was just about to quit; but on asking about the train, we learnt to my dismay that the mail now left at 6 p.m. instead of eight, as we had

214

been told; and there was only one daily. There was nothing for it but to search for quarters in the town.

Archangel was crowded—my companion was to occupy a bathroom at his friend's house, and where I should obtain a bed appeared problematical. We went to the Troitka Hotel. It was full to the cellars, and so was the other hotel—a one-horsed place at the best. This exhausted the hotel accommodation. I remembered I had a card of an acquaintance on me, and we went to his flat. A dark, low-browed, typical northern Russian appeared. " No, the owner of the flat was out, and he had several gentlemen staying with him." It was impossible to spend the night walking about the streets of Archangel; it was already bitterly cold and raining, and I refused to trouble my companion's friends, who were already, I had gathered, overcrowded. We therefore harangued the man in front of us. Yes, there was a kitchen, but it was already occupied. There might be room for another. There was also a fuel-shed. I readily agreed to occupy either, and left the choice to him. If my acquaintance turned up I would discuss the matter with him later. I left my bag with the man, said good-bye to my companion, and made for the Café de Paris, a very fair restaurant in the main street, with good cooking, where most of the commercial element of the town and the foreign officers appeared to take their meals. Our men, in our insular fashion, have messes of their own. The café was crowded, but, as it happened, the first man I saw was my acquaintance of the flat. I sat down at his table and explained my predicament. He said he would probably be able to arrange matters for me. The dinner was good, and there was white bread and thin beer—both luxuries nowadays.

I had seen, coming down the river, that a big saw-mill, the Imperial mill originally belonging to the Czar, which I was to have visited, had been recently burnt down. We had noticed it on our way up-stream, with a big ocean-going steamer alongside loading up sawn timber for a British port. I asked my companion about this fire. It was the usual tale. The steamer was hauled out into the stream in time, but the mill was gutted and a lot of the sawn timber burnt. The place had been intentionally fired by the workmen, which is on a par with the insensate folly of the Russian lower classes—to destroy what belongs to the capitalist even though it provides themselves with work, and in spite of the fact that, as in this case, the capitalist was their own Government.

My companion told me a great deal of interest and importance to us in this country on the subject of the saw-milling industry in Archangel, and of the great future in front of it. In this business he was an expert, and had no doubts whatever that Archangel in the future was going to take the place of Riga in the western European markets, and especially in the British ones. In ordinary years the bigger mills here saw up from 250,000 to 300,000 logs in a season. This year's average would, my informant told me, be only 30,000 to 40,000, and then the mills will have to shut down, as they will have finished their stocks. The closing, however, depended on the amount of felling done during the winter, and that a certain amount would be done I had ascertained up the river. It is considered that the labour required for undertaking the felling operations in the forests on a large scale will not present insuperable difficulties; but the matter of tonnage to carry the sawn material will prove more difficult. There were a few big steamers loading up with timber in the river or at the wharves of the mills, but the available tonnage for this export is now extremely restricted, and most of the mill yards are full of sawn material.

I was leisurely finishing dinner when my acquaintance, who had gone out " to fix me up," as he expressed it, returned. He said that it would not do for me to occupy either kitchen or fuel-shed at his place. A member of the Staff had offered to put me up; that my host to be was dining at the Admiral's and would be home at about eleven, and would I turn up at his place then ? My acquaintance said he had instructed the man at his flat to take my bag and myself to my destination at that hour. Before the war one might have felt some surprise and diffidence in

descending upon an unknown man at this hour of night.
But those who knock about nowadays so often find themselves in the most extraordinary positions that one ceases
to feel surprised and takes what the gods send with thank-
fulness. As I now had plenty of time and no further care
as to my night's lodging, I sat on in the café and watched
my fellow-guests. It was a contrast, this well-lighted and
rather garish northern café restaurant, to Flocca's and the
Tour Blanche of Salonika, where I had a year ago watched
the fighting men of a dozen nations in varied and often
brilliant uniforms making merry in the brief intervals
of leave obtainable between the more serious business all
were engaged upon—British, French, Italians, Serbians,
Russians, Roumanians, French Zouaves and Colonial
regiments, Indians, Armenians, Greeks, Albanians and
Annanese. In the brilliant colouring of the Eastern
Mediterranean they were an extraordinarily interesting
crowd. Here the atmosphere was very different. There
breathed over the place a blast from the Arctic Ocean,
exemplified by a beautiful model of an old northern ocean
three-masted wind-jammer on the bar. The majority of
the men present were sailors—officers of the British, French
and Russian navies and merchant services, with Norwegian
and Swedish merchant skippers. Junior naval officers
of our own and the other nations sitting cheek by jowl with
rugged ships' captains who had spent their lives in the rough
boisterous waters of the Arctic Ocean and the White and
North Seas. Pretentious as this Café de Paris is, with an
external appearance which would not disgrace a capital
of Europe, there pervades it an atmosphere such as I
personally had never encountered before in my wanderings.
Over in a corner sat two of our naval men, a lieutenant-
commander and lieutenant. They had come in at ten
o'clock. Foreigners of several kinds were still eating heavy
meals, and I idly wondered what these two had ordered
at this hour, as I saw they had not come for a drink only.
I should never have guessed. Two boiled eggs apiece with
bread, butter and coffee was their meal—eminently British,
and, I suppose, seaman-like, for I do not think it would

have occurred to any landsman to order so curious a meal at that time of night. In front of me sat a Norwegian skipper with brick-red face and clear, steady eyes. He sat stolidly drinking coffee for a couple of hours, reading a creased, well-worn and well-thumbed paper, which had evidently passed through many hands. There was no whisky, rum, gin or liqueurs to be had. The old merry, early days of the war in Archangel, when whisky, brought out by the ships' captains, was plentiful, are a memory of the past. A bottle of whisky was a rare bird now, and tobacco had almost given out. Our people struggled along with what they could get from the ships, and that was precious little. As one red-faced, burly ship's captain said disgustedly: "On leaving England I was only allowed to take three bottles of whisky with me. And what's the good of that to me?" To a man accustomed to take his whisky neat in a tumbler with the merest dash of water, small good indeed, with a two months' voyage before he would see home again. A small table by the wall was occupied by two youngsters in Russian naval uniform. Both had square, rather heavy features, and the piercing eyes one associates with the seaman. The gold braid on the sleeves is similar to ours but heavier. In fact, our men stood out as the quietest and neatest dressed of the crowd; for although all the foreign sailors' uniforms one saw here were copies of ours, they all carried more gold braid, and often the less dressy high collar buttoned to the neck. A Russian flag-lieutenant came in to give some order to the youngsters, wearing shoulder-knots of heavy white cord which almost covered his breast. On the left sat two old grizzled sea captains, heavily bearded, in thick pea jackets and peaked caps. Their nationality I did not discover. It was not British. They smacked of stormy oceans and the life of the tramp steamer. Sipping *café au lait* in that restaurant they looked very out of place, as also did a Jack tar and petty officer who were demolishing a heavy hot supper and did not appear quite certain whether they ought to be there. There was a sprinkling of military officers—French in their pre-war uniforms, not in the blue one has come to associate with this nation in war time ; and Russian—mostly dug-outs or very junior subalterns. None wore medals, and were chiefly, if not entirely, on transport work here. The handful of civilians were either timber or flax men, the two main export industries of Archangel.

After a tramp through the wet, deserted streets of Archangel, we knocked up the house we imagined to be that of my host. The front was dark and silent, but after knocking and ringing several times an upper window was partly opened and the quavering voice of a woman asked us what we wanted. My guide explained our purpose, and the voice in a tone of relief said that the captain's house was next door. They are very frightened of burglars nowadays in Archangel, as elsewhere in this country, and so the lady up above had reason for her fear. I met my host with several other men on his own doorstep, and he welcomed me with the hospitality so characteristic of the Britisher abroad. We sat up for an hour or two discussing the present situation in Russia. There had been no communication with Petrograd for several days, he said, and beyond the fact that the news had come through that Korniloff was marching on the capital they knew no more. But the wildest rumours were afloat. " We think up here, or a good many of us," he continued, " that if the Allies sent 100,000 men here and railed them to Petrograd it would be sufficient to give the necessary stiffening to the loyal Russian troops and finish off the Bolsheviks. As long as they are allowed to play their present game, the Provisional Government have not a chance of reintroducing discipline into the army. We have been pulling along all right with the Russian staff up here, but the working classes are getting out of hand. They are not so bad, of course, as further south, but they are difficult enough to deal with. You may have heard that the powerful ice-breakers we have keep a fairway open in the river during winter. Well, every one here is aware that if the ice-breakers cease patrolling the fairway the ice banks up in the latter, forming a ridge, and this constantly increases in height across the river, thus damming up the water and flooding the country above the ice dam. Higher up the river there were large accumulations of wheat, sugar and matches last winter, running into many millions of tons. The crews of the ice-breakers joined in with the rest in neglecting their work after the Revolution in March; the fairway froze over and the ice banked up, with the result that these large dumps of stores, so badly wanted by northern Russia, were flooded and ruined. No one," said my friend, "expects the matches one buys now (in the middle of September) to light. The surprise occurs when one does. They come from the flooded stores."

I woke up next morning in a soft bed with that feeling of bliss known to all travellers. I heard a good deal about Russia from the captain, who, previous to the war, had spent a number of years in business in the country, which he knew thoroughly. One cannot help forming the opinion after hearing men of this type talk, men who had made a life-study of the people, and I had heard many by now, that had they been listened to and their advice been taken, Russia might have been in a different position, and the Allies in a different position, to the one which now confronts her and us. Men of this type should not have been allowed to join the army. The Foreign Office is the department which should have recruited and made use of them. They maintain, many whom I conversed with to-day, that it is not yet too late. But after my residence in Petrograd I fear it is now too late to do anything to stave off what appears to be certain disaster—unless Korniloff can do it. Such papers from the south as have arrived here say nothing of what is really happening. A *New York Herald*, dated the 12th, which was given me to-day (13th), has great head-lines saying that "Civil war has broken out in Russia, and Korniloff is marching on Petrograd to assume power." The crisis, says this paper, is graver than any that has occurred since the Revolution. Korniloff, it is stated, has been dismissed his post of Commander-in-Chief, and the Members of the Provisional Government have resigned in order to leave Kerensky liberty of action to deal with the extremely dangerous situation. Little hope, it is said, is entertained of a pacific solution to the conflict, a collision between the rival parties being looked upon as a certainty. The Council of Workmen and Soldiers are supporting the Provisional Government, as also are the Committee of the Peasants' delegates. Petrograd appears to be in a great state of excitement.

My first step to-day was to ascertain at Government House whether I should be allowed to return to Petrograd and to procure the necessary permit. No permit, I found, was necessary, which seemed strange. A coupé in the sleeper was easily procured, as few wished now to travel south.

These matters settled, I was able to make further inquiries on the subject of the saw-mill industry of the place. Its past history and present position is, as has been shown, of the very first importance to us in this country, and this point cannot be too strongly insisted upon in view of the fact that this part of Russia is almost unknown in Great Britain. It was about the middle of last century that the saw-milling industry had its first beginnings on the shores of the White Sea. By the eighties about 1,250,000 roubles' worth of timber was being exported, only the largest sizes being used for the purpose, the rest being left to rot in the forests. With the increasing demand in Western Europe, however, the timber industry in the northern regions began to expand. By 1900 the number of saw-mills had increased to 32, with an annual turnover of about 13,000,000 roubles, some 9000 men being employed. There are at the present time 55 mills in the Archangel and Vologda Governments, employing some 15,000 men before the war. Fifty of these mills are at Archangel or in the Archangel Government, and they saw up about 10,000,000 logs annually. As the work done never amounted to more than 60 to 65 per cent. of the possibility, this amount, with better supervision and work, could easily be increased. It is now a certainty that this business will be enormously expanded in order to supply the very large demands which will arise in Western Europe with the termination of the war.

A consignment of 1,500,000 barrels of smoked herrings had just arrived here from Scotland, and a second lot of the same amount was expected. The Russian peasants eat them. In fact, my friend remarked, " Give them plenty of rye bread, with herring, tea and sugar " (and he might have added the universal cabbage soup), " and there would be no food riots or any other, and they would soon settle down again." It is a pity we or America could not have imported some of these deficiencies earlier in the year, instead of continuing to send Russia munitions and guns long after the possibility of the Russians being able to utilise them had become well known. The river is full of craft, including some 5000-ton vessels, tramps of every description, trawlers, etc. I believe there are at the moment about fifteen of our ammunition ships in the river besides a few Russian and French; and this in the middle of September, when the Russian front has almost disappeared ! We have some submarines here, of course, and others at Reval. Four of the latter were taken to Reval by canal via Petrograd. They tied the submarines to barges and sank the latter to a level, which left the submarines awash. The barges were towed by tugs. I was told that it was a curious sight to see the submarines proceeding down the Neva through Petrograd in this novel fashion, with the British officers and crews on deck.

The labourers on the coal wharves at Archangel were threatening to strike. They received thirteen roubles a day and a bread-card, which enabled them to buy two pounds of bread a day instead of one pound, the ordinary allowance of the civil population (Russian 1 lb. = $\frac{3}{4}$ lb. British). The men were now demanding two and a half pounds of bread per day. Bread is, of course, the chief staff of life to the Russian peasant, just as it is to the Serbian and most of the Eastern Europe peasantry.

The wires opened before I left Archangel, and I was able to send off a telegram home to relieve anxiety and a second to Petrograd. My friend took me across the river in a Government tug. When we boarded the latter the crew were below. At our shout they came up smiling, four men and a boy. In reply to a question, we elicited the fact that they had got hold of a bottle of cognac for which they paid thirty-five roubles. I expressed surprise at their being able to pay the price. " Why," said my friend, " the skipper of this tug gets 700 roubles a month and has only to buy his food, as he lives on board. The men get 300 to 350 roubles a month and also live on board. They are as rich as Crœsus." We backed out and went up the river. It was an interesting and busy sight. Two tramps were completing with deck-loads of timber, being boarded up to a considerable height. The sides of these vessels were painted in the most extraordinary geometrical patterns to render the boats invisible. But the effect close by was that of an appalling nightmare of the worst efforts of futurist art. We passed great iron munition ships, whose work during the past couple of years has been one record of risk and hardship, and all, one fears, for naught.

The Moscow *wagon-lit* was full of people, but that for Petrograd almost empty, there being but five of us. This in itself was sufficient testimony to the uncertainty of affairs in Petrograd; as for long now it has been difficult to secure seats in this train without several days' notice. The first man I met was my companion. He had heard that Korniloff's " Savage Division " of Cossacks were leading the van in the march on Petrograd, and that their advance posts had reached Pavlost, where he lived. He was, therefore, hurrying back. With him was one of the English chaplains at Petrograd, who had been on several months' duty up here with our fleet. A most entertaining companion he proved. He was most amusing, too, in his efforts to collect food *en route* to take to Petrograd—butter, eggs, and so forth. The peasants bring these articles for sale to the passengers in the trains, and thus, if you keep your eyes open on a journey of this distance, you may lay in quite a fair stock of these commodities. The parson, well versed in the ways of the country, did not do badly. But he missed one chance. At a small wayside place where we halted a bare minute, he was offered three hares for eight roubles—a gift. He hesitated—one of the hares was covered with blood. They were newly shot or trapped. It would be a messy addition to his rather neat baggage. The train started. Still he remained undecided. The train was gathering way. Too late he made up his mind and shouted to the man. The latter turned a dull expressionless face on us and remained staring, rooted to the spot, until we lost sight of him. He is probably still wondering what the " Barin " meant by shouting at him after refusing to take his hares. But the parson bewailed his indecision for the rest of the journey.

He told us a good deal about the trawlers out in the White Sea and Arctic Ocean, and the appalling life of hardship these men lead—almost incredible tales to a landsman. He had visited one of them recently to see the men, and of course was asked to stay to tea or tea-supper. This is what it consisted of : a large salmon pie, fine white bread, quantities of beautiful butter, apricot and strawberry jam, rock cakes and strong black tea *à l'Anglais*. It makes your mouth water, does it not ? But one likes to know that these brave, hardy fellows are done well.

At Vologda we got the Moscow papers. But they were quite indefinite on the Korniloff business, having large blank areas where the Censor, presumably recently reestablished, had excised paragraphs.

The queerest part of this journey back to Petrograd was its ending. All the way up to Archangel we were constantly pestered for our passports. The examining officials were illiterate militia soldiers and sailors who could not make head or tail of the passport when offered them. Can one wonder, therefore, at German spies being everywhere ? On the return journey we were never once asked to produce the passports. On arriving at the Nicholas Station at 10.30 a.m. (our tickets had been given up the preceding day), we quitted the carriage, called porters, and, following our luggage, walked out of the station absolutely unquestioned.

Truly Russia is a land of surprises !

CHAPTER XIV

SEPTEMBER 3RD—15TH

THE LOSS OF RIGA AND THE KORNILOFF AFFAIR— THE SOUKHOMLINOFF TRIAL

On my return to the capital I lost no time in picking up the threads of the chief events which had taken place during my absence. The two weeks had witnessed the fall of Riga and the march of Korniloff on the capital.

The offensive which resulted in the capture of Riga, of which rumours had been prevalent in Petrograd at the time of my departure, commenced at the beginning of September. It had been fully expected, but the Commander of the 12th Army, during the last week in August, stated in the *Novoe Vremya* that his defences were storm-proof. The German 8th Army, under von Hutier, forced a passage of the western Dvina on both sides of Uexküll, an important bridgehead about eighteen miles up-stream from Riga. By the evening of September 2nd the Germans had penetrated the Russian positions at several points on the Jaegel river line four to five miles beyond the Dvina and from twelve to fifteen miles south-east of Riga. With the Riga–Dvinsk railway cut and the Riga–Petrograd railway directly threatened, the Russians had to relinquish the last remaining section of the Riga–Windau railway west of the city. Riga was evacuated on the 3rd, the fortifications at the mouth of the Dvina and the bridges across the river being blown up. At the time of the Russian withdrawal the town was being heavily shelled by the Germans and was on fire in several places. The Russians retreated in fair order and continued this retreat on a fifty-mile front for several days along the shores of the Gulf and to the south-east, finally taking up a position on the line of the Mlupe river, with Friedrichstadt on the left flank. Here the army made a stand. The Germans claimed to have taken 9000 prisoners and 325 guns, besides machine-guns and other booty.

The Council of Workmen and Soldiers endeavoured without success to make use of the fall of Riga to obtain Korniloff's dismissal—in spite of the fact that the General had predicted its loss at the Moscow Conference. The loss of the town was taken quietly in the capital. It had been regarded as a certainty in view of the well-known fact that the 12th Army was infested with German spies and permeated with their propaganda. Few expected them to stand when the test came. The Germans also had an easy task, as they were able to denude with safety other parts of the front in order to concentrate on Uexküll.

At the beginning of September Nekrasoff told the Press that the Government had the fullest confidence in Korniloff, who they were aware had no connection with certain political intrigues which were being carried on round him. They had every confidence in the political neutrality of the Generalissimo. The only matters in dispute between the latter and the Government were in connection with the discipline of the army and were not political. Some of the General's stipulations had been already given effect to. The rest would be shortly. Savinkoff, he said, will shortly confer with Korniloff and will draw up a report for presentation to the Government. The Government denied that Korniloff was to be suspended, and were at one with him that serious and energetic measures must be taken at once to re-establish the fighting efficiency of the army.

Nekrasoff's reference to political intrigues was in connection with a counter-revolutionary plot which had been hatched in Petrograd during the Moscow Conference in which well-known politicians, members of the Cadet party, and officers, were said to be implicated. It was also evident that the Government had reason to suspect that the Cossacks were giving it support, for it was rumoured that the Government had threatened to withdraw the privileges of the Cossacks. There can be little doubt that this was a most short-sighted move, for the Cossacks had been the one absolutely loyal military unit since the Revolution.

Shortly after his return to the front from the Moscow Conference, Korniloff took matters into his own hands and gave orders for the forcible seizure of cereals from the peasants within the war zone. He also opened direct negotiations with the railway servants with the object of satisfying their requirements and reducing the disorganisation of the railways.

Meanwhile the Soviet rejected by a large majority any attempt to introduce the death penalty either at the front or rear. The loss of Riga had, however, momentarily aroused the Government to the increasing danger, since, with the 12th Army still in retreat, the capital was now within the war zone. On the recommendation of a special Commission they accepted Korniloff's proposals and reintroduced the death penalty at the front and rear for soldiers and civilians alike, the penalty to be inflicted for treason, desertion, cowardice and military insubordination. It has been a belated move. The Petrograd Soviet also came out in a new light, and called upon all soldiers and workmen to carry out their duties ! The capital during these days, as may be imagined from the mercurial temperament of its cosmopolitan population, was in a state of tense excitement, fully expecting the Germans to march into the city. The usual exodus took place daily, the Government at the same time closing the capital to all who had no fixed abode or residence in the city. My own return showed how this order was being carried out !

Before the public had recovered from the excitement engendered by the fall of Riga and the German advance towards Petrograd, a bombshell fell in their midst with the news that on September 8th Korniloff had called on Kerensky to resign and give place to a military dictatorship which the General proposed to set up. Kerensky had at once dismissed Korniloff from his post of Generalissimo, proclaiming him and his Chief of Staff, Lukomsky, who refused to take up the command, traitors. Korniloff, refusing to accept his dismissal, arrested the Commissary-General, Filonenko, and marched on the capital. The Soviet at once issued a manifesto calling on all to offer armed resistance. Kerensky placed Petrograd under martial law and made preparations to resist Korniloff's advance, ordering the railway connections with Petrograd to be torn up. The capital was thrown into a state of great excitement and, with the General's Moscow speech and the Government's recent assurances that they were in complete accord with Korniloff still ringing in their ears, the public could be pardoned for its state of total bewilderment at this amazing whirligig. Another surprise, an unwelcome one to the Germans, was added by the action of the 12th Army, some of whose rearguards took this opportunity of turning on the Germans, counter-attacking in the neighbourhood of the Pskoff road, driving back the enemy and making prisoners. Generals Denekin and Erdeli and the whole of the Headquarter Staff were arrested. The Baltic Fleet and its officers sided with the Government. The latter, and the Council of Workmen and Soldiers sent delegates to discuss matters with and suborn Korniloff's advancing troops. Efforts were also taken to place the capital in a state of defence.

It was V. Lvoff who brought the ultimatum from Korniloff in which the latter demanded to be appointed Dictator in conjunction with Kerensky and Savinkoff, Assistant War Minister. The Cadet Ministers resigned, thus throwing the Government once again into the melting pot. This news left me wondering with whom I should now have to deal with in Petrograd.

It is openly said here that Korniloff had numerous sympathisers amongst the *bourgeoisie*, since they considered that his attempt was made with the object of instituting a strong authority. Exactly how great this support was is not known. The excitement grew in the capital with the announcement that the vanguard of Korniloff's army consisted of the " Savage Division " of the Cossacks, and that they were within thirty miles of the city. As the rival troops approached each other, with Kerensky and Korniloff at their heads, the leaders issued stirring manifestoes and appeals after the Russian manner. Kerensky temporarily assumed the post of Generalissimo and issued passionate and frantic appeals for support to the army, navy, the Ukraine, Mussulmans and every political party in Russia. The Soviet also deluged the capital with appeals, calling upon all to support the Government. The last thing they wished to see was a Military Dictator who would restore discipline into the rabble army at the rear. Korniloff issued a proclamation, suppressed by the Government, declaring that his only desire was to bring the country out of the present impasse and lead it along the road to order and victory. He swore that he would only hold the power till the Constituent Assembly met.

Korniloff's advanced troops reached Gatchina, twenty miles from the capital, with outposts at Pavlost, but he got no further. The envoys of the Council of Workmen and Soldiers did their work too well. The General's troops fell away from him. There was no fighting. With the defalcation of the soldiers the attempt collapsed.

During the period when a conflict between the rival forces appeared imminent the diplomatic representatives of the Allies met in Petrograd and a Verbal Note was presented to Tereshchenko by Sir George Buchanan, the doyen of the Diplomatic Corps, offering the good offices of the Allied representatives with the sole aim of serving the interests of Russia and the interests of the Allies (in order to prevent a conflict and civil war).

Alexeieff was appointed Chief of the Staff and proceeded to Headquarters to arrest Korniloff, who returned there, and Lukomsky. Krymoff, commanding the Savage Division, ordering his troops to yield, proceeded to Petrograd, where, after an interview with Kerensky, he shot himself.

It has been an ill-starred affair, which had it turned out otherwise, might have resulted in a strong Government taking the reins and saving the army. This is the opinion of many in Petrograd and elsewhere, so I am informed.

That there was a widespread counter-revolutionary plot involving some of the Grand Dukes, who have been arrested, and other personages in the entourage of the Czar, is now made public. All the big towns, including Petrograd, Moscow, Kieff, Odessa, and even Siberia, are said to be involved, and wholesale arrests are being made throughout the country.

Meanwhile in the midst of the alarms and public excitement the course of justice proceeded on its way undisturbed, and evidence of an important character was given at the Soukhomlinoff trial.

Rodzianko stated that the Duma had been greatly alarmed at the defects in the Russian artillery and had repeatedly addressed the defendant on the subject. The General opposed the activities of the Duma in this direction. In March 1915 the Grand Duke Nicholas intimated that the continuation of the war under the conditions then existing was becoming impossible. " I then went," said Rodzianko, " to Galicia, and what I saw there filled me with terror. I affirm that the responsibility for the enormous losses which we suffered during the retreat entirely falls upon the defendant. On my return I appealed to the Czar and persuaded him to dismiss Soukhomlinoff."

Miliukoff confirmed the above evidence, and said that in February 1915, when the deplorable results of their weakness in artillery and munitions had become evident, the defendant at a meeting of the Duma had made an optimistic speech saying that all the necessary steps had been taken to plentifully supply the army.

Gutchkoff said that in 1908 the Members of the Duma realised that Russia was on the eve of great events; for the reports of all their military attachés agreed as to the war preparations of Germany and Austria. But in spite of this all efforts to organise the artillery and commissariat were opposed by Soukhomlinoff. "Russia," said the witness in conclusion, " entered the Great War entirely unprepared, and that fault was the defendant's." (Great sensation in the Court.)

GENERAL RIVERSIDE VIEW OF ARCHANGEL

A DETACHMENT OF SAILORS FROM THE BALTIC FLEET ADDRESSING THE POPULACE IN PETROGRAD

General Manikovsky, Commandant in Kronstadt in August 1914, said " the shortage of munitions was so great that, by order of the Generalissimo, we had to borrow large quantities of projectiles from the fortress, thus reducing its fighting value." Other witnesses gave evidence that Madame Soukhomlinoff spent enormous sums of money.

General Alexeieff said that lack of munitions made itself felt from the outset of the war and that the defendant ignored all demands. Atschiller and defendant were on the best of terms. For a considerable period before the war Austrian spies infested the whole of the Kieff military district, the Austrian Consulate at Kieff being their headquarters. Makaroff, former Minister of Interior, stated that he had been obliged to write officially to the General on the subject of the spy Miasoiedoff, then attached to the Ministry of War.

A letter written to the ex-Czaritza on September 27th, 1916, by Prince Andronikoff, who is described as an " influential political adventurer," was read. It says that Soukhomlinoff is the victim of his love for his wife, who spends money recklessly on dress and foreign travel, living at the rate of £15,000 a year. Although a faithful subject of his Czar, the General, in order to satisfy his wife, had to increase his income by taking bribes from contractors.

Stuermer, Prime Minister in the old regime from January to November 1916, and probably one of the most hated men of his time, is dead. He died in prison on September 3rd.

CHAPTER XV

PETROGRAD IN SEPTEMBER (*continued*)

September 16*th*.—The Korniloff affair has frightened what
remains of the Coalition Government, and they took the
bold step to-day of anticipating the decision of the Constituent Assembly by proclaiming Russia a Republic.
This historic proclamation is as follows :

" The revolt of General Korniloff has been suppressed.
But the mischief which it has brought into the ranks of
the army and into the country is great, and has once more
increased the danger which threatens the country and
liberty. Considering it essential to put an end to the
indefinite nature of the political regime, remembering the
unanimity and enthusiasm with which the idea of a Republic
was greeted at the Moscow Conference, the Provisional
Government hereby declares that the political regime of the
Russian Empire is a republican regime and proclaims the
Russian Republic. The urgent necessity of taking immediate and decisive measures to establish political order, have
led the Provisional Government to the decision to place the
whole executive power in the hands of five of its members
with the Minister-President at their head. The Provisional
Government considers the re-establishment of discipline
and the fighting value of the army as its essential duty.
Convinced that the only way to bring the country out of
its present precarious situation, is by a concentration of all

the living forces of the country, the Provisional Government will increase its power by bringing to its bosom representatives of all parties who place the general and permanent interests of their country above the temporary and private interests of their parties and classes. The Provisional Government hopes to complete this work within a few days.

(Sgd.)   " MINISTER-PRESIDENT KERENSKY.
(Sgd.)   " MINISTER OF JUSTICE ZAROUDNY."

The Council of Five consists of Kerensky, Tereshchenko (Foreign Affairs), Admiral Verderevski (Marine), General Verkhovski (War), and Nikitine (Posts and Telegraphs). Kerensky is Generalissimo of the land and sea forces. So this man has now been Minister of Justice, War, Marine, President of the Provisional Government and finally Generalissimo in the space of six months !

The proclamation of the Republic is considered to end the life of the fourth Duma appointed by the old regime, which thus automatically ceases to exist.

Petrograd has been uneasy and restless for some days, as can be well imagined with the excitement which the Korniloff affair gave rise to. The latest cause has been due to the big sailors' demonstration which was to have taken place to-day, and the threatened outbreak which was to be feared from it. The sailors arrived from the fleet, but the demonstration was prohibited, and the town packed with the militia police with orders to fire if necessary. Whether the militia would have been of any earthly good had the sailors persisted in carrying out their object is open to doubt, but the latter were either overawed, or, which is far more likely, listened to reason—not the persuasions of the Government, it is said, but those of the Council of Workmen and Soldiers, who do not want an outbreak just yet. Whatever the plans of the Bolshevik portion of this dark body may be, they are not matured, and it is becoming increasingly evident to all here, that the masses will be kept in leash· till the auspicious moment arrives. No one dares to conjecture what will happen if that moment does arrive. But we all seem to be living in a fool's paradise, sitting on top of a powder magazine. Korniloff, being a man of war, at least knows what a spark to a powder magazine results in.

The day being fine, and a Sunday, the streets of the capital were filled with the pleasure-seeking cosmopolitan crowds, and the hordes of ruffianly loafing soldiery, now more numerous than ever.

There was no ceremony at the proclamation of the Republic, and no sign of a popular demonstration. Under happier auguries how different would have been the conditions ! Representatives of the whole civilised world would have assembled to give the blessing of their Governments to the new infant Republic, the youngest and yet one of the mightiest on earth. Walking across the Troitka Bridge over the Neva somewhere about midnight, whilst the capital lay asleep, I mused, and it would have been difficult not to muse, on the contrasts which so notable a day in the history of Russia presented—the reality with the might-have-been. All those who have her well-being at heart must hope that that reality will dawn over this harassed land some day.

The reasons for the Government's determination to proclaim the Republic are not difficult to appreciate. The fear and state of indecision aroused in the Ministers by the march of Korniloff, and the threatened capture, or entry into the capital precipitated an acute Cabinet crisis. As was to be expected, and in fact had become customary, the Provisional Government consulted the Council of Workmen and Soldiers, a body who, as we shall see, is now itself torn with dissension, and also the Moderate Socialists. All Friday the *pourparlers* with the latter continued. Some of the members had emphatically protested against the continued presence of Cadets in the Government, as had also the Council. The situation was complicated by the fact that General Alexeieff, appointed Chief of the Staff, had only accepted the appointment on the condition the Provisional Government continued to number some of the *bourgeoisie* amongst its members.

During the night of September 15th–16th, Skobeleff, Avksentieff and Zaroudny resigned. By 2.30 a.m. the Ministers had decided to extricate themselves from the dilemma by appointing a council of five members only, the other ministries remaining under the charge of assistant ministers without portfolios. That the Government remained in power at all was a close thing.

The Soviet Executive Committee was in session, and a meeting was to take place on Friday evening at seven o'clock. It was not opened, however, till ten o'clock, when the ex-Minister of Labour, Skobeleff, who had just resigned from the Government, spoke. " The Russian Revolution is a revolution of the *bourgeoisie*, and I think that the Coalition Government has been justified. Russia remains a democratic country in spite of all. All the *bourgeois* elements did not side with Korniloff. You say that all but ourselves are counter-revolutionaries. It is not so. If it is so, let us seize the power. We can do so—and set up a Soviet Government in the Winter Palace. It will be the certain road to a counter-revolution. This time Korniloff's soldiers fraternised with us—but when we are at the Winter Palace they will not do so. Do not forget that Petrograd is not Russia. Before the Petrograd Soviet takes such a step it must consider the feeling throughout the country. I have been twice at the front. I saw there strong dissatisfaction, and even indignation against Petrograd, even amongst soldiers who were fraternising. Petrograd stands near the source of power, and the temptation to stretch out a hand and grasp it is strong. But it would be our ruin."

Bogdanoff did not agree with the last speaker. " The Korniloff movement was not at an end. Kaledin on the Don was raising troops to support the counter-revolutionary movement. It was not by chance that Korniloff and Kaledin had been such conspicuous figures at the Moscow Conference. They led a group inspired by Rodzianko, Miliukoff, and others."

At the sitting of the next night, four former Ministers, Avksentieff, Skobeleff, Tseretelli and Tchernoff, were present.

The Bolshevik Riazano said : " We require a Minister who will be responsible to the unified will of the people, not to a private foolishness of his own " (meaning Kerensky and his conscience).

Tchernoff, whose one theme is the division of all the land among the people, from which he derives his popularity amongst certain parts of the masses and incurs the hate of the *bourgeoisie*, said it was impossible for the Soviets to work with the Cadets. He ended by saying, " We must organise a democratic congress. Without it I am not sure that the country can survive."

Liber said the Korniloff plot was provoked by the weakness of the democracy. " All the elements which were seeking to bring order out of chaos were grouped round Korniloff. That movement has been suppressed, but another danger lifts its head and it comes from the left. You think yourselves sufficiently strong," he said, turning to the Bolsheviks, " to give the people bread and peace ! If we reject the Cadets they will join with those at the other end of the revolutionary scale and we shall be left isolated. If you think, you Bolsheviks, that all Russia will follow you to Cronstadt and Viborg " [alluding to the officers massacred at these places], " organise a Government, but remember that we shall prove implacable and shall exact to the uttermost from you bread and peace."

Avksentieff said they should support the Government, for if the Government were not supported and thus able to put an end to the chaos and strengthen the army, Russia was finished.

Skobeleff : We have come here with one object, to save Russia and the Revolution. If we do not join up and organise, Russia will become the prey of civil war, which will open our gates to the Germans.

Tseretelli : The new Government was not constituted without our aid. Kerensky consulted us and we gave him full liberty to construct a Government capable of fighting against counter-revolution. As long as the democracy is powerful, coalition is not a danger, but a valuable aid. It is only when the democracy is weak that coalition becomes dangerous.

The Bolshevik motion which was adopted yesterday was put to the meeting and thrown out by a very large majority, and the following motion put and passed almost unanimously :—

1. To call a general democratic congress, who will decide the question of the ruling authority.

2. Until this congress is opened the present Government to remain in power and fight against counter-revolution. The democracy should support the Government in its effort to organise the country.

3. To prevent the commission of acts by Government agents likely to irritate popular opinion, the Government should act in consultation with the committee which is fighting the counter-revolutionaries.

It is of interest to see how the opinions of some of the best men amongst the Socialists have become greatly modified. Tseretelli, Skobeleff, Avksentieff, even Tchernoff in some respects, are now all of them far nearer the Cadet party and the opinions held by a large number of the *bourgeoisie* than a couple of months ago, and the breach is rapidly widening between them and the utopian and German-inspired leaders of the Bolsheviks and the majority perhaps of the Council of Workmen and Soldiers. It looks now as if the great fight will be between the two great Socialist parties. If the Moderate Socialists unite with the Cadets, it may not yet be too late to get rid of the Bolsheviks and the Council.

The preliminary investigation into the Bolshevik rising of the 16th–18th July last is completed. There are eighty-seven accused, and they have commenced to read the charges to them. They will come before the court towards the middle of October unless their comrades get them out before then. If the Provisional Government kept this matter pending, in the hopes that they might attain a stronger position from which to deal with it, they have made a bad mistake. But it is only a further example of the vacillation which has pervaded their councils and acts.

A wave of horror has passed through Russia with the revelations which have come to hand on the Viborg massacres. Apparently the General and Staff who were murdered had just previously telegraphed to Kerensky, placing themselves entirely at the disposition of the Government, having no complicity in the Korniloff movement. The trouble commenced by the crowd seizing from their guards two Generals and a Colonel, who had been arrested by the representatives of the Council of Workmen and Soldiers, as being implicated in the Korniloff rising. Other officers were also taken. These were first beaten and then forced into the river. About fifteen officers were killed in this fashion. Further excesses are still apprehended. Few can refrain from commiserating the Russian officers in these days. All the more honour to them that so large a number continue to wear the uniform, which proves their continued readiness to serve their country, and brave the grave risk which that act involves.

We have got absolutely sick of orders and notifications which result in nothing and to which no one pays the slightest attention. Will this one have a better fortune ? It is Generalissimo Kerensky's first order to the army and fleet.

As a result of General Korniloff's affair (he does not call it " revolt "), the normal life of the army is completely disorganised. " To re-establish discipline I order :—

" 1. All political strife is to cease in the army. All efforts are to be concentrated in re-establishing our fighting force, on which the safety of the State solely rests.

" 2. All army committees and commissaries are to confine themselves strictly within their jurisdictions; they are not to concern themselves in any way with the orders given by the military chiefs with reference to their duties and military operations.

" 3. Re-establishment under the orders of their chiefs of the regimental transport.

" 4. Immediately cease from placing their chiefs under arrest. This duty is confined exclusively to the judicial authority, the Procurator-General and the Extraordinary

Commission of Inquiry I have appointed, which has already commenced its duties.

" 5. The removal or discharge of persons placed in command is to stop at once. This duty, which only belongs to the competent agencies appointed by Government, does not fall within the powers or duties of the committees."

In one form or another we have had all this before. Two months ago Kerensky might have been able to enforce the order. Now most are sceptical.

The Soukhomlinoff trial has reached its twenty-second day, and the long list of witnesses is nearing its end. A significant incident took place at this hearing. The guard on the Navy and Army hall is from the famous Preobrajensky Regiment. Three companies of this regiment marched down to the building and asked to speak to the commandant of the draft who were on guard within. When the commandant appeared the soldiers said that they did not understand why the court were so long over their debates (many more educated than these Preobrajensky soldiers are equally in the dark in this matter). In the opinion of the soldiers Soukhomlinoff's guilt was not in doubt. They asked, therefore, that he should be delivered into their hands to be judged by the Committee of their Regiment. The commandant had some difficulty in explaining to the men that the debates must be surrounded with every evidence of impartiality, and that justice must be allowed to take its course. The soldiers accepted the point of view. But they insisted that the Soukhomlinoffs should be subjected to prison regime. That they should not be allowed to obtain their meals from restaurants, but that they should be given meals from the nearest barracks; that they should not have dessert or be allowed mattresses. The accused had been living in the Navy and Army building. To satisfy the soldiers they have been incarcerated in the Fortress of Peter and Paul. And the guard is now drawn from the Volynia Regiment.

And the ink not yet dry on Kerensky's army order !

September 18th.—There is some talk of Japan coming to Russia's assistance. It is said that Lansing has had a conference with Count Ishia in Washington, and come to an agreement under which Japan is to place her naval and economic forces at the disposal of the Allies, for the purpose of transporting war materials from the United States to Russia. The expression " war material " is ambiguous. In face of the state of the Russian front and the congestion of munitions and war materials at Archangel, where they are still from some incomprehensible cause continuing to arrive, the needs of Russia consist chiefly of the necessities of the peasants—agricultural implements, cloth, leather and so forth.

Rumour has been rife that Sweden is to join in the great war on the side of the Central Powers and attack Russia. Of course this has been a danger from almost the commencement of the war, and it has not been Germany's fault that it has not come about. But since it is not apparent that Sweden would gain anything by letting herself be dragged into the European furnace, but would have a good deal to lose, at the least all the money she has made out of the war, it is difficult to imagine her being capable of such suicidal folly. Tereshchenko has now given an official denial to the rumour.

It is also said that the Government are going to quit Petrograd and make their headquarters at Moscow. It would be a good thing in many ways, but the rumour is denied. Kerensky in his capacity of Commander-in-Chief has gone to the front with the War and Navy Ministers, and will be away for two or three days. The remaining two of the Council of Five are sitting under Tereshchenko, Vice-President, but nothing of importance will be done till Kerensky's return.

We ought to be thoroughly tired of conferences, but the reverse is the case. As shown yesterday, a democratic conference is the next one to make its appearance here. It is fixed for September 25th.

The conference is to consist of 100 delegates of the Council of Workmen and Soldiers, 100 from the Soviets, 50 from the district committees of these bodies, 84 from the military organisations, 20 from the railways, 10 from the posts,

10 from the employers of commerce and industry, 150 from the co-operative societies and representatives from lawyers, doctors, journalists, zemstvos, employees, etc.

The ultra Socialists, who a few days ago voted against the death penalty and were endeavouring to force Kerensky to withdraw it, are now shouting for the blood of Korniloff, and of every one who had any connection with the outbreak.

The explanations of Kaledin, who is safe with his Cossacks on the Don, that he had no complicity with the Korniloff plot, have been apparently accepted by the Government, the Cossacks having refused to give him up until he has appeared before a congress of their own, and this affair is considered to be at an end. One of the papers says, however, that Kaledin is preparing to cut the Moscow railway in the south, and so stop food supplies reaching the north. Food is already far shorter and much more expensive than it was last month. All the prices have gone up at the Hôtel Europe and the amount of food one receives down.

The Government seem to be playing to all sides, for Trotsky, the Bolshevik implicated in the July rising, has to-day been liberated with a caution. It is supposed he will now join his fellow conspirator Lenin.

The occupant of the post of Governor-General of Petrograd having sooner or later proved a thorn in the side of the Provisional Government, the post has now been abolished—taken over by Kerensky himself it is supposed. But there must be a limit to what one man can undertake !

Being under the impression that in the absence of a Governor-General the Government would have too much to do at present to bother about rounding up deserters and thieves, etc., I went to the Alexandra Market this morning with the object of trying to obtain an ikon or two. For the curio-hunter this market is a most interesting place, consisting of a four-sided glass arcade with an open court in the centre filled with booths. Shops with a part of their contents displayed outside line both sides of the arcade, a large percentage owned by Jews. Articles from all over the East find a more or less temporary lodging here ; and

R

at present not a little of the loot from Petrograd houses, though we were not likely to be shown that. Unfortunately, I had not the time, or in fact inclination, for curio-hunting. That must wait till the Germans' account is settled. Although the place was fairly crowded, soldiers, I noticed, were most conspicuous by their absence.

In spite of the strange days Petrograd has been passing through, and the upset and anxiety of the Ministers, the reconstruction work in their departments is making progress. An important economic meeting was held the other night in the Department of Agriculture, at which, amongst other things, the timber matter was fully discussed. Although nothing eventuated that I did not already know, it was of interest to note that sub-committees were appointed to deal with certain branches of economic work connected with the development of Russia's unexploited wealth, with trade and export questions and so forth. I had an interesting and important interview with one of the two Assistant Ministers at the Commerce and Industry Ministry, and another with the official of that Department, with whom I have already discussed the question of opening out the forests of the north-east region. Many matters we had left over for discussion until my return from the north were gone into in detail. It was of interest, and also a hopeful augury of the future recovery of Russia, to find that these officials were quietly continuing their work and preparing for the day at which it would be possible to put into action the schemes, the details of which they were now engaged in working out. It behoves us at home to be equally prepared to seize the auspicious moment, and not, owing to our want of careful forethought, let others step in before us in markets in which it is of paramount importance that we should have a place.

As evidence that there is hope yet for parts of the army at the front if only the rot at the rear can be stemmed, the recent advance at Riga is to the point. In its way it is somewhat remarkable, for it is only a fortnight ago that the twelfth army was hurriedly retreating before the

Germans. It shows once again that Russia is a country of surprises and unlimited possibilities. The twelfth army has turned and has made a three-days' advance. On September 9th fights between outposts of a local character occurred, and in some places these encounters were of a stubborn nature. The success so obtained led to bigger enterprises by the Russian commanders. On the 11th and 12th an offensive was developed on the whole front between Friedrichstadt and the Gulf of Riga. Such a change from a hasty retreat to a tenacious offensive is peculiarly characteristic of the Russian temperament, and has entirely disconcerted the Germans and probably upset their plans. Any check now, with the rains already setting in, will necessitate their remaining at the point they have reached till the winter frosts make the ground practicable. The failure of the Germans to push home the Riga success is attributed here to a desire to regroup their armies with a view to striking a fresh blow, perhaps at Dvinsk. They must have thought that this operation could be carried out with impunity in view of what their spies had told them of the disorganisation in the Russian Army. And few here would have considered such an advance by the Russians a possibility. The Russian Staff on the Riga must have had confidence in their men to have risked taking the step which has turned out so successful, and must, amongst other things, have increased the *morale* of the twelfth army. If the contagion will only spread to the south and is not interfered with from the rear, there is still hope. But it is a big " if."

The Provisional Government have confirmed the Ukraine Secretariat on the motion submitted to them by the Rada. The General Secretaries consist of Oukrayna, Vinnichenko (Finance), Shoulgine (National Affairs), Zaroubrin (General Controller), Stoshenko (Public Instruction), Lotetzky (General Clerk), Savtchenko-Belsky (Agriculture), and Stembitzky (Commissioner for the Ukraine with the Provisional Government). The next step in this drama now lies with the Ukraine, for few imagine that they are yet satisfied.

Events in Finland are assuming a grave complexion, and will scarcely be stopped by the rescript of Kerensky as Supreme Commander of the Fleet, that the violence and anarchy exhibited by the sailors of the fleet at Helsingfors are disgracing the navy and must cease at once and that order is to be restored. A general convention has been held at Helsingfors in which the Soviets, local committees, garrison and fleet committees, internationalists, *et hoc genus omne*, took part. The resolution adopted is briefly to get rid, by wholesale murder, of all the *bourgeoisie*, reorganisation of the staff of the army, the arrest of the Central Committee of the party of National Freedom and Provisional Committee of the Duma, suppression of all the non-Socialistic Press, full satisfaction to be accorded to the demands of both Finland and the Ukraine, the arming of all workmen, and so forth. The resolution was carried by a large majority. Telegrams will not stop this kind of thing.

The massacres of the officers at Viborg have aroused so much feeling that even the Council of Workmen and Soldiers here have deemed it necessary to address an appeal for moderation to those whom they address as, " Comrades, Soldiers."

Kerensky has also addressed to Viborg a telegram of a similar kind to the one despatched to Helsingfors.

Tseretelli telegraphed : " The Soviet considers the recent acts of violence and assassination as a mortal blow to the Revolution. The power of the Government and that of the democracy is sufficiently strong to try before tribunals all those who are enemies to the new regime."

Tchernoff, formerly Minister of Agriculture, who received strong support from Kerensky when the Cadets tried to have him turned out of the Ministry last month, but who was ultimately forced to resign, has now turned against his former comrade and chief, the President of the Cabinet. He has been publicly accusing Kerensky in the Socialist Press of all sorts of acts supporting the counter-revolutionaries. These accusations Kerensky has now publicly repudiated. Tchernoff is playing his own hand

and trying for the Presidency in the future. The majority here think that it would be a bad thing for Russia if he were successful. But whether consciously or unconsciously, he is also playing the Bolshevik game, and it is not apparent at present that this will help him personally.

September 19th.—I had occasion to go to the Headquarters Staff Offices, situated next to the Foreign Office, to-day in connection with an inquiry. I went up a narrow, squalid, dirty stone stairway, which led by an equally dirty passage to a great, handsome circular hall with a high domed roof. This hall had numerous marble plaques let into the walls inscribed with names and dates in gold lettering. Comfortable lounges were placed round the walls on which couples and parties of officers were sitting and conversing, all smoking the inevitable cigarette. As I waited there, hundreds of officers must have passed through the hall, most with bundles of papers or memoranda in their hands. An officer of high rank, engaged in animated or grave conversation with a companion, would walk up and down the tessellated floor for a few minutes and then say adieu and disappear. It was of considerable interest in view of existing conditions to watch the different types of officer, passing and repassing. Some were very immaculate, with spruce uniforms and beautifully fitting highly polished top boots, their tunics ablaze with medals. But others were of a very different type—the new officer, obviously elected by the soldiers —their uniforms ill-fitting and slovenly worn, and boots dirty and uncared for. The Headquarters Staff do not say much, but it is easy to see what they think of these new recruits forced upon them under the new condition of affairs—absolutely useless of course, so far as the assistance they can give, and only set there for the purpose of spying. Many of them are probably in German pay and account for the fact that the Staff find it almost impossible to keep army secrets from becoming known to the enemy within a very short time after the staff schemes have been conceived. My friend here gave me a good deal of information on the possibility of holding up the eastern front (their western front). " I am certain that we could do it still," he said. " Many of us think it—if only the Allies could give us assistance to stiffen our line. Our Ministers do not appear to see it. They have not the technical knowledge, of course, and fear that damnable Council of Workmen and Soldiers too much. But we have lots of good men yet, uncontaminated men, if we could only isolate them with a backing of Allied troops. It ought to have been done two months ago. Look at Riga and what we have recently done there ! "

Of course, this was the view of a purely military man, but it is of interest to record it.

I was talking to a French journalist here, and we discussed the question of Japanese aid to Russia, which interests many at the moment. His opinion was, that it ought to be tried at as early a date as possible before matters get worse. But he went further, and said he thought that the Western Allies should ask Japan to lend a hand in Europe with her armies. Where ? I asked. And his first instance was not Europe at all. He said the full weight of Japan ought to be brought on to one front only, and it would entirely change the face of the war. Supposing, he said, a strong Japanese Army appeared alongside the British Army in Mesopotamia. The Turkish goose would be cooked in a few weeks. They would march on Constantinople via Asia Minor. The Balkan front would be paralysed and smashed, and the Central Powers would be deprived of Bulgarian and Turkish aid and would have to capitulate. A Japanese army in Mesopotamia he averred would decide the war. There may be something in it, but as a Britisher I confess to a feeling that I should like us to finish up the Mesopotamian stunt ourselves and not confess to defeat by calling in Japan. And we shall do it. And the Russian front is the one which cries aloud for assistance and stiffening before it is too late.

People here are not altogether satisfied that the declaration of a Republic is sufficient. A Republic, they say, should have a President, and some recommend that the Provisional Government themselves elect a President.

which would, of course, be Kerensky. The present idea is
apparently on the lines of the Swiss Republic, the Prime
Minister being invested with supreme authority. The
decree states that the Council of Five would invite such
persons into the Cabinet who place their country before
their private interests. It is said that the Government
will not wait the meeting of the Democratic Congress
before taking this step.

Kerensky has reported to the Cabinet that the Korniloff
rising is now over and is under investigation. Besides the
four Generals confined at Mohileff, Aladin and Zavoiko have
been arrested. The Cossack Staff have denied that General
Kaledin was concerned in the rising, but the General
has resigned his position as Hetman of the Cossacks; it
is said that the order issued for the arrest of the General
has been rescinded. General Shablovesky is president of
the commission of inquiry into the Korniloff revolt,
and the question of committing the latter for trial will
be shortly decided. There appears to be some legal
difficulty with regard to the prosecution of offenders who
committed acts against the old Government, now that a new
form of Government, the Republic, has been proclaimed;
but the nature of these difficulties does not yet appear to
be clear. As Korniloff is an honorary Cossack, the Cossacks
have demanded to be given full details of the trial. The
Ministers have, however, been forced into a step which
appears unwise. Having appointed a commission of inquiry
of their own into this affair, they have now approved
of the formation of a special, a second, commission of
inquiry on which members of the Council of Workmen and
Soldiers are to be represented. This commission is to act
independently of the Government one. The members of
the Council state that it is their intention to conduct an
impartial investigation of the conspiracy, and to discover
who are at the bottom of the rebellion. Naturally there
is a great outcry on the part of the Cadet party, although
the Council state that it is not their intention to try the
Cadet party. They entertain no enmity towards that
party, but only wish to get at the whole truth. In other

words, they do not trust the Government or their commission. The Cabinet are surely riding for a fall, and they
are likely to get a bad one unless a miracle happens.
Seventeen fresh officers, including Prince Dolgorukoff,
commanding the 1st Cavalry Corps (who has been brought
from Reval to Petrograd), have been arrested as implicated or concerned in the Korniloff affair and interned in
the " Kresty " prison.

A party of us, consisting of a Russian officer and civilian,
two French officers, an American (a civilian), and myself,
were dining together last night. The conversation turned
on an article which has recently appeared. The article
begins with the quotation, *Quem Jupiter vult perdere
dementat prius*, so its tenor can be guessed at. It is re-
freshing to remember sometimes that it is not only the
Allies who have made mistakes in this war. Some of the
German *faux pas* are first dealt with : their belief that
England would not come in if they invaded Belgium, and,
almost as bad a lapse, that Italy would fight on the side of
Austria. Their attack on Russia in the spring of 1915, an
advance on an unarmed army who, in spite of appalling
losses, retreated in an orderly fashion and lured their enemy
on into the marshes. The Russian officer present had been
in this retreat, and said that they were aware that the
Germans had confidently averred that this was to be the
end of the Russians in this war. " And we had a very
bad time of it," he continued, " but the marshes helped
us. We knew them and the Germans did not." If the
Germans had thrown 2,000,000 men on to the Western
front that spring they must have broken through, for the
French were not at their full strength yet, and the British
were only at the initial stage of raising and training their
new armies, continues the article. But the gods blinded
the Germans, and at the same time opened the eyes of the
French and British to the real position. " Lloyd George
did that," said one of the French officers; " he told you,"
turning to me, " and us that the war would be lost unless
we concentrated on making shells. And the Bosches have
seen those shells since." The Germans, says the writer,

recognised their fault almost as soon as the Allies, and the assault on Verdun in February 1916 was their effort to retrieve it. After that failure they gave up the Western front and betook themselves to secondary ones—Serbia, Roumania and so on. They started fighting all over the world, losing hundreds of thousands of men. The further they got involved in the Russian marshes the more men they lost. " Yes, and a far greater number than our Western Allies have any notion of," said one of the Russians. " The Austrians lost enormously, but we do not count them. But so did the Germans, and some of the flower of their armies." The article then deals with the future, and this was our chief interest. Next spring when the great, the first real, campaign on the grand style, commences on the Western front the Germans will not be able to face it. They won't have the men. And the British Army has only just reached its full strength, an army of millions, fresh, young and equipped as no army has ever been, impatient to come to grips with the Germans. The last mistake of the latter was to break with America. That mistake is not only financial or economic, but a military one. The millions of men America will throw into the fray will entirely change the present method of warfare. The war will be finished in the air. Tens of thousands of aeroplanes will fly over the German lines. No German aeroplane or balloon will be able to leave the ground. The German gunners will no longer have aeroplanes to direct their fire. The whole of the German rear will be bombed from north to south. The allied infantry will only have to stroll forward behind the barrage, accompanied by an army of tanks, and sweep up what is left of the Germans ! A most comfortable feeling for us all pervades this forecast. But the American demurred somewhat. " We can't do quite all that by next spring, you know." " But you are making thousands of aeroplanes, are you not ? " said one of the Frenchmen excitedly. " Wal, yes, I guess we're doing that all right. And we're building a damned fine engine, too." " What for ? " I queried. " So as to fly higher and faster than any Hun, I guess. They'll pepper him all right." " But if the planes are wanted for bombing chiefly, won't any old bus with a less highly powered easily made engine do, if you have enough of them ? " " Yes, they would do. I don't know which they are turning out most of." " We spent months over our high-powered engines," I remarked. " We had to make them. Now that we have got them it will be a pity if you go and waste more time in turning out one of your own pattern when what is wanted is apparently thousands of easily made planes which will carry a load of bombs." " Our losses in men," said one of the Frenchmen, " and those of the Russians, French, Italians and British have been incurred in going over the top. Yours should be in the air, but it ought to finish the Bosche."

At the forthcoming Democratic Congress which is to consist of 800 delegates, members of the Duma and the propertied classes are not to be invited. The Cossacks have asked the Provisional Government whether the conference is a private affair or a State one. If the latter, they demand to be represented by a number of delegates proportionate to those of other organisations attending.

The President and office-bearers of the Central Executive Committee of the Council of Workmen and Soldiers have resigned as a protest at the passing of the resolution by the Council last Thursday that the full power belonged to the Soviets. This vote commits the President and office-bearers to a political policy for which they do not wish to be responsible. Therefore, the President Tchkheidze, Vice - President Anissimoff, and Gotz, Dan, Skobeleff, Tseretelli and Tchernoff tender their resignation. In order to test the feeling of the Petrograd Soviet in the matter the seven members intend to put forward their names for re-election to the executive committee collectively. It is regarded as a clever move.

Another echo of the Stockholm Conference reaches us with the returning Russian delegates—Rozanoff and Erlich. This " international " conference has again been postponed, this time until January. The Dutch-Scandinavian Committee are going to send out another invitation throughout the world asking for a reply by December 1st, and explaining the postponement. " From August to September, and now to January. How hard these people are working to be sure to win the war for the Germans," remarks a paper here.

Minister of War Verkhovsky issues a statement for publication stating that the Government have already worked out the details of measures to raise the fighting force of the army. These measures will be introduced in the very near future, but the plans must remain a secret for the present. The Minister says he is confident that complete order will be restored in the army by these measures. The commanding officers will regain full authority. Can he really believe this, as an army man ? A civilian might, but scarcely a military officer in high command.

A big demonstration had been organised for to-day, which was to include thousands of armed soldiers and workmen. It was intended that the resignation, under threat of a rising, of the Government should be demanded. It was countered, however, through the influence of the more moderate amongst the Council of Workmen and Soldiers, of which the Bolsheviks have not yet obtained the mastery, and only isolated groups of armed men proceeded to the Smolny Institute, the headquarters of the council, where they were bidden to disperse.

An Arms Act, or rather notification, has been issued here to-day, and it was time. Every person found carrying fire-arms without a special permit after October 3rd will be punished with imprisonment up to three months, or a fine up to 3000 roubles. But why the long notice ? A week should have been enough notice in the capital.

The accounts of the Viborg massacres become yet more nauseating. The bodies of twenty-two officers killed have been already identified, whilst sixty more are missing. A committee of inquiry has been opened with the Central Committee of Soviets represented on it.

From Helsingfors comes the news that four officers of the cruiser *Petropavlosk* were butchered by sailors last night. These men are pirates pure and simple, and should be treated as such.

But it is not only at Viborg and Helsingfors that matters are in a serious state. Throughout Finland the situation becomes daily worse. With others it has been mishandled from the first and its gravity misjudged. Propaganda against the Provisional Government is becoming intensified, nearly all the parties now taking part in it, a complete separation from Russia being demanded. Nekrasoff is being sent to Helsingfors to relieve Stakhovitch as Governor-General, but no one apparently envies him his job, and few would accept it.

September 20*th*.—The Democratic Congress appears likely to precipitate another Government crisis. The resignation of the officers of the Soviet, headed by Tchkheidze, has caused considerable anxiety in ministerial circles. They fear the increase in power and activity of the Bolsheviks. The Provisional Government, it is said, have learnt that they will be subjected to severe criticism at the conference, and that it is possible that resolutions will be adopted which may make it impossible for some of the Ministers to remain in power. This information was given them at the time Tchernoff was conducting his campaign against Kerensky in the Press. And it is from the action of Tchernoff and his following that the possible crisis is feared. During the last Government crisis it was some of the Soviet groups who persuaded Kerensky to remain President, and reform the Government; but these groups are now, it is said, losing ground in the Soviet. If Tchernoff and his Socialists support the Bolsheviks at the Conference, and vote for the Bolshevik resolutions, they are likely to outvote the Socialistic groups of Tchkheidze, Skobeleff, Tseretelli, etc., who have more or less consistently, and especially latterly, supported the Kerensky Government. It is for this reason that the resignation of the Soviet officers is considered to portend a change in the political situation for the worse, owing to the increasing influence of the Bolsheviks. The attitude of the Conference, or the probable attitude, it is thought will be known if the new elections of the Soviet officers are held before the Conference meets on September 25th. If Tchernoff, who is a candidate for the Presidency of the Soviet, is elected, it is probable that he will use every effort to force Kerensky to resign by siding with the Bolsheviks at the Conference. He then, doubtless, hopes to find his way clear to the post of Minister-President. Kerensky is to make a speech to the Conference, and this time the speech is not to be an oratorical effort merely, but will be carefully considered beforehand by the Council of Five. It would be something new to see Kerensky reading a typed speech.

Generals Denekin, Markoff, Erdeli and Vannoysky, arrested in connection with the Korniloff affair, have been removed to Jitomir, where they are to be tried by a military court, consisting exclusively of representatives of the local garrison of the south-west army, who insisted that the Generals should be sent for trial to their front. These men are, of course, hostile to the Generals, who, they say, were trying to restore the monarchy.

Until Kerensky's return from the front no meetings of the Government will take place. The Ministers in Petrograd are mainly occupied with the food problems of the capital; a daily report of the amounts of food is to be presented. Scarcity has already made itself seriously felt. There is also anxiety as to whether a sufficiency of fuel, chiefly wood, has been got in to tide over the winter in spite of the fact that the capital at present presents the appearance of a gigantic fuel dépôt. All the squares, as for instance, the Winter Palace Square, St. Isaac's, the Champ de Mars and all the yards of private dwelling houses contain enormous stacks of firewood billets—fine parapets to man and hold if serious outbreaks occur in the capital during the winter. For it would require a very large number of machine-guns mounted on the roofs to dislodge determined men who took cover behind the stacks.

The Times appears to be one of the few home papers to have obtained the proper view-point of Korniloff's attempt to coerce the Government into taking the necessary measures to restore the discipline of the army. For that is what the effort was intended to bring about. What the failure of that effort is likely to mean to Russia cannot yet be accurately forecasted. The Democratic Conference may give us a line to go upon, but the increase in strength of the Bolsheviks in the Council of the Workmen and Soldiers, and in Petrograd and the army, is most alarming. Government Prikazes and resolutions will not deter them from striving to attain their ends.

Kaledin has been exonerated by an assembly of 203 Cossack officers' which met at Novo Tcherkask, so this terminates his complicity in the Korniloff attempt so far as the Government are concerned. They must, however, be aware that there is much more behind this than appears on the surface.

The Press is engaged in discussing very freely and openly what Russia is doing in the war, and the help they consider the Allies should give them, and it is of interest at this juncture to have their point of view. It is notorious, it is asserted, that on the Anglo-French front the Central Powers have concentrated about 150 divisions, on the Italian front 36, and Macedonian 10–11 divisions. On the Russian front there are 135–140 divisions, and on the Asiatic fronts 28–30 divisions, of which 20 are facing us (the Russians). So Russia is holding up 160 divisions, whilst the rest of the Allies have 200 divisions against them. So that Russia has against her nearly half the enemy forces, whilst the three Great Powers—England, France and Italy—are only dealing with the remainder—a little over half. This comparison, they say, is not made in disparagement of her Allies, who have long accepted the principle that each ally is to do her best for the common good of all, but the comparison is useful when we hear people say without reflecting, that Russia is not fulfilling her engagements. Even during the turmoil aroused by the Korniloff affair, they point out that the Russians were able to obtain small successes on the Riga and Roumanian sectors. We do not find in the Allied Press any expectation of any large movement to be delivered against the enemy, and it is just such a movement that we now in our distress and disorganised state most require in order to give us a breathing space to reorganise discipline.

I merely quote these extracts to indicate what is being said. Certain answers are easy to give in favour of the Western Allies. But it is not easy to believe that the real situation here is fully realised in either France or Britain. For what is going to happen to those 140 German divisions if the Russian front breaks up altogether ? Have the Allied statesmen considered this point of view ? Or did they take it into account three months ago ?

CHAPTER XVI

PETROGRAD IN SEPTEMBER (*continued*)

GROWING POWER OF THE BOLSHEVIKS—THE TRUTH ABOUT
THE KORNILOFF REVOLT—END OF THE SOUKHOMLINOFF
TRIAL

September 21*st*.—I had a most interesting talk with a
compatriot this evening. He has spent most of his life
in Russia connected with timber interests. He told me
that although he was trying to wind up his present business
it was not with any intention of dissociating himself
from business affairs in Russia. With the new ideas
amongst the workmen and the new methods of running
the works and so forth it would be easier, he held, to wind
up existing concerns and start afresh than to try and
carry on an old business which had been run for years on
definite lines, under the new conditions which would obtain
when matters had settled down. "Others," he said,
"are acting in the same way. As to the stuff and nonsense one hears and reads of in the foreign Press and in
our own Press at home of Russia going under and being
finished, it is, of course, rubbish. A country of this size
and population could not go under; and many of the wider
awake continental nations, Norwegians and Swedes and
also the Americans, are well aware that this is so. Most of
these yarns are started by Germany. It is pure bluff with
which they hope and intend to frighten off the big capitalists
of Western Europe. Germany does not intend to let
them in here. Her propaganda in the army has as much
to do with her economic intentions in Russia as to release,
she hopes, armies to be transferred to the Western front.
If we let ourselves be fooled by this rot we shall be even

more timid than I take our own capitalists at home to be. And in the past they have always played the German game by waiting too long! Things are getting pretty bad here, as you know, and will almost certainly get far worse. Petrograd is, of course, mainly responsible with a few of the other large towns behind her. They are the centres of this damned Bolshevik crowd. But Petrograd is not Russia, and those of us who really know Russia, not your publicists who have talked such a lot of nonsense and misled our people at home, do not fear for Russia when the people really perceive where they are drifting. And there are plenty of good men in Russia too. They want backbone, that is all." "What do you make of the present position?" I asked. "Well, it is somewhat difficult to say. My own Russian people, those who have worked with me and my father before me, in some instances, and are devoted to my interests, say that the Bolsheviks are far stronger than the Provisional Government think, or will admit to themselves at any rate. They say that a very short time now will see them get the upper hand. If that happens they want to get out of Petrograd into the country and sit down and wait. There won't be anything to do here, they think, as the Bolsheviks will soon stop all the work that is being done. They don't think that a Bolshevik Government will last long, as the food question will become so difficult that the people will be likely to rise against any Government which is in power. They fully expect the Germans will come to Petrograd." "Good Lord!" I ejaculated. "Oh, yes, they think that is certain, but they don't believe they will remain, as there won't be any food for them. And they can always return again when the war is over. Every one now thinks Germany will come back into Russia after the war and be more domineering than before." "But that is pretty bad, is it not?" I queried. "Oh, I don't know. What can you expect? These people have lost faith in the Allies. They expected them to come here early in the summer and help the army and the Government. As they did not appear they naturally think the Allies have

s

left Russia in the lurch. They are so ignorant and this statement of the position has been repeated so often by the German spies and propagandists that one can't be surprised that the Russians have come to believe it."

" But out in the districts," he continued, " the real Russia, things are by no means as bad as they are painted or as they are believed to be by the people here in Petrograd. The latter never go out into the districts. Even at our Embassy few go out into the districts. Perhaps they have enough to do without that. Every one in Petrograd in time comes to see Russia through Petrograd spectacles and from the Petrograd point of view, and in the end lose sight altogether of the real Russian point of view. The system wants changing somehow ! "

I told him how surprised I was to find the Dvina and Vichegda rivers still lighted throughout. " Yes, that is an illustration in point. They are lighted by Government, not by the river companies. Of course the population up there is a sparse one and they are far off and care little for the Revolution or the war either. But a great part of Russia is in much the same condition. It won't have been affected at all or very little by either, and still less probably by all this froth and effervescence of the towns and more densely populated centres.

" The Russian is a very nice fellow, peasant and *bourgeois*, when you come to know him, much too good to go under to a lot of Zimmerwaldists, Internationalists and Bolsheviks, the bulk of whom are Germans or Jews or both, who make a business of this kind of thing. Russians indeed ! They are not Russians. They are the scum and agitators of Europe who will sell themselves anywhere. In the end it will probably be the food question which will settle the problem here. Anyway, that is my opinion for what it is worth."

In ministerial circles there is a tendency to try and deal leniently with Korniloff on the ground that his exploit was undertaken with honest intention and from a mistaken idea that it was to the interests of his country. He did not, it is said, wish to depose the Provisional Government, but only to influence it into taking stronger measures with regard to the army. Korniloff's aims are known to have a strong backing in the country and amongst the Cossacks, and the Government wish to conciliate his supporters if they can do so without breaking with the Council of Workmen and Soldiers.

The Cadets have adopted a resolution calling upon members of the party not to attend the Democratic Conference, because it will only reflect the views of one political set, and therefore cannot have any influential political effect. Or so they think. But this appears extremely doubtful.

All the higher educational establishments, including the Petrograd University, are to be closed during the current school year with the exception of the Faculty of Medicine. This order may be taken as significant of the way the wind is blowing.

Sweden, I see, is bringing in new passport regulations under which the wretched traveller has to fill in a sheath of forms attaching a photograph of himself to each. Truly travelling has become a difficult matter. Will it ever become a luxury and pastime again?

The usual skirmishes are commencing in the Press on the subject of the Democratic Conference. The Cadet Press say that if the Democrats do not give up their proposal to attack the Government a definite rupture is inevitable and Kerensky will have to declare himself definitely against those who represent organised democracy. The Bolsheviks, on the other hand, say that the parting of the ways has been reached and the Government must throw over the *bourgeoisie*, and, in fact, every one who is not of their way of thinking, or the Government must go. I suppose this Conference, as a counterblast to the Moscow one, was inevitable; but it becomes increasingly apparent that Russia is hopelessly lost in the mist of class warfare. We are only now repeating what went on during the second half of last month. In this connection the action of the Cossack Union is of interest. The Union has addressed a document to the Provisional Government requesting it to put an end to the agitation being carried on by the agents of the Council of Workmen and Soldiers amongst the Cossack troops against their officers. It is pointed out that the propaganda is causing grave unrest amongst the Cossack soldiers and will lead to the weakening of the army.

The number of commissions at present conducting investigations on behalf of Government with reference to retreats, assassinations, and so forth, would be ludicrous were it not so serious. There is the investigation into the retreat of the Russians which left the Roumanians in the air, two inquiries into the Korniloff affair, another into the Viborg matter, and a fifth at Helsingfors, and a host of smaller ones too numerous to mention. Even the Cabinet itself can have little faith in the results of their deliberations. It keeps a certain number of hot-heads quiet, though—for a time. The Ukrainian peasants are holding a congress of their own at Kieff, this disease being so infectious. By all accounts the sittings are something out of the ordinary uproarious, even for Russia at the present moment. The congress is exhorting their Secretariat to conduct a more energetic fight against the Provisional Government in order to obtain full liberty for the Ukrainians.

We have reached the twenty-fifth and twenty-sixth days of the Soukhomlinoff trial. I am not sure that the soldiers of the Preobrajensky Regiment had not some reason for their complaint as to its length. The General is engaged in making his defence. On the question of his order to dismantle the fortresses in the west of Russia and Poland he said he was justified in the step he had taken. That in modern warfare the old type of fortress was useless, as had been demonstrated at Liége, Namur, and Verdun, and elsewhere. They were only death traps for the troops defending them. He had substituted trenches and modern fortifications for the old type. Verdun had only resisted the attacks of the enemy by being protected in time by the modern system of defence this war had shown to be the only possible one. The old type of fortress also cost an enormous amount of money, and after the edict forbidding the sale of vodka the financial resources of the country were greatly curtailed and there was no money for the upkeep of these costly and useless means of defence. He had wished to increase the heavy artillery, and for that reason undertook to erect works for this purpose alone. He concluded by stating that he had not mixed in political matters and had only worked for the good of his country.

The following day the Prosecutor-General commenced his harangue. In addressing the jury he said, " You are not here to deal in vengeance, but in justice. Society asks for your complete impartiality, and for this you must rise above parties, above class, and put out of your mind politics. Remember that even the Revolutionists must pass bareheaded before the Temples of God and of Justice." The speaker then proceeded to examine the charges on which the accused is arraigned for high treason. He said it was not by accident that Soukhomlinoff had been surrounded by spies such as Altchiller, Miassoiedoff, Gochkivitch, and many others who were condemned as spies; Altchiller was a secret agent of the Austrian Government. Miassoiedoff had been executed as a spy. The latter was in the service of the accused, and he must have known his character. Madame Soukhomlinoff received these men in her salon. It was impossible that she did not know their characters and work. The accused were in league with them. He alluded to the distinguished military career of the General. He had been decorated with the Cross of St. George for bravery, and he was still wearing it. He had had a brilliant career before him and became eventually Minister of War. Prince Andronikoff was the first to approach him, one of the flowers bred of the fœtid atmosphere of the last days of the aristocracy. Russia trembles with horror when it remembers that men like Andronikoff governed their great country. They did not govern because they possessed talent or energy, but because they were obsequious servants and pandered to the tastes of the monarch as a man, and not as a ruler. The disasters of Russia are due to this fact.

The prosecutor pointed out that the Director of Artillery never, as the accused asserted, appealed to private industry for help, although this would have been superfluous, as even the State factories were decaying for want of orders whilst the large credits allotted for arming and provisioning the army remained unutilised. In spite of the anxiety displayed by the Duma and public opinion, which openly and constantly proclaimed the dangerous shortage of munitions, the General remained deaf, and thus sanctioned by his criminal negligence the inactivity of the Director-General of Artillery. The accused lied each time when it was a question of Russian armaments; but in addition to lying, he insulted his country when, in reply to Marshal Joffre, he said that the situation of Russia, though bad, was not desperate, and that Russia would triumph by her own efforts over all the difficulties with which she was faced. The ex-Minister's sole and only thought was how to maintain himself in power.

Petrograd appears to be gloating over the fact that Turkey is bankrupt. I fancy Turkey has been in this condition before and Russia herself must be perilously near it. Turkey's financial position was by no means bright at the outbreak of the war. She is now said to owe Germany, in debts incurred between 1914 and 1917, £142,000,000, and has other commitments amounting to £28,000,000 or about £170,000,000. Germany, it may be surmised, will have to wait some time before she sees her share of this sum, especially as she practically forced the Turks into this war. I have heard it said that Turkey would have let us into Constantinople and elsewhere for a cool £100,000,000 down; it would, as we now know, have been a good bargain for us.

The ex-Czar is asking where the bulk of his baggage, which was to have been sent after him to Tobolsk, has got to. He makes a special application for the furs and books it contains. His daughters have applied for permission to proceed to a convent in the neighbourhood. How appallingly pitiable !

The real position of affairs regarding the Korniloff march

on Petrograd is leaking out. *Pourparlers* were opened by wireless between Savinkoff and Korniloff. The latter clearly states that N. V. Lvoff was sent to him by Kerensky in order that the latter might have the General's advice on three propositions put forward by the President : (1) Kerensky would resign the Ministry; (2) Kerensky would remain in the Government; (3) Korniloff to accept the post of dictator which the Government would proclaim.

" I declared," said Korniloff, " that I considered it my sincere conviction that a dictatorship was the only possible issue out of the present position, a state of siege being proclaimed throughout the country. I begged Lvoff to repeat to Kerensky and to you that I considered the participation of both of you in the Government as absolutely necessary and to ask the former to come to us at the headquarters, so that a definite decision might be taken; I added that, from positive information which I possessed of a Bolshevik rising in preparation at Petrograd, I considered the situation extremely serious and that it was dangerous for both of you to remain in Petrograd. For that reason I asked you both to come to the headquarters, giving my word of honour as to your safety. After an examination of the general situation with the Commissary-General (Filonenko) we both arrived at the conclusion that in the interests of the welfare of the country it was necessary to establish a Collective Dictatorship or a Council of Defence in which it would be obligatory on Kerensky, yourself, Filonenko and myself to join."

Lvoff is now alleged to have a softening of the brain !

" Under the Bolshevik Mantle " is the title of a short article describing the present political situation. If the revolutionary democracy, it says, go to the Democratic Conference it will mean that they are on the road towards forming a Coalition Government. It is impossible to bring together the two problems—the fight against coalition and the fight against Bolshevism. They are antagonistic. If the coalition with the middle classes is foregone the Bolshevik programme is fulfilled. On the other hand, if a coalition plank is accepted, the chief Bolshevik plan fails. That portion of the revolutionary democracy which has as yet only adopted half of the Bolshevik programme and which is ready to proceed to the formation of a homogeneous Government should take into consideration that the first half of the programme will be followed by the second; that after the formation of a Socialistic Government, we shall assuredly proceed to a Dictatorship of the proletariat, and that then it will only be possible to terminate the alliance with the Bolsheviks by Civil War.

One has lost count of the number of times the railway men have threatened to strike unless their pay was immediately increased. The strikes have been averted by the simple but weak policy of giving in, which has, of course, resulted, within a brief space, in fresh demands. Another threatened strike is now engaging the attention of the Ministry. The total new demands would amount to an extra expenditure of five and a half milliard roubles, and this burden the country could not support. But what opinion can any one have of men who will act in this fashion whilst the enemy are invading their homeland and their brothers at the front are entirely dependent on the railways for their means of existence? They will have a rude and hard lesson if the Germans should ever reach these railways.

The peasant problem grows no easier. The Central Committee of the Peasants' Council have notified the Government that the peasants must be supplied with iron and manufactured goods. Serious trouble is, the Committee say, a certainty if the peasants become disappointed in the Revolution.

The Government are taking steps to prevent the population of Petrograd increasing. No one will be allowed to enter the capital without a special permit. Residents and business men will be given certificates. Foreigners will enter on their passports, if in order. The order is to come into force on September 23rd.

Siberia is in the enviable position of being one of the very few countries having a superabundance of food supplies, which are to be had at exceptionally low rates.

It is said that there will, therefore, be no difficulty in solving the local food question in the Ural regions. They should be a happy and contented people.

General Alexeieff has resigned the post of Chief of the Staff to which he was appointed when Kerensky assumed Korniloff's post of Generalissimo. The resignation was announced by the War Minister, Verkhovsky, at a meeting of the Executive Committee of the Council of Workmen and Soldiers to whom he was explaining the army situation and his programme for dealing with it. He said there were two ways of regenerating the army—the first was to re-organise it by repressive and sanguinary measures, and the other was to implant in its ranks healthy ideas of discipline. " General Korniloff had tried the first way. It is a false and dangerous way, because the present army consists of a whole people under arms. The second way is mine. I applied it at Moscow, where it produced excellent results. I am about to bring it into operation on all the fronts and in the rear." The speaker then referred to the " foolish enterprise " of General Korniloff which had compromised afresh the relations between commanders and their men. The Government had decided to replace all commanders who had not the confidence of their men, by others, independently of their rank, provided the latter possessed the experience necessary to conduct military operations and were free from political suspicion. The Minister added, " General Alexeieff does not understand the psychology of our present troops and therefore cannot remain in his post. The whole of the main headquarters will be reformed and an officer enjoying general confidence will be placed at its head." He also dealt with the problem of reducing the strength of the army, pointing out that the country could no longer support the great burden. " Only one-tenth of the mobilised army is at the front," he said, " the other nine-tenths are at the rear, requiring enormous supplies for their maintenance. We are going to reduce the effective army by one-third, without interfering in any way with the troops on active service at the front or touching the artillery or machine-gun sections."

All this has a dangerous appearance of pandering to the Bolsheviks, and is the more to be deplored when the uprightness and love of country known to be so characteristic of Alexeieff are taken into account. His resignation is said to be entirely due to his difference of opinion on this question of the removal from general headquarters of all generals and officers suspected of complicity in the Korniloff movement. Alexeieff holds that such a step will be suicidal, as it will be impossible to effectively replace these men. Fears are openly expressed here that this will mean the end of the army from the point of view of its fighting value. It is said that General Tcheremisoff, a former commander-in-chief on the south-western front, will be Alexeieff's successor. Also that Savinkoff, the former assistant Minister of War, is to enroll himself as a private in a " Shock " battalion.

News comes from Odessa that Kaledin, who is once again Hetman of the Don Cossacks, has seized a number of railway lines in the valley of the Don with the object of cutting off the coal supplies sent to Petrograd and Moscow from this region. The Provisional Government have ordered that all the Cossack detachments, which were withdrawn from the western front by Korniloff and were proceeding eastwards, are to be stopped and sent back to the front. As the Cossacks have been absolutely loyal to the Government since the Revolution, in fact, the one redeeming feature of the army, it is difficult to say how far this news is true or false; but it is understood that they are very anxious about the possible fate of Korniloff. And the extremists are known to be carrying on an active propaganda in the south which is distasteful to the older men amongst the Cossacks, although it is said that some of the younger have become inoculated with the Bolshevik creed whilst at the front. The local committee at Odessa has passed a series of resolutions denouncing the Government negotiations with the anti-democratic groups, refusing to accept the exclusion of the political influence of the revolutionary committees from the army.

September 23rd.—The public prosecutor concluded his

summing up at the Soukhomlinoff trial by stating that he upheld the whole of the charges brought against the ex-Minister and asked that a severe punishment should be inflicted, as all the prisoner's crimes had been committed in a time of war and had led to incalculable disasters.

The Provisional Government have issued a Prikaz to the army and the fleet.

The Korniloff revolt, the document reads, has given rise to a feeling of distrust of their chiefs amongst the soldiers and sailors which is subversive of the unity of the army. The Government proclaims that whilst the majority of the officers are faithful to the Republic, a small group have betrayed the confidence of the Government.   Inasmuch as any movement calculated to cause distrust in the leadership of the army is a danger to its fighting strength the Provisional Government declares—

(1) That all chiefs who are not capable of commanding troops in such a way as to strengthen Russia shall be removed.

(2) The high command of main headquarters in so far as it was implicated in General Korniloff's revolt shall be superseded.

(3) The troops who took part in the revolt shall be removed from the neighbourhood of the headquarters and relieved by faithful troops.

(4) All who were guilty of disaffection during the Korniloff revolt shall be handed over to justice.

(5) The Government demands from the army and navy a return to normal life, with full liberty of action for their chiefs in all questions of military operations and all questions of army and navy discipline.

(6) The Government orders that all persons arrested in the recent crisis should be handed over to the authorities and the administration of severe punishment in all cases of assassination of military chiefs.

(7) All the prisoners who have been arrested on the charge of putting their officers to death shall be handed over to justice.

It is reported that the Helsingfors Revolutionary Committee have set at liberty the sailors who killed the officers of the *Petropavlosk* and that that inquiry will therefore be suspended.

Since his arrest Korniloff has been living in an hotel at Mohileff under the guard of what is known as the " Korniloff battalion." The Council of Workmen and Soldiers sent an intimation to Kerensky that they did not consider that this guard was strict enough and that the battalion sympathised with the General. They, therefore, demanded that the latter should be imprisoned. In deference to this request Kerensky has ordered Korniloff's removal to the municipal prison and the guard has been relieved by a battalion of the Knights of St. George.

In connection with the numerous arrests of officers supposed to be in sympathy with, or to have openly aided, the Korniloff affair, the Minister of the Interior (Nikitini, Posts and Telegraphs, is now also Minister of the Interior) reports to the Ministry that after investigation the majority of these officers are innocent, and their release is therefore probable.

No less than 90,000,000 persons in Russia are to be nominated as possessing necessary qualifications for electing the delegates to the Constituent Assembly. The enormous amount of work involved in the electoral campaign can, therefore, be to some degree estimated. The expenses are placed at the large figure of 100,000,000 roubles (£10,000,000 at a 2s. rouble, its pre-war figure). The Government are likely to have some trouble in providing this sum, even with the paper currency.

The Russian Army has suffered another reverse in the Riga region. The Germans, under Count von Schmettor, have, it is reported, captured the bridge-head of Jakobstadt, seventy miles up-stream from Riga on the western bank of the Dneister. Thus the invasion of Lithuania is being continued. After the taking of Riga and the subsequent advance into the province made by the Germans, the latter had remained quiescent. The Russians held a large bridge-head in the corner of Courland which they had fortified. With this they held a twenty-five mile front, having a depth of several miles strongly fortified. This front, having been pierced in one or two places, the Russians apparently evacuated the whole position. The loss of this bridge-head exposes the railway to Dvinsk, which is on the opposite bank of the river. They say that the position was very strong and should have been easily held.

Rumours are circulating in Petrograd, the people in their present state will believe anything, that the Allies are considering the question of concluding a separate peace with the Central Powers. These fantastic stories are known to have a German, and probably Bolshevik (which amounts to the same thing, it is said), origin. The educated smile at them, but nevertheless such rumours are doing a great deal of harm and are making the Allies more disliked than ever.

Kieff is now imitating the capital and Moscow, and is indulging in a conference of its own—a nationality congress in which Tartars, Georgians, Don Cossacks, Letts, Lithuanians and Jews are amongst the nationalities present. Forty different nationalities inhabiting the Russian empire are said to be represented. The principal subject debated at the first meeting was autonomy; and the best method of obtaining autonomy for all these races under a federal system was considered. Other questions are to receive consideration, such as the general principles of self-government. At the second meeting of this Conference the Crim Tartars declared that they would never submit to external rule of any kind.

There is other news from Kieff to-day. The university students of that town, disapproving of their rector's attitude with reference to the Ukrainian question, have deposed him and demanded a new election, declaring the position vacant. The students are, it appears, against the Ukrainisation of South Russia. This Ukrainian question is by no means settled yet.

The Germans appear to have played a wrong card recently at Riga. They have shown the Soviets the treatment they may expect if Russia, or rather Petrograd and neighbourhood, ever come under the German heel.

Some workmen, who have escaped from Riga and recently arrived here, report that the Germans shot out of hand six members of the executive committee of the local Soviet at that place because they refused to work on the construction of German military defences.

September 24th.—The first meeting of the Democratic Conference arranged for to-morrow was yesterday announced as postponed till 27th inst. It is said that in view of the insinuations to which his revelations on the subject of the Korniloff revolt have given rise to, Kerensky will shortly publish a statement in which he will make known the actual facts of that affair.

An official dementi has been issued by the Minister of Foreign Affairs to the rumour that the Allies are proposing to make a separate peace with the Germans. This step has certainly not been taken before it was time. I have myself been subjected to the most absurd cross-examination on this subject. In view of the silence maintained by the Government here even intelligent men commenced to grow anxious. Were we really going to throw the Russians over in their hour of peril and leave them to be overrun by the Germans has been the burden of the questions. I have been bombarded by men who should really have known better. But it is admittedly difficult for the most sane amongst Russians to maintain a cool head and a level vision in the midst of the chaos at present reigning, when every hour produces its new quota of German lies and disquieting reports.

The Minister of Marine was sent to speak at a meeting of the Central Executive Committee of the Council of Workmen and Soldiers. He said that the distrust of the sailors for their officers was unjustified, as the officers were a fine body of men and constituted the fleet's last resource. Full confidence should be accorded them or the way would be opened to the enemy. He asked for the assistance of the Council in order to achieve this end and restore the fleet's efficiency. Every effort should be made to fight against the noxious propaganda which was spreading through the fleet.

A discussion took place, after which the Committee passed a resolution to the effect that they recognised that the situation was a menacing one and was a danger to the country and to the revolution. They would, therefore, despatch to Helsingfors a deputation of five members with the object of putting a'stop to all arbitrary acts and violence; to assist in the inquiry into acts of assassination; to co-operate in the re-establishment of the normal working of the naval committees; to re-establish the authority of the commanders in regard to naval operations, and to inquire into the reports of German activity in the Baltic Fleet.

With reference to the Finnish question the committee passed a resolution welcoming the proposal of the Social Democracy of Finland to establish a common committee to devise ways and means to smooth over the difficulties existing between Finland and Russia, and appointed as delegates to that committee three of their members: Lunatcharsky, Posern and Tchernoff.

From their past records it does not appear very probable that these persons will be likely to influence the Finnish Socialists or any of the other parties in Finland. In Finland, at least, the Council of Workmen and Soldiers of Petrograd have little influence, nor would it appear that they have much chance of establishing their authority at Helsingfors or elsewhere in the country, even with the fleet at the Finnish capital to help them.

September 25th.—Savinkoff, former Assistant Minister of War, has allowed the following statement, in which he retraces the history of the Korniloff revolt, to be published in the Press to-day. The statement is being discussed with great interest, as it clears up so much which had remained dark in this, to us, mysterious affair; and incidentally exonerates Korniloff from much of the odium with which he has been stigmatised.

" It is alleged," Savinkoff says, " that a counter-revolutionary plot was being hatched at Main Headquarters and in the country generally, but I am profoundly convinced that General Korniloff did not take part in the movement.

I am no less convinced that his Chief-of-Staff, General Lukhomsky, and the other principal instigators, obstinately tried to influence General Korniloff, who was very dissatisfied with the over-weak policy of the Government, as he had declared on several occasions. Nevertheless, it would certainly have been possible to work conscientiously with General Korniloff for the good of the country."

" As far as I am concerned, I have always been of the opinion that liberty can only be assured by a powerful army, and that a German victory would put an end to liberty in Russia. I have always held the view that measures, even severe measures, were necessary to re-establish discipline and to restore the fighting efficiency to the army, but always provided that such measures had the support of Kerensky and the authority of his name."

Savinkoff proceeds to explain how he strove to act as a connecting link between Korniloff and Kerensky, in order to bring about an effective agreement between them, but these efforts were set at nought by the counter-revolution which was discovered five weeks ago.

" Filonenko," Savinkoff continues, " the Commissary-General at Main Headquarters, who was watching the plot, asked for authority to take all necessary steps to put an end to it. Kerensky, believing in the loyalty of General Lukhomsky and the other army chiefs, who were suspected of complicity, opposed their arrest as suggested by Filonenko." In spite of the difficulties created by the plot, Savinkoff declares that his collaboration with General Korniloff resulted in the drafting of a plan for the re-establishment of the death penalty in the rear, the militarisation of the railway and war industries, and, in the event of Maximalist disorders, the proclamation of martial law in Petrograd and Moscow.

As Kerensky did not approve of this project, Savinkoff was compelled to resign. Shortly afterwards, however, Kerensky recalled Savinkoff, informing him that the plan had been approved.

Having received satisfaction on this side, Savinkoff directed his efforts to saving Korniloff from the plot in which Main Headquarters was trying to involve him, and with this object in view he left for Main Headquarters on September 4th, taking with him the scheme approved by Kerensky, and bearing instructions from the Minister-President to ask for the despatch to Petrograd of a cavalry corps for fear of Maximalist disorders.

" At Main Headquarters," Savinkoff relates, " I found the Commander-in-Chief in a very excited state of mind, heaping reproaches on the Government, and declaring that he had no more faith in it, that the country was going to the dogs, and that he could no longer work with Kerensky. As soon as he had calmed down, I informed him that his plans had been approved by Kerensky, and at the same time I transmitted to him the request for the despatch to Petrograd of a cavalry corps. I specified, however, that he should not send the ' Savage Division ' of Cossacks, nor entrust the command of the troops sent to General Krymoff, who was suspected of counter-revolutionary tendencies. On learning that the measures urged by him had been approved, Korniloff altered his tone, agreed to all my requests, and stated that he now thought it would be possible to work with the Government.

" I left Main Headquarters on September 6th. Korniloff, who saw me off, bade me convey to the Government the expression of his satisfaction, and the assurance of his perfect loyalty.

" I carried away the impression that an agreement between Korniloff and Kerensky had been practically accomplished. Unfortunately, the events which occurred between September 6th and September 9th completely changed the situation.

" While I was returning from Main Headquarters to Petrograd, V. Lvoff, the former Procurator of the Synod, was on his way from Petrograd to Main Headquarters. Before leaving Petrograd he had had an interview on the general political situation with Kerensky, such as any politician might have. Arriving at Main Headquarters on September 7th, Lvoff went to Korniloff and informed him that he had been personally instructed by Kerensky

T

to ask him to choose one of the three following alternatives, in view of the fact that it was impossible for Kerensky to continue any longer in power :—

" (1) Kerensky to resign, and Korniloff to become head of the Government, and to form a new Cabinet, of which Kerensky should be a member.

" (2) The whole Government to resign and hand over the power to General Korniloff, who should proclaim himself dictator until the Constituent Assembly meets.

" (3) The Government to resign in order to form a Directorate, the principal members of which should be Kerensky, General Korniloff, and Savinkoff.

" After thinking it over Korniloff chose the third alternative.

" Lvoff left Main Headquarters the same day, and on the following day called on Kerensky at the Winter Palace, and informed him that he had been instructed by General Korniloff to demand that the whole civil and military power should be handed over to the Commander-in-Chief, who would then form a new Cabinet. In confirmation, Lvoff handed Kerensky a document to this effect written by Lvoff on behalf of the Commander-in-Chief. The document was in the nature of an ultimatum.

" Kerensky, surprised at this unexpected act, especially as I had assured him of the loyalty of General Korniloff, got into telephonic communication with the General : ' Do you subscribe to the words which Lvoff has addressed to me ? '

" Korniloff replied in the affirmative.

" Filonenko, to whom Korniloff related his conversation with Kerensky, expressed his astonishment that the Commander-in-Chief should have thoughtlessly confirmed on the telephone a statement which had never even been read over to him. But it was too late. A fatal misunderstanding had already been created. Kerensky relieved General Korniloff of his command, summoning him to Petrograd.

" Korniloff replied (and here it is that the misunderstanding ends and the rebellion begins) that he did not consider himself relieved of his command which he would continue to hold. He then ordered the arrest of Filonenko and at the same time gave instructions to the ' Savage Division ' to march on Petrograd, under the command of General Krymoff.

" At my own request I was authorised to converse with Korniloff on the telephone. I spoke to him twice, trying to point out the inadmissibility of his acts. I explained that there had been a misunderstanding, and I urged him to agree to stop the march of his troops and come himself to Petrograd in order to clear up the incident; but Korniloff answered that he no longer recognised the Government."

Savinkoff, in conclusion, repeats that, although he considers Korniloff's behaviour unpardonable, nevertheless he still persists in the view that the ex-Commander-in-Chief had, down to the last moment, been no party to the plot of some of his Generals.

The following memorandum prepared by Korniloff for the inquiry held into his actions during the revolt, describes in soldier-like fashion events in his career during the war which preceded the step which brought about his downfall.[1]

Korniloff briefly sums up events and his attitude towards them from the moment in the earliest days of the Revolution, when the Provisional Government recalled him from the front to take command of the Petrograd military district. This post he resigned because " he could not remain a passive witness of the evil influence of the Committee of Delegates subverting the army," and took command of the 8th Army. When the demoralisation on the south-west front was at its height (during the Tarnapol retreat) Korniloff was appointed to the command of this group of armies, but he made it a condition that he should have a free hand. Without waiting for superior orders he resorted to the death penalty for insubordination and

---

[1] This is the only liberty I have permitted myself to take with this diary, which in all other cases records events as set down at the time. The General's memorandum was not published till October. For convenience, and in justice to a brave man, I have recorded it here.—E. P. S.

desertion, and forbade the troops to hold meetings. Following on his success in dealing with this terrible situation he became Commander-in-Chief, but he accepted only on condition that the Government did not interfere with his military instructions, dispositions, and appointments, and that the death penalty should be re-introduced. Korniloff refused to start for headquarters till his demands had been conceded.

On arrival at Mohileff he set to work immediately to draft a series of instructions and orders for the re-establishment of discipline in the army, and these he brought to Petrograd. Korniloff bluntly says here that while he thought that Kerensky had lost much of his authority at that time, yet he saw no one else who could take his place. At a meeting with the Government Savinkoff, the Acting War Minister, reported on the proposed measures for raising the discipline of the army. The General then warned the Government that the Germans were preparing a blow at Riga, and that counter-measures had been launched, but that in view of the indiscipline in the army, especially on the northern front, where demoralisation was greatest, the probability of the Russians keeping Riga was remote.

Korniloff goes on to say that when he touched upon the possibility of attacking the enemy on another front, Kerensky, who was sitting next to him, whispered : " On this question it is necessary to be careful." A few moments later he received a scribbled note from Savinkoff, who was also sitting at the council table, with the same warning. After the end of the Conference, " from words uttered by Savinkoff, it became clear to me that the warning had in view the Minister of Agriculture, Tchernoff."

His second journey to Petrograd, where he arrived on August 23rd, was made at the suggestion of Savinkoff, but on arrival he found Kerensky was against his being present when his proposals for strengthening discipline in the army were being discussed by the Government. Notwithstanding Kerensky's attitude Korniloff submitted his memorandum at a private sitting of the Government at which Kerensky, Nekrasoff, and Tereshchenko were present. His suggestions were accepted. The only question the Government reserved was the date on which these measures were to be enforced.

The Cabinet never redeemed in full its promise to Korniloff. It was this vacillation and inability to face the position, even with the enemy invading their country, which exasperated the General. With his temperament it was a certainty that sooner or later he would be forced into an open effort to save the army before it was too late. It was the last chance. That it was the last chance was not apparently realised by Russia's Allies.

Korniloff and some of the other generals and officers who took part in the revolt were transferred last night (September 24th) by special train to the town of Bykhoff in the province of Mogileff, where they will be detained till their trial. The military organisations on the south-western front, in agreement with the Kieff Soviet, have refused to hand over to the Commissioners charged with the investigation of the Korniloff affair, his supporters, Generals Denekin and Markoff and others, and have decided to try them before a military revolutionary tribunal. The Commissioners entered into negotiations with the organisations, but the only result as yet is that the latter have undertaken to postpone action for a week.

The " Shock " battalions are now receiving the attention of the Soviet, the military section of which has passed a motion demanding their dissolution. The Soviet's reasons are, to say the least, curious when the majority of them are very far from being oppressed with the desire to die for their country. Here are the reasons :—

(1) From the point of view of principle it is inadmissible that there should be in the army groups of privileged soldiers who arrogate to themselves the right to die for the liberty of the country, when that right belongs to all soldiers.

(2) The " Shock " battalions place the Russian Army in the position of an army which refuses to defend its liberty.

(3) The " Shock " battalions diminish the capacity of the army by creating, on the one side, a category of heroes, and on the other, a mass of conscienceless soldiers.

This is another effort on the part of the Council to weaken the army and so render it powerless to interfere with their actions when the Bolshevik sections make their bid for power.

We had hoped we had heard the last of the Finnish Diet question, but it has cropped up again. In spite of the Government's proclamation, which dissolved it on July 31st last, the President of the Diet has convoked a sitting for the 28th inst., in order, he says, to vote several urgent financial, economic, and labour bills !

Kerensky returned to Petrograd from Main Headquarters to-day.

September 26th.—Kerensky has been giving an interview to the Petrograd correspondent of the *Figaro* in which he declares that Russia will never make a separate peace. He is reported to have said, " I maintain hope and confidence that the country will revive. The time has come when we are going to re-climb the slope, and we shall get to the top. I know that in France public opinion is growing impatient, but the Allies must understand that what is our misfortune is also our pride—that is to say, that we have attracted to our front rather more than half the total forces of the Central Empires. We had to confront a tremendous effort on the part of the enemy, but we have pulled ourselves together, and we shall do everything to face the formidable situation in order to attain the success of our armies.

" The Allies must know that, if cases of weakness and faint-heartedness have occurred in our ranks, we are ardently determined to make them good and to take full revenge.

" The enemy has made skilful use of the circumstances in order to throw suspicion on our faithfulness and loyalty as an ally. Only the German Press could have spoken

of a separate peace. Russia will never make a separate
peace. No man would ever consent to put his signature
to such a treaty. Such an idea must be excluded alike
from the hopes of our enemies and the fears of our Allies."

But how Kerensky, with an army totally incapacitated
and the Bolsheviks growing more openly defiant daily,
imagines he is going to re-climb the slope, passes comprehension. Only an unpractical idealist could place faith
in such a miracle.

There was a rumour in the capital to-day that Tereshchenko had resigned. As he is the one non-Socialistic
member of the Cabinet all the moderate people were alarmed
at the news. Later on it turned out that he had not
resigned, as he considers the present international situation
so delicate that it is impossible to relinquish his position
till a new Foreign Minister is appointed. At the same
time he says that he is unable to remain in the Cabinet
unless a free and firm Government is established. He is
a good man, and we shall now see whether his plain speaking
will stiffen up Kerensky into taking the only possible step
to ultimately save his Government—if it be not already
too late to do so.

The Cossacks have decided not to take part in the
Democratic Conference, which it considers to be merely a
party meeting. The Minister of War has telegraphed to
Kaledin to come to headquarters in order to explain the
movements of the Don Cossacks. The Cossack Congress
of Novo Tcherkask say that it is impossible for the General
to comply with the request, as his safety could not be
guaranteed at the headquarters. What a comedy this
would all be were it not so serious !

The Central Committee of the Soviets has adopted by
119 votes to 101 a resolution urging that the Government,
when reconstituted, shall be in the nature of a Coalition
Government in which the Cadet party should not be
included.

Kerensky has at last taken a step which many here
think he ought to have taken two months ago. He has
informed the Council of Workmen and Soldiers that he

resigns his membership, thus keeping company with the officers who have already resigned.

The Ministry of Finance has issued a statement explaining the financial position of Russia, which shows that the expenses caused by the war, which amounted on September 14th to 41,000,000,000 roubles (over £4,000,000,000 at pre-war rates) are still increasing, owing to the demands for increased wages which contributed to the increase in the price of necessities and to the high cost of living. The Ministry calls upon the people to postpone all further demands until the end of the war.

The newspapers announce that the financial year will henceforth begin on July 1st, instead of on January 1st.

The Soukhomlinoff trial has come to an end. The court have found that General Soukhomlinoff, ex-Minister of War, is guilty of high treason, fraud and breach of trust. The jury returned a verdict of " guilty " on twelve out of the thirteen charges against the accused and a verdict of "not guilty " on the first charge, accusing him of inaction and inertia during the war with the object of assisting the enemy by weakening the Russian armed forces. Madame Soukhomlinoff is acquitted.

The accused has been condemned to hard labour for life. Madame Soukhomlinoff has asked permission to accompany her husband. The General's Counsel has appealed to the Court of Cassation.

Thus closes a remarkable trial, in its way one of the most remarkable Petrograd has ever witnessed. Many here think that the General should have been shot.

CHAPTER XVII

PETROGRAD IN SEPTEMBER AND OCTOBER

THE DEMOCRATIC CONFERENCE—THE FINNISH QUESTION—
THE PRELIMINARY PARLIAMENT—AUTONOMY FOR THE
UKRAINE

September 28th.—The *Izvestya*, the official organ of the
Council of Workmen and Soldiers, said yesterday, " The
Democratic Conference which opens to-day will have
to deal with the following : 1. Devise methods by which
a frank union between the Government and democratic
organisations may be secured. 2. Settle the form which
the Government should take up to the meeting of the
Constituent Assembly. 3. Decide on the political composition of the Government."

The Soldiers' section of the Council of Workmen and
Soldiers have elected its executive committee. The
Maximalists obtained nine out of nineteen seats. The
Workmen's section of the Soviet elected their executive
committee on the 22nd inst., on which the Maximalists
obtained six seats out of nine.

The Government, in view of Lenin's probable presence
at the Democratic Conference, have announced that
although they will not arrest him in the Conference Hall
they will do so if they catch him anywhere outside. As he
is said to be a careful man where his own skin is concerned,
this will probably have the desired effect of keeping him
away. But, it is asked, why not have let him attend and
made sure of bagging him ?

It was not at first proposed that the Diplomatic representatives should be present, as the Conference is not considered a State one. Its character has, however, gradually

undergone a change, and now to all intents and purposes, although not officially recognised, it amounts to a semi-official Conference. Boxes will accordingly be reserved for foreign diplomats.

The Democratic Conference met at five o'clock yesterday evening in the municipal theatre, the large hall being decorated in the favourite revolutionary colour, red. Twelve hundred delegates from all parts of Russia were present. The Members of the Provisional Government occupied the Imperial box, and several members of the Diplomatic Corps were present.

Tchkheidze declared the Conference open. He explained the reasons for calling the Conference in the grave position of the country, and the urgent necessity which faced them to constitute a revolutionary authority responsible to all elements of society on which reliance could be placed.

Avksentieff, President of the Peasants' Council and now the new Minister of Agriculture, declared that the moment had arrived when the democracy must concentrate on the work of saving the Revolution, which was menaced by a catastrophe which would be irreparable unless avoided in time.

A committee was then elected consisting of thirty-three members, including Tchkheidze, Tseretelli, Avksentieff and Tchernoff. Kerensky (who was received with prolonged applause by the majority present) then spoke.

He welcomed the Conference on behalf of the Russian Government and of himself as Commander-in-Chief. The Government, he said, had already declared its programme at the Moscow State Conference. He would therefore confine himself to a few remarks in his own defence, particularly in regard to the Korniloff affair. He said that he had received information a long time before that a *coup d'état* was being prepared, and he daily took all the necessary steps to counteract it. From the time of General Korniloff's appointment as Commander-in-Chief, Headquarters had begun to address ultimatum after ultimatum to the Provisional Government. The Government had realised that events in Galicia necessitated fresh efforts to counter the disorganisation in the army, but he had worked out his own plans for the emergency, while Headquarters was endeavouring to impose on the Government entirely different plans. For some time it was a struggle between two systems, and Headquarters took advantage of every misfortune at the front in order to immediately despatch a fresh ultimatum to Petrograd. Shortly before the Moscow Conference another and still stronger ultimatum was sent from Headquarters which threatened, if consent were not given to its proposals, to wreck the Conference; but the Government, in spite of the threat, rejected the ultimatum. After the Riga disaster the demands of Headquarters became still more pronounced. Government was even told that from henceforth no rearrangement of the Cabinet should be made without the sanction of Headquarters. In view of the fact that Petrograd was now so much nearer the war zone, owing to the fall of Riga, Korniloff further demanded that all the troops in the Petrograd district should be placed under his authority. The Government refused this demand, foreseeing the dangerous consequences of such a measure. Kerensky explained that it became ultimately necessary to act promptly and vigorously in view of the sudden and unexpected movement of Korniloff's army towards Petrograd.

On the subject of the programme before the Conference his Government charged him to say that the Government ought now to make a greater effort than had yet been made, as anarchy was reaching a serious point and spreading throughout the State. He quoted a telegram from Helsingfors warning the Government that the local revolutionaries would not allow the Government to stand in the way of the reopening of the Diet, which had been dissolved. (Applause from Nationalists.) Facing towards them, Kerensky continued : " Citizens, all who have not yet lost their reason will value that applause, especially at a moment like this when we have just received a telegram announcing the approach of the German Fleet in the Gulf of Finland." If the Government and the country did not hear the Conference speak firmly and concisely the cause of the Revolution was irretrievably lost. This is the more necessary because we are expecting great events at the front, and do not know with what resources we shall be able to oppose them. In concluding Kerensky said : " I have been speaking as a citizen, and now will speak as your President and Head of the State, to declare once again that whoever attacks the Republic of Russia will be faced with the whole might of the Revolutionary Government." (Loud applause.)

Verkhovsky (War Minister) said that Germany, seeing the weakness of Russia, had made efforts towards a separate peace with France and Great Britain, offering them all they wanted at the expense of Russia. But Russia's brave Allies had indignantly rejected her proposals, believing firmly, in spite of all, that the Russian Army would do its duty. The army and navy were not refusing to fight, but they were not animated with the spirit of victory, that spirit which could alone save Russia. The chief reason for this was to be found in the relations between the soldiers and their officers, which were not normal and had become worse since the Korniloff affair. The officers who had taken part in this affair had been removed, and the choice of their successors was now engaging the attention of the Generalissimo. The war must be carried on till they were certain that the peace would be a peace of freedom for all nations, and to this end he insisted on the re-establishment of discipline even, if necessary, by the most stringent measures.

Tchernoff declared himself as strongly opposed to a coalition with the Cadets.

Kameneff protested against a coalition with the Cadets, or with any of the *bourgeois* parties, with whom, he maintained, the Socialists could never agree.

Tseretelli (greeted with loud cheers and cries of " Long live the Revolutionary Leader ") said that an exclusively socialistic Ministry was impracticable. Such a Ministry could never survive long. On the other hand, the *bourgeois* elements would have to give up their struggle against the democracy, which had been considerably strengthened as

a result of the Korniloff revolt. " Therefore," he ended,
" the principle of coalition is imperatively forced upon
us."

The Minimalist Social Cadets voted (81 to 77) in favour
of a coalition Cabinet to include representatives of the
bourgeoisie, but voted against the inclusion of Cadets by
91 to 87.

Kerensky has had a conference with the representatives
of Commerce and Industry of Moscow. He sounded the
men of Commerce on the question of their being willing to
enter the Cabinet. They agreed to do so on the sole condition that the Cabinet became entirely independent of
parties or associations.

Lenin did not appear at the Conference ! The reason
given is that the Bolsheviks would not allow him to do
so in the face of Government's refusal to guarantee him
from arrest, save within the hall of meeting ! A cunning
fox this Lenin. Many are wondering where his earth is
in Petrograd.

Tereshchenko has been talking to the Press representatives here, and his remarks, intended for publication, are
of considerable interest. " Russia," said the Foreign
Secretary, " has made known the principles for which the
free people of Russia are fighting. Germany in reply
continues to proclaim that might is greater than right,
awaiting the time when she may be able to consolidate
the conquests she has made by force." He referred to
Germany's latest acts in regard to the Polish question,
and especially the declaration of the Governor-General
of Warsaw and the new administrative statutes for Poland.
These were concessions to the Poles—concessions made by
Germany owing to her weakness. They would not satisfy
the Poles, whose country still remains disunited. Russia
offers, in contrast to the German proposals and acts, the
principle of free development of all nations, and the Russian
Government reiterates its unalterable resolution to carry
into effect its proclamation to the Poles of March 30th,
1917, especially in regard to the free reconstitution of the
free Polish people.

" The Provisional Government has made a proposal to the Allied Powers to issue a joint decree notifying the above-mentioned proclamation. At the same time Russia will take care that the future independent Polish Kingdom shall enjoy the necessary conditions for its economic and financial regeneration, while leaving open the greater question of indemnities for the losses caused by the enemy's invasion.

" The Foreign Minister said he hoped that in future Russia's general policy would no longer be ' a policy of paradoxes, which has cost Russia so much during the last few months.' In fact he said we acted nominally on behalf of peace, but our actions have resulted in creating conditions which tend to lengthen the war; we ought to expend our energies in reducing the number of the war's victims, but in truth we have made the bloodshed yet more terrible; we laboured for a democratic peace, but in reality we brought the triumph of German Imperialism nearer. These misunderstandings must no longer be allowed to continue. In order to end the war in accordance with the principles laid down by the Government, it is necessary that all the live forces of the country should unite to assist the Government to carry through a purely national policy."

Matters in Finland are becoming graver and more difficult for the Government to handle every day. The Finnish Governor-General recently ordered seals to be affixed to the doors of the Diet, attaching to them the following notice : " The President of the dissolved Diet having summoned the Members of the Diet to meet to-day for a continuation of the session, I order, with the object of protecting the rights of the Finnish people who are to elect their legal representatives in three days' time, seals to be affixed in order to show the illegality of the assembling of the Diet."

Southern Russia appears to be loyal so far to the Government. Odessa is reported quiet. The Korniloff movement does not seem to have roused much feeling in the town, the Government having taken full precautions. It would not appear that they knew much more down in the south of what was actually taking place than we did in the north at Archangel, or in fact than did the Petrograders themselves. In Odessa the factories continue working. A proclamation has been issued stating that any reactionary movement will be repressed by force. The people are said to sympathise with the Government.

Kieff is also tranquil. Excitement was as high there as in Petrograd during the Korniloff advance on the capital, but precautionary measures were taken by the Government. A large crowd had assembled at the theatre to celebrate the six months' anniversary of the Revolution. The Commander-in-Chief, General Oberutcheff, in a speech announcing the news of the Korniloff rising and its result, said they were all loyal to the Government and the Revolution. Loud cheers for Kerensky greeted the speech from every corner of the theatre, and cries of " Down with Korniloff."

September 30th.—In spite of the Governor-General of Finland's order affixed to the doors of the Diet, the President of the latter carried out his intention of holding a session. He proceeded to the Chamber and broke the seals on the doors. The Diet then opened the sitting, eighty Socialists and Democratic Deputies being present. The members of the Centre and Right were not present, but in their absence several Bills were passed. The chief of these were measures regarding the eight hours day, the equal rights of Jews, the exercise of the Sovereign power by the Diet, and the responsibility of the Finnish Senate to the Diet. The sitting began at 12.45 and ended at 2.30. The prosecution of the President and Members of the Diet who made their way in this fashion into the Chamber and held a sitting has now been ordered by the Governor-General. Few here appear to be able to form an estimate as to how the matter will end.

The Democratic Conference met at 6 p.m. last evening, instead of at the advertised hour of 11 a.m. The change of hour was made in order that the various parties might have the day for deliberation in order to settle on their lines of action.

Skobeleff, former Minister of Labour, was the first speaker. He said he was in favour of coalition with the industrial *bourgeois* party and even with the Cadets, with the exception of those of that party implicated in the Korniloff affair. We must show ourselves statesmen, he said, honest and practical, if history is to recognise our revolutionary services.

Zaroudny, ex-Minister of Justice, protested against the charge made against the Cadet party as a whole, which stigmatised it as implicated as a party in the Korniloff revolt. The party had acted honestly, he said, and were the first to say that a Kerensky dictatorship was the only way out of the impasse they had all got into. He suggested that the Conference should open negotiations with the Government for the establishment of a preliminary Parliament representing all parties to which the Cabinet should be responsible.

Pietchekaneff, an ex-Minister, said a coalition was a necessity since a Workers' democracy, should it grasp the power, would not be able to keep it for long; he explained the absolute necessity of co-operation with the Cadets.

Avksentieff pointed out the necessity of having some body who would be able to maintain a check on the Government, a body, he said, whose members should be united to the country by indissoluble ties. This body, which would be a forerunner of a future parliament, should be composed of democratic representatives; but in order to have the necessary authority it must represent all classes, and therefore the middle classes would have to be in it.

Tseretelli agreed that the Conference ought to fix a new basis for the Government and that it was necessary to create a body capable of controlling the Government; the latter would then enjoy the confidence of the entire country and would be able to give its whole energies to the work of saving the country from the abyss into which it was falling.

Kutchin, a delegate representing all the Military Committees at the front, delivered a really strong speech, which had a faint echo, whether the orator intended it or no, of

General Korniloff's address at the Moscow Conference. The speaker declared that the country could not be saved unless the fighting capacity of the army was re-established and the soldiers' distrust of their officers, which was still great, was uprooted. He added that this task would be greatly facilitated if the army learned that the New Government had the whole-hearted support of the democracy.

Voytinsky, a Military delegate, described the precarious position of the army, especially as regards its food supplies. He recommended certain measures for the re-establishment of discipline and reorganisation in the army by the removal from it of injurious elements. This should be done with care and tact so as not to increase the number of deserters. But above all, supplies must be properly organised. " You cannot expect starving troops to fight."

Verkhovsky, speaking for the War Ministry, drew attention to the fact that although this year's harvest was better than that of last, the army was still in need of bread and other vital necessaries, the cause being, of course, defective transport.

Several Army and Navy delegates subsequently spoke on behalf of their own services and insisted, with a rather remarkable unanimity, on the necessity of re-establishing a stable Government which would have the power and strength necessary to reintroduce discipline at the front. The emphasis laid on this point indicates that at last even the soldiers' delegates, or some of them, have realised that this is the one outstanding factor if Russia is to be saved from anarchy and from Germany's clutches.

It is impossible, however, not to feel in strong sympathy with those here who say that it will need a miracle now to bring discipline into the Russian Army.

A Cossack delegate, for the Cossacks have not stood entirely aloof, said the Cossacks would defend the Russian Republic and support the Government.

The next meeting of the Conference took place at five o'clock yesterday (29th) when the Alexandrina Theatre was crowded for a full sitting. It has been shown that the Thursday's (27th) sitting concluded with three speeches

U

made by Tchernoff, Kameneff, and Tseretelli in which semi-coalition, purely socialistic, and full coalition forms of Government were respectively advocated. The coalition doctrine was further expounded to-day. The first five speakers were the ex-Ministers Skobeleff, Zaroudny, Piet-chekhaneff, Avksentieff and Tseretelli. They favoured a Coalition Government, but Zaroudny and Avksentieff added the proviso that some form of Provisional Government, which neither clearly defined, should be amenable to the organisation elected or appointed by the Democratic Conference.

All the subsequent speakers, representatives of the Army and Navy, Military Committees, and the Cossacks, took their stand on the coalition form of Government, in some cases without any reservation, in others with reservations.

It is impossible to deal at any length with the individual speeches, nor would it be of value here. For the Russian is so addicted, when once on his legs orating, to wander from the point and discuss in a loose disjointed manner matters in heaven, earth and beneath which have no relation to the point at issue. The time limit imposed at Moscow showed how aware the Russians themselves are of this national proclivity, and *du reste* this diary exhibits the national trait without further insistence being necessary. In spite of all the unnecessary verbiage in which delegates wrapped up their meaning, it has become clear that the aim of the Conference is definite enough, and is restricted to an effort to decide upon the form of Government which should remain in force until the meeting of the Constituent Assembly. The appalling and menacing dangers threatening their country, which have now become visible to the most blind, have brought the parties together to this extent, with the exception of the Bolshevik visionaries and internationalists who are more concerned about their own programme and its advancement than the safety and rehabilitation of their own country.

The policy, then, which the majority appear to favour is a Coalition Government, responsible to an organisation elected or appointed by the Democratic Conference, and this policy seems likely to be given effect to within the next few days, if no unforeseen contretemps supervenes. The Bolsheviks have so far remained quiescent. Whether they will move or await a moment which appears to them more opportune, no one appears able to foretell. But it is held on all sides to have been a wise move to have summoned to the Conference representatives from the towns, the Zemstvos and other democratic organisations, thus out-numbering the Petrograd extremists and preventing their displaying the force, and consequently the power, which would have been otherwise possible. The danger of a purely socialistic Provisional Government is already being discounted. A Coalition Government, provided it is strong enough to be independent of the Council of Workmen and Soldiers, would obtain a large support and might be able to bring the country through yet; and to this end, as has been shown, the more reasonable of the Socialists are willing to compromise on almost any point to retain the Coalition. They now realise that representatives of the *bourgeoisie* are essential if the Government is to have the necessary weight and authority. It is perhaps not too optimistic a forecast to predict that the Conference has reached a point at which it may find salvation in this way out.

Verkhovsky spoke again yesterday. He said measures now being taken were restoring confidence in the army, shaken by the Korniloff revolt. But the army was insufficiently supplied with clothes, food and fodder for a winter campaign. They hoped to alleviate the situation by a partial demobilisation of the men in the rear. For every man in the trenches, owing to the exaggerated scale on which the original mobilisation had been carried out, Russia now had from six to ten men in the rear. This was a needless burden to the country; the more so as a considerable proportion of these men had received no training whatsoever.

The Conference has as yet made no declaration on the subject of peace, although yesterday's speakers talked round the subject, saying that Russia, in conjunction with the Allies, should make every effort to bring about peace.

It is natural that Russia, faced with so many grave internal problems, should look forward to peace as a solution of the external one. The ultimate decisions of the Conference, if inspired with the spirit of true statesmanship, may tend to accelerate the fruition of the people's wish for peace and order; and should this eventuate the Conference will prove of even greater historic importance than the one at Moscow.

But, as many point out, peace can only be secured by a strong army. How a strong army is to be obtained, in reality one of the most important questions of the hour, and one which, if we omit the general statements of the War Minister, the Conference has not dealt with at all in a practical fashion, passes comprehension. All its valued and experienced Chiefs—Alexeieff, Brusiloff, Ruzsky, Ivanoff, Korniloff, Yudenitch, Gurko and many others are of proved competence in the field, but they are not in the active ranks at present, so far as is known. Socialists and Maximalists may be all right as politicians (although they have not shown themselves very able ones as yet), but they cannot be made into Generals if success is to be achieved at the front. One of the first acts taken after the Revolution was the declaration that all soldiers should be allowed free political opinions, and this is still permitted to the rank and file, but not to the officer, if his politics is of the wrong kind. It is now held by many that the politicians should allow the Generals to retain their political opinions, replace them in command, and by means of a strong Central Government see that they stick to the job they are given to do for the good of their country. This ideal could, so many think, have been realised two months ago if the Provisional Government had taken a firm stand against the Council of Workmen and Soldiers; if in fact, with the fear of this body in their hearts, they had not been so afraid, as Nekrasoff put it at the beginning of August, of stepping on a piece of orange peel. [How far away that day appears now! And what an opportunity still lay open then—had it only been grasped!] Russia has, it must be admitted, done as well as any of her Allies almost would have done during August, and even September, given the same conditions. In fact, had the Allies afforded her practical support then, many think she could have pulled through and been able to hold up the Eastern front. But, it is asked, is not this the end ? Without Generals what is going to happen on the fronts ? This is the most burning and crucial question of all. Even at the eleventh hour it is hoped that the Democratic Conference will give attention to this point, for few think now that Kerensky has the firmness to deal with this army matter. And, it is being asked, what will Germany do if things do not improve on the Russian fronts and all Russia's best Generals remain on the retired list ? What proportion of her army will Germany transfer to the Western front against the Allies ? She has five railways for this purpose, and by commencing early she will be able to transfer most of her picked troops to act against the British, French, or even the Italians. Russian military experts say that Germany has already commenced this operation, but it is not being openly said here to any extent.

October 1*st.*—The second plenary meeting of the Conference took place yesterday. Speakers representing the municipalities said the economic condition of the towns was deplorable; the majority of these, as also of the Zemstvos speakers, were in favour of a Coalition Government. The fact that the majority of the better disposed lower classes are in favour of the coalition idea is scarcely surprising. Bad as the old regime was in many ways, order at least was maintained, personal property was safe, and the law was respected. With the coming of the Revolution order and respect for authority and the law have disappeared, as these pages depict, and the more socialistic the Government in power, the greater has been the spread of anarchy and disorganisation. It was undoubtedly the desire of large masses of the people for a return to order which gave Korniloff a very considerable support among them, and had he won through to Petrograd many think that he would have had the masses of the population on his side at once. The Cossacks and the military organisations are also in favour of coalition, but the co-operatives and Trades Unions are against it.

At the early sitting the representatives of the nationalities spoke, and they devoted themselves chiefly to their own national affairs, and paid but little attention to the larger issue before the country.   The Ukraine, Poland, Esthonia and others were, generally speaking, as was to be looked for after the past months, against coalition.   A strong Coalition Government would be the more capable of dealing with them and preventing the dismemberment of Russia.   A purely socialistic or Bolshevik Government would probably have enough to do coping with its own internal difficulties, and would be unable to maintain a strong hold over the activities of the Separatists.   The one exception to this generally expressed view turned up in the Caucasian Highlanders who, whilst admitting that the question of nationalities was most important, declared that the present was not the moment to discuss it.   A united Russia to carry on the war was what was required at the moment, said the Caucasian Highlander, and to secure it he voted for the coalition.   As a result of the day's work coalition still appears to be in the ascendancy.

An incident which has its ludicrous side as well as the graver one is reported from Kharkoff.   The employees of the electric light company demanded higher wages. The request, the wages having already been raised several times since the Revolution, was refused.   The employees thereupon arrested the directors and managers and imprisoned them in their own board-room.   They then proceeded to hold a meeting.   The first proposal was to execute summary justice on their prisoners.   This was rejected, probably because the employees realised that they would not be able to lay hands on the money for their pay if they made away with the heads of the concern.   A vote was carried unanimously, however, to keep the directors and managers prisoners till the increase demanded was granted.

I could multiply this story by dozens of a similar character which have taken place during the past few months.

On the subject of the rumours already alluded to that the Allies propose making a separate peace, the Petrograd News Agency has now been authorised to give a direct denial to this false report, so persistently kept alive in parts of the Press here.

Our Ambassador states officially that Great Britain would never agree to such a policy. The French Ambassador has informed the Provisional Government that a personage holding an important diplomatic post in Germany recently made overtures to some French politicians with a view to a discussion of questions of interest to France, but the overtures were indignantly rejected. The Italian Ambassador here has declared that Italy would continue her co-operation in the common cause, and that she rejected all thoughts of peace negotiations which neglected Russia's interests. But the rumours had then some ground to go on, and many wonder why they were not categorically denied at once. Germany makes great capital in this way here.

Tashkent (Russian Turkestan) is now in a ferment. A revolutionary committee of political agitators has been formed who obtained the support of portions of two local regiments, and then took over the administration of the town, stating that they did not recognise the Provisional Government. They have not had things all their own way, however, as the Mussulman population would not recognise the committee, and were joined by the Cadets of the Military School who occupied the fortress of the capital. An encounter appeared probable between the rival forces. On learning of the event the Provisional Government sent one of their telegraphic ultimatums which, as has been their usual fate, was rejected. The Provisional Government have now appointed General Korovnitchenko, who commands the troops in the Kazan district, Commissary-General of Turkistan and given him a sufficient force to repress the committee.

The Government have denied the rumour, which has been going the round of Petrograd, that British armoured cars took part in the Korniloff revolt. The rumour, it is said, is an invention (of the Germans ?) intended to sow discord between Russia and Great Britain.

October 2nd.—Considerable excitement was shown at the third plenary sitting of the Democratic Conference, but it was kept in hand by Tchkheidze, who is showing himself a very able Chairman. The divergence of opinion has now developed on two main lines. The one for coalition, with the participation of the *bourgeoisie* and Cadets (save those who are implicated in the Korniloff revolt), the Government to be responsible to the projected Assembly in which the *bourgeoisie* and Cadets are to be represented by one-third; there is a minority who wish a Coalition Government with no responsibility to any Assembly. The other main division appears to be about equally divided between the supporters of a purely socialistic Ministry responsible to a Democratic Assembly, and those who want all the power and authority to pass into the hands of the Council of Workmen and Soldiers.

Before the day was over, however, the chaotic state of public feeling and ideas, even on questions they have most at heart, was to be well exemplified by the action of the Conference itself. It first passed a resolution in favour of a Coalition Government by 766 to 688 votes. It then proceeded to contradict its own act by voting the following amendments to the resolution—

1. Against the inclusion of *bourgeois* elements in the coalition, particularly of persons implicated in the Korniloff movement.
2. Against a coalition with the entire Cadet Party.

A heated discussion took place amongst the members after the amendments were carried. A further vote was taken, and the Conference took the extraordinary step of going back on its own act and voted by 813 to 180 votes against a coalition of any kind. So now nobody knows where he is or what will be the next step in the whirligig.

A railway strike is again threatened, and the Government are apparently preparing to give in to a certain extent and grant a portion of the increased wages demanded.

The increase to be granted amounts to R1,400,000,000 (£140,000,000—two shillings to rouble). This, it is hoped, may avert the strike for a time. But where is the money to come from?

October 3rd.—The Conference settled down a little after the display above described and proceeded to vote that its Executive Committee (thirty-three in number, elected on the first day) should be increased by members from all parties, and that it should hold a special sitting this afternoon in order to elaborate a scheme for reconciling the different views expressed at the Conference and securing unity amongst the members.

At the meeting to-day Kerensky made an impassioned speech. He said that a purely socialistic Ministry would be a danger to the country both from a domestic and foreign policy point of view. Only a Coalition Government could save the country. If, therefore, it was decided to appoint a socialistic one, whilst submitting to the decision he would resign his position, in order to put an end to the struggle for power.

The Conference voted unanimously their intention not to dissolve until an Authority had been constituted in a form acceptable to the democracy.

This is an evidence of a real earnestness of purpose, at any rate. But how the Russian loves a Conference ! The Press are amusing on the subject, but most of what they write appeared in its columns in much the same form throughout August. It is merely a *réchauffé*.

The Executive Committee of the Petrograd Soviet has emulated the example of the Democratic Conference. After passing a resolution against handing over the Governmental power to the Soviets (by 91 to 86 votes), they then voted against coalition *with the bourgeoisie* (127 to 47). So they are very much where they were at the start, and the Press point out that they have not helped the situation in any way.

The Germans are initiating operations in the Baltic in the neighbourhood of the island of Oesel, where some trawlers and air scouts are at work. Whether this is evidence of a serious movement is unknown, but most here think that it is unlikely at this season.

October 4th.—At three o'clock this afternoon the members of the Government, under the presidency of Kerensky, conferred with a delegation of the Democratic Conference, and with representatives of the *bourgeois* elements. After an hour and a half's discussion, complete agreement was reached on all points.

The Minister President declared that the Government proposed to immediately form a complete Cabinet, so that the reconstituted Coalition Government should be able to get to work at once on the basis laid down by the Government and the representatives of democracy and the *bourgeoisie.*

In view of the Government's objections, the representatives of the Democratic Conference have renounced the plan to ask one of their delegates to take part in the Inter-Allied Conference in Paris.

Speaking to representatives of the *bourgeoisie* and the Democrats, M. Tereshchenko spoke strongly, favouring a Coalition Government, a strong and disciplined army, and the re-establishment of order in the country, which could only be effected by a Government responsible to a legally elected legislature, and not to a legislature elected by itself.

The Democratic Conference having fixed the number of representatives in the Preliminary Parliament at about 305, and the Government having given a hundred and twenty seats to the non-Democratic parties, the result is that the latter will, if the composition of the Parliament is not altered, have only twenty-eight per cent. of the votes. The Maximalists, on the other hand, will dispose of sixty-six seats.

The fact that the reconstruction of the Cabinet on a coalition basis is being satisfactorily accomplished is the subject of lively comment in to-day's papers. The *Retch* is of opinion that the coalition now forming is in the nature of a final experiment, which, if it proves abortive, would make the country the scene of a cannibal banquet for Lenin and his friends on the ruins of Great Russia. The paper considers the creation of the Preliminary Parliament a decisive attempt to transform what has hitherto been a merely nominal coalition into an organic body.

The *Izvestia*, the organ of the Soviet, notes with satisfaction that the *bourgeois* elements have at last shown a serious wish to arrive at an understanding with the Revolutionary Democracy, and to abandon their extreme policy.

The *Rabotchaye Gazette*, the Socialist Democrat organ, trusts that the Preliminary Parliament will get rid of the great evil of irresponsible power, and will get closer to the heart of the country.

The *Volya Naroda,* the organ of the Popular Socialists, says that in spite of all its defects, the Preliminary Parliament ought to be able to carry out a great, real, and salutary work.

When the Democratic Conference met to-day the President announced that the Executive Committee, which now comprised members of all the different parties, had completed the work delegated to it of co-ordinating the views of the majority of the Conference, and he trusted that the report would be accepted by the Members. The report was then read to the meeting by Tseretelli.

The document set forth and defined the principles which it said animated (in spite of the contradictory voting) the large majority of the members, and which had been accepted by them; and he therefore submitted on behalf of the Committee a resolution declaring that it was indispensable to constitute a strong revolutionary authority, which would carry out the programme of the Moscow Conference, and initiate an active policy in order to obtain a general peace.

The Conference then voted that the Committee should select five of its members, who should proceed immediately to draft a scheme for the formation of such an authority. The President, remembering preceding incidents, then called upon the Assembly to vote that the discussion should not be reopened. This was passed unanimously. The resolution was carried by 839 to 106 votes. The Bolsheviks then withdrew from the hall in a body. For the present they had lost the game.

The Conference confirmed the assurance given to the Government by the delegates that the responsible democratic political parties would free themselves from the anarchist influence.

The Constitution of a Preliminary Parliament was decided upon at the night session, and the Press this evening say that it will be a provisional body consultative in character but having no legal powers. It is stated that it will, however, have authority to consider questions of foreign policy. The Government will be called upon to supply the Parliament from time to time with information concerning internal matters affecting the country.

This happy outcome is hailed by most of the Press as a great forward step, and they consider that if the parties mainly responsible do not withdraw there will be hope of Russia extricating herself from the position she is in.

But outsiders, not so concerned with the domestic politics, ask, What about the Army ? And the Germans ?

October 5th.—The Democratic conference closed yesterday after approving of a first list of delegates to the Preliminary Parliament, and authorising the Committee to sanction the rest. This last sitting ended with the delegates standing up and singing the " Marseillaise " and the " Internationale."

The Conference has proved a conference of surprises. It has been impossible to forecast from day to day what would be the ultimate outcome. Behind the scenes the influential leaders worked extremely hard. Kerensky has had interviews with representatives of most of the parties, the various Democratic sections, the Cadets, Moscow Industrialists, and many other *bourgeois* elements. Finally Kerensky's threat to resign if the idea of excluding the Cadet party, which embraces some of the most experienced and thoughtful men in Russia, politicians and business men, were persisted in, brought the majority of the Conference to acquiescence. But even at the end there was not complete unanimity. That was impossible from the start, and the extremists remain irreconcilable. In how far they will have to be reckoned with later it is too soon perhaps to forecast, but of course no one imagines that we have heard the last of them. But the Conference has made a practical certainty of two things : a Coalition Government, and the formation of a Preliminary Parliament. When one comes to look back on the past three months, this is really a wonderful achievement in itself. The foreigner is justified in his complaint that it is impossible to make head or tail of Russian politics, with their hairsplitting division of parties and their peculiar shades of opinion; though most countries can show very much the same thing. But the foreigner has at length something concrete to hold on to, and should now be able to follow the trend of the situation far more clearly. For although unanimity is by no means attained yet, the sharp cleavage between the moderates of all parties and the Bolsheviks is at length definitely apparent.

The Cadets' conditions on which they are willing to join the Coalition were accepted to-day by Kerensky. There is little doubt that the Cadets and *bourgeoisie* generally have been placated by the Government's decision that Korniloff will not be prosecuted for high treason.

The Preliminary Parliament had its first meeting this evening, Tchkheidze being elected President, the Maximalists disapproving. A Committee of the Preliminary Parliament, consisting of six members, who included Avksentieff, Tchernoff, Trotsky and Kameneff, was then elected.

It is proposed to hold a secret sitting to discuss the negotiations which had taken place between the delegates of the Conference and the Provisional Government on the subject of the formation of a Coalition Government and other matters.

The organisations represented in the Preliminary Parliament and the number of delegates are as follows : The Executive Committee of Peasants Delegates 38, including Kerensky, Tchernoff, Avksentieff and Madame Bréshkovskaya; Zemstvos, 27; Co-operative Societies, 17; Non-Slav Nationalities, 7; Agrarian Committees, 7; Economic organisations, 5; Cossacks, 4; Mussulmans, 4; Fleet, 3;

Alliance of Towns, 3; School Teachers, 2; Socialists, 2; Ukraine, 2; Feminine organisations, 1; Orthodox Clergy 1.

October 7th.—The railway-men have struck, and the Press is pretty severe in its comments on their action. It is pointed out that in 1905 the railway strike decided the fate of the Revolution, whereas in 1917, says one paper, it is aiding the cause of the counter-revolutionists. The action of the railway men is, says another, really directed at Russia herself, and will directly benefit the enemy, and this to obtain more money for themselves, money which the country has not got to give them. That the strike should come just now, when so great a stride towards harmony and fusion has been made, is considered to be all the more unjustifiable.

On the motion of Tseretelli, the Preliminary Parliament is to be styled the " Provisional Council of the Russian Republic." It is to be accorded the right to ask the Government questions but not the right to interpellate the Government; also the right of initiation in constitutional questions and the right to discuss measures and Bills which have been submitted for the consideration of the Government. In practice it is held that no Government will be able to remain in office if a vote of want of confidence against it is taken in the Provisional Council.

The business of the elections for the Constituent Assembly progresses. The total number of electoral districts has been fixed by Government at 730. The more important electoral districts are Petrograd with 20 members, Moscow 29, Kieff 22, Caucasus 36, and the Valley of the Don, 17.

The autonomy of the Ukraine is announced. The Ukraine Secretariat-General has issued a proclamation to the people, in which it declares that as its internal organisation is now complete it enters on its task of governing the country. The proclamation adds that notice of the fact has been communicated to all public institutions.

The Ukraine has had able men to guide it in its determination to secure autonomy. Finland in the absence of such has degenerated into lawlessness, in which bloodshed and

anarchy at present form the prevailing features in parts
of the country, to which are added overtures to the enemy.
How the Finnish matter is to end seems at present an
insolvable puzzle. The punishment to be meted out to
the Diet for assembling in direct opposition to the orders
of Government has not yet been decided. And Finland
now proposes to set up an autonomous Republic !

The Government have taken action in the direction of
fixing prices for some of the articles of food. The price of
bread being fixed, it is said that the peasants are now fur-
nishing abundant supplies of wheat to the railway dépôts
throughout the country. In how far this is the actual truth
it is difficult to discover, for the peasant can still only
be paid for his supplies with the paper rouble, and he
could have obtained this for his wheat any time during the
last few months. His reason for holding up his grain is,
that he could not purchase his necessities, and his power
of being able to do so is no greater now than it has been for
the last several months; for the available supplies of iron,
cloth, etc., he demands are non-existent.

There is a big conflagration taking place in some of
the Baku oil reservoirs, where several million poods of oil
are burning. More German handiwork, says the Press.

Lvoff, who played a chief part in the Korniloff affair,
has been transferred to the Petropavlosk Fortress. Investigation has established the fact that Lvoff acted as an
unauthorised and untrustworthy intermediary between
Korniloff and Kerensky. Korniloff, it is now said, never
entrusted any specific mission to Lvoff. It transpires
that Kerensky had a private interview with Lvoff, the
conversation being of a character to which the Premier
attached no importance. But Lvoff, without any authorisation, repeated the whole conversation to Korniloff under
the form of an official commission. It has been further
established that Korniloff only saw Lvoff once in his life.

In discussing the outcome of the Democratic Conference
with a Russian diplomat, an astute man with a considerable
reputation, he said : " Yes, for the present, the Bolsheviks
are beaten. The Democratic Conference was a nasty blow

for them, and it may appear to foreign eyes that they are finished. The matter now rests, if the parties carry out their Conference policy, on the army. If the better elements in the army can be kept together and reinforced in time by troops holding moderate socialistic opinions they will be strong enough to overawe and render powerless the *canaille* whom the Bolsheviks have at their backs. But you are probably correct in fearing that it is now too late. The greater bulk of the fighting army is far too demoralised to enable it to be got in hand again. The Allies, France and England, lost their chance last July and August. They should have treated the fronts as a whole and sent—insisted on sending if necessary—troops to the Eastern front. Now, even if the army could be rehabilitated sufficiently to try and hold the front, unless I am very much mistaken, another factor will then appear in the situation. And that factor will be Germany. It is not for nothing that Lenin went to Berlin. If Russia appears to have the slightest chance of combining, and really starting the work of rehabilitation, Germany will play another card. Having failed with her spies and her propaganda, she will start open warfare on a considerable scale again, hoping thus to bring about fresh panic and disorder in Petrograd and elsewhere. In this way she will try to carry out her designs by means of her partners Lenin and his associates."

The extracts from my diary end here.

CHAPTER XVIII

THE FALL OF THE PROVISIONAL GOVERNMENT AND ADVENT OF THE BOLSHEVIKS

THE NEW COALITION CABINET—THE GERMANS IN THE
BALTIC—OPENING OF THE PRELIMINARY PARLIAMENT
—THE ADVENT OF THE BOLSHEVIKS

October 8th to November 8th.—To bring my narrative up
to the era of Lenin and Trotsky, the last month of the life
of the Provisional Government will be briefly dealt with.

The new Cabinet was formed on October 8th. It con-
sisted of six Socialists : Kerensky (President and General-
issimo), Nikitini (Interior and Posts and Telegraphs),
Maliantovitch (Justice), Prokopovitch (Food Supplies),
Avksentieff (Agriculture), and Gvozdeff (Labour). The
Non-Socialists were Tereshchenko (Foreign Affairs), Kono-
valoff (Commerce and Industry), Bernatsky (Finance),
Salazkin (Public Instruction), Kartasheff (Religion), Kish-
kin (Public Relief), Smirnoff (State Controller), Tretiakoff
(President of Economic Council), Liverovsky (Ways and
Communications), General Verkhovsky (War), and Admiral
Verderevsky (Marine). The formation of this Government
entailed the dissolution of the Council of Five. The
Government at once issued the customary Proclamation
calling on all to rally round it and save the Revolution,
which was in extreme peril.

Before this Government got into its stride they were
faced with a new menace. This cloud suddenly appeared
in the Baltic and furnished direct evidence of the clearness
of vision of the Russian diplomat, with an expression of
whose views I concluded my diary. On the 12th a large
German force, covered by a fleet of sixty warships, effected

a landing on Oesel, a fortified island on the north side of the Gulf of Riga, and rapidly overran a considerable part of it. Oesel is less than eighty miles from Reval, the supposed German objective. The Russian Baltic Fleet was engaged, but the comparative facility with which the landing, effected with remarkable despatch, was carried out, was obviously due to the utter lack of discipline in the fleet and the negligent outlook kept by the patrols. Kerensky sent one of his telegrams to the fleet threatening punishment for any desertion, and so on. The German *coup* threatened the loss of the whole Gulf, the Finnish ports, and the capture of Reval, thus opening out a direct road to the capital. The usual controversy broke out in the Press, each organ accusing its opponents of being directly responsible, but the *Volya Naroda* recalled Kerensky's warning at the Moscow Conference, that just such a *coup* was to be anticipated, a warning characterised by Trotsky as an unworthy political manœuvre. By the middle of the month the Germans had obtained the mastery of the Gulf and were proceeding to sweep up the mines. They had secured most of the Oesel; had fought an action with the Russian Fleet, during which the Russian battle-ship *Slava* was sunk, and captured Moon and Dagö Islands. At the end of these operations the Germans announced that they had captured 20,000 prisoners and 100 big guns, besides other booty, especially stores.

The Central Committee of the Council of Workmen and Soldiers, thoroughly alarmed, adopted a resolution, declaring that the epidemic of disorders throughout the country was bringing the State to anarchy and ruining it.

The naval operations and the increasing disorder in the capital decided the Cabinet to make arrangements to remove the Government to Moscow, a decision vehemently opposed by the extremists for obvious reasons. It was also ordered that the civilian population should evacuate Reval.

The Preliminary Parliament was formally opened on October 20th in the Marie Palace. In his inaugural speech Kerensky said : " For the first time since the Revolution the Government finds itself in a position to work in concert with the representatives of the organised forces of the Russian people, which has become its own master. We hope that the arbitrary power which has been overthrown will never be restored. Two simple and yet very difficult problems must fix your attention and that of the Government : the defence of the country, and the restoration of the fighting force of the army." After paying an enthusiastic tribute to the navy, a tribute he regretted he could not pay to the army, he dealt at length with the growth of anarchy throughout the country. Kerensky then offered the Presidential chair to Madame Bréshkovakaya, who was installed amidst tumultuous applause. Avksentieff was elected President of the Assembly by 288 votes.

Trotsky, President of the Petrograd Soviet, then spoke, and violently attacked the Government, especially the *bourgeois* Ministers. " The Maximalists cannot," he said, " work with the Government or with the Preliminary Parliament, which I am leaving in order to say to the workmen, soldiers and peasants, that Petrograd, the Revolution, and the people are in danger." The Maximalists, or Bolsheviks, they were practically the same thing now, then left the Chamber shouting, " Long live a democratic and honourable peace ! " " Long live the Constituent Assembly ! " This action on the part of Lenin's accomplice amounted to a declaration of war, and it is almost incomprehensible that Kerensky, even at the eleventh hour, did not make a stand to save his Government. Instead, he ordered the dissolution of the Duma, in view of the elections for the Constituent Assembly fixed for November 25th, and the 4th Duma thus officially disappeared. It had made history, but with a display of more firmness on the part of its leaders it might have gone down through the ages as the real and undisputed mother of the infant Russian Republic.

The Council of Workmen and Soldiers selected Skobeleff as their delegate to the Inter-Allied Conference at Paris. His instructions at first covered a wide field, by now fairly well known, comprising such matters as a *plébiscite* to decide the fate of Alsace-Lorraine and other parts, in Austria and elsewhere; the return to Germany of all her colonies; neutralisation of all straits leading to inner seas, Suez and Panama Canals, etc.; general disarmament on sea and land, and so forth.

The second meeting of the Preliminary Parliament took place on the 24th. Verkhovsky made a statement on the army, merely reiterating the points he had dealt with in his public utterances last month, and making promises he had not as yet been able to fulfil. The Minister of Marine and Alexeieff spoke in the same strain, the latter saying that the army was incapable of doing its duty. Kerensky followed, and laid the blame for the present state of the army on Korniloff, attributing it entirely to his action. He protested against Alexeieff's statement about the army. He declared that the Government had done all they could, and that they were not to blame if the prestige of the Revolution had diminished amongst a section of the people. He said that on all the fronts they would not find a single commander who was hostile to his system of military administration. He said nothing, however, about the fighting capacity of these officers ! " You will see," he concluded, " that the co-ordination of the General Staff, the Military Commissaries and the Soldiers' Committee, can create an army whose martial and fighting spirit will enable us to say to the people at the Constituent Assembly that the enemy's offensive will be stopped." The members then proceeded to elect a Committee of National Defence, comprising forty-one members.

Tereshchenko announced, with reference to the instructions given by the Soviet to Skobeleff, that their views would not be binding on the Russian official representatives at the Inter-Allied Conference.

Towards the end of October the officers of the army made a last effort, in which they were supported by a congress of politicians at Moscow, to get the Government to really attempt to restore the efficiency of the army. The Petrograd meeting of officers, after examining the matter, declared there was now no army, nor had its chiefs any authority. The Congress at Moscow was addressed by Generals Brusiloff and Ruzsky and others. It instructed its representatives in the Preliminary Parliament to insist on the Government placing the army outside politics, to restrict the activities of the Soldier's Committees to exclusively economic duties, and to restore discipline.

Alexeieff refused the offer to go to the Inter-Allied Conference at Paris as Russia's military representative, so the Government did not get rid of him in this fashion. The Soviet, in view of the openly expressed dissent from the views contained in their memorandum for Skobeleff, set about revising it.

The Provisional Government still had the Ukranian and Finnish questions on their hands. Owing to the separatist tendencies of the former, which daily became stronger, the Government, as a measure of repression, decided at the end of the month to refuse to the Ukraine all the monetary contributions which it had hitherto received for its administrative expenditure.

In Finland they had got as far as naming an individual as President of the proposed Finnish Republic. But at this time Germany was already threatening Helsingfors. The latter power had been evacuating the Verder Peninsula (Esthonia) after acting in his usual barbarous fashion and laying waste the whole country. At the beginning of November Kerensky was reported (from America) to have said that Russia had entered the war at the start and was now worn out by the strain, and claimed that the Allies should shoulder the burden of the war. He was also reported to have said, " Where is the great British Fleet now that the German Fleet is out in the Baltic ? " This announcement gave rise to considerable feeling in the Allied Press, and Kerensky gave an interview to a correspondent of the associated Press. " Is Russia out of the war ? " he was asked. Kerensky declaimed on the enormous part Russia had played in the war. " We were fighting when England was preparing. We have fought since the beginning," he said, " we are now worn out and have the right to claim that the Allies should take the heaviest burden on their shoulders. At present Russian public opinion is greatly agitated by the question, ' Where is the great British Fleet now that the German Fleet is out in the Baltic ? ' " " Could an American army be of use if sent to Russia ? " " It would be impossible to send one," Kerensky replied. " It is a question of transport. The difficulties are too great. The greatest help America could give would be by sending boots, leather, iron and money. The masses of Russia are worn out economically," he concluded; " they doubt the possibility of attainment."

The first rumour of the plot by the Bolsheviks to seize the power appeared at the beginning of November. An armed demonstration was to take place, it was said, on a date kept secret. Preparations to counteract it were said to have been already taken by the Government of Petrograd. The Press apparently openly discussed the matter, and several Bolshevik journals were suppressed, so that the Government had ample time, had they possessed the initiative and power, to put it down. But they had alienated the Cossacks, who dealt with the July rising. The Government now had only the useless militia in Petrograd, who had replaced the police, a force, as has been shown, quite incapable of performing its duties. Petrograd at this time was already subjected to all the horrors of lynch law.

The last change in the Cabinet was made a few days before its fall : Verkhovsky, who had disagreed with his colleagues, being replaced as Minister of War by General Manikovsky.

The Council in Petrograd had recently appointed a Military Committee, whose duty it was to maintain close relations with the troops in the capital. Trotsky, President of the Council, sent a request to the garrison on November 5th, asking the soldiers not to obey any orders unless signed and approved by this Committee. The latter then sent special military commissioners to all important points in Petrograd. These proceedings were looked upon, as well they might be, as the first attempts of the Bolsheviks to seize the power. The Government, it was believed, had decided to deal vigorously with this open defiance. The British Press had head-lines describing this as a " Firm Government stand." Those who knew the real position of affairs were fully aware that it was only a matter of a few days or weeks before the weak Provisional Government must be swept away.

There was a skirmish between Skobeleff and Tereshchenko in the Preliminary Parliament on the same day. The former said that the Allies ought to co-ordinate the aims for which they must continue the war and invite the enemy to enter upon a discussion of the conditions of peace. Tereshchenko in reply said, " The whole world desired peace. We must work for a peace without annexations on either side. That is what each side must declare. To obtain this we must first re-establish discipline in the army; and secondly, those taking part in the Inter-Allied Conference, whether the Minister of Foreign Affairs or the Delegate of Democracy, or both, should feel that they had the whole nation behind them."

At the meeting of the Parliament the following day Kerensky, alluding to the Bolsheviks' attempts to seize the power and declare civil war, said, " People who dare at this time to raise their hands against the will of the Russian people threaten at the same time to open the front to Germany. All acts of this kind will be immediately suppressed." This was almost his last public speech. He had gone on for so long threatening without acting that by now he had lost all power of taking the initiative, although he must have known the perilous position of his Government. He asked the Parliament whether the Cabinet could rely on its support. A resolution was passed, amidst intense excitement, by 122 to 102, promising to support the Government if it proceeded to carry out immediately the programme of the Revolutionary Democracy.

A dispute which had arisen between the General Staff of the Petrograd military district and the Revolutionary Military Committee came to a head on the 6th. The Committees wished to increase the democratic element on the Staff. They also wanted to control all the orders issued by the Staff and participate in its military deliberations. These demands were refused, whereupon the Council of Workmen and Soldiers convened a meeting and telephoned to each regiment announcing that the staff having refused to recognise the military committee, the Council henceforth considered the Staff as an anti-democratic organisation. The troops were, therefore, requested to only obey the orders of the military committee in future. The Provisional Government then decided to regard the Revolutionary Military Committee as an illegal organisation, and ordered that its members should be prosecuted. The military authorities were instructed to take the necessary measures in case of a revolt against the Government. The Military Governor of Petrograd, in view of the possible action of the Committee, summoned troops into the capital from the environs, an order which the Committee instructed the troops to disregard. In the afternoon the Government had the bridges across the Neva disconnected, thereby stopping the tram service. By the evening the city was said to be under the guard of troops loyal to the Cabinet.

On the 7th an armed naval detachment, acting under the orders of the Bolshevik Revolutionary Committee, occupied the offices of the official Petrograd Telegraph Agency. The Bolsheviks also occupied the Central Telegraph Office, the State Bank and the Marie Palace, where the sittings of the Preliminary Parliament had, in view of the gravity of the position, been suspended. No disorders took place. But it was the beginning of the end. The weak vacillating Provisional Government had vacillated and temporised too long. The difficulties they had to face were admittedly enormous. But from the first they displayed weakness in permitting the existence of a rival authority, and this could have but one outcome in the long run.

The following day the blow fell. The Bolsheviks, under Lenin, who suddenly appeared from his lair, and Trotsky, deposed the Provisional Government and assumed the power " until the creation of a Government of Soviets," whose function would be to offer " an immediate democratic peace," and to promote " an honest convocation of the Constituent Assembly." In view of subsequent happenings the word " honest " seems peculiarly misplaced in this announcement. The *coup d'état* was the work of the Petrograd garrison and proletariat, and was accomplished with little bloodshed at the outset. Kerensky fled. The Ministers Tereshchenko, Konovaloff, Kishkin, Maliantovitch, Nikitini and others were arrested.

Lenin, Trotsky and the Extremists had triumphed, and the Bolshevik sway commenced.

So ended one of the most tragic periods in the history of Russia, a period which, commencing with bright promise, might so easily have led to a prosperous, contented and happy Russia.

But the reins fell into weak hands, and Russia's Allies, for reasons which to many at least appear inexplicable, remained aloof from the new and struggling Republic, born in such troublous and perilous times.

Why did her Allies remain aloof? Was their information as to the real happenings in Russia during the first half of 1917 at fault? Was Russia's position really understood by France and Great Britain?

Why was the Eastern front sacrificed when at least an attempt might have been made to save it—an attempt which some, qualified to speak, think would have been certain to have met with success?

And with the front the infant Republic might have been saved from the iron heel of the German.

INDEX

315

Printed in the United States
31033LVS00001B/20

9 780898 754506